Charles Newhall Taintor

The Hudson River Route

New York to West Point, Catskill Mountains, Albany, Saratoga Springs, Lake George, Lake Champlain, Adirondack Mountains, Montreal and Quebec

Charles Newhall Taintor

The Hudson River Route
New York to West Point, Catskill Mountains, Albany, Saratoga Springs, Lake George, Lake Champlain, Adirondack Mountains, Montreal and Quebec

ISBN/EAN: 9783742866479

Manufactured in Europe, USA, Canada, Australia, Japa

Cover: Foto ©ninafisch / pixelio.de

Manufactured and distributed by brebook publishing software (www.brebook.com)

Charles Newhall Taintor

The Hudson River Route

HUDSON RIVER ROUTE.

NEW YORK TO WEST POINT, CATSKILL MTS.
Albany, Saratoga, Lake George,
LAKE CHAMPLAIN, ADIRONDACK MTS.
Mt. Mansfield, Green Mountains,
MONTREAL AND QUEBEC.

TAINTOR BROTHERS, MERRILL & CO.
758 Broadway, New York.

LARGEST HOTEL IN BOSTON.

THE ST. JAMES.
FRANKLIN SQUARE.

DOYLE & MEAD,
Proprietors.

Accessible by Horse Cars from all Railway Stations.

INDEX.

ADIRONDACK MOUNTAINS.	121
Adirondack R. R.	83
Acra	58
Albany	63
Albany Junction	70
Albany Rural Cemetery	69
Andre and Arnold	29
Athens	60
Ballston Spa	76
Barnegat	46
Barrytown	50
Benson Landing	114
Big Indian	56
Boiseville	56
Brandon	100
Brosseaus	126
Brooksville	103
Burlington	116
Cairo	58
Caldwell	105a
Cambridge	91
Capture of Stony Point	34
Carmansville	21
Castleton, N. Y.	62
Castleton, Vt.	89
Catskill	52
Catskill Mountains	54
Catskill Mountain House	57
Centre Rutland	100
Charlotte	103a
Clarendon Springs	90a
Coeyman's	61
Cohoes	69
Cold Spring	40
Columbiaville	60
Comstock's Landing	89
Cornwall Landing	41
Coxsackie	61
Croton Point	32
Crown Point	115
Day Line Steamers	12
Del. & Hud. Canal Co's R. R.	67
Dobb's Ferry	26
Dunham's Basin	88
Eagle Bridge	91
East Windham	58
Essex	116
Fairhaven	89
Ferrisburg	103a
Fishkill Landing	42
Fort Ann	88
Fort Clinton	36
Fort Edward	87
Fort Lee	22
Fort Montgomery	36
Fort Ticonderoga	114
Fort Washington	21
Fox Hollow	56
Freehold	50
Gansevoort	87
Garrison	39
Germantown	51
Glens Falls	105
Grand Ligne	126
Grand Trunk R. R.	125
Granville	93
Greenbush	62
Green Island	73
Guigou House	57
Hadley	84
Hastings	25
Haverstraw	33
Hoboken	20
Hudson	60
HUDSON RIVER	5
Hunter	58
Hyde Park	47
Hydeville	89
Irvington	27
Jersey City	20
Jessup's Landing	84
Jewett's Heights	59
Kingston	49
Kings	84
Lacolle	126
LAKE CHAMPLAIN	111
Lake Champlain Route	110
Lake Dunmore	101
LAKE GEORGE	106
LAKE GEORGE ROUTE, Via Adirondack Railroad	83
LAKE GEORGE ROUTE, Via Glens Falls	104
Laurel House	57
Leicester Junction	103b
Lexington	53

Low Point	45	St. Lambert	126
Luzerne	85	St. Johns	126
Manhattanville	21	Salisbury	101
Marlborough	45	Sandy Hill	105
Mechanicsville	73	Saratoga Springs	82
Middlebury	102	Saugerties	51
Middle Granville	93	Schenectady	80
Middletown Healing Sp'gs.	97	Schodac	61
Milton Ferry	46	Shandaken	56
Montreal	127	Shoreham	103b
Moreau	87	Shelburne	103a
Mt. Pleasant	56	Shokan	55
New Baltimore	61	Shushan	92
Newburgh	43	Sing Sing	31
New Hamburgh	45	Smith's Basin	88
New Haven	103	South Corinth	84
New Paltz	47	Spuyten Duyvil	23
North Creek	86	Staatsburg	48
North Ferrisburg	103a	Stony Creek	85
Nyack	31	Stony Point	33
Orwell	103b	Stotesville	126
Overlook Mt. House	55	Stuyvesant	61
Palisades Mt. House	24	Summit Station	57
Palenville	58	Sutherland Falls	100
Pawlet	93	Tannersville	58
Peekskill	35	Tarrytown	28
Phœnicia	56	Ticonderoga	103b
Piermont	26	Teller's Point	32
Pine Hill	57	The Glen	86
Pittsford	100	Tivoli	50
Plattsburgh	119	Thurman	86
Poughkeepsie	46	Tremper House	56
Poultney	95	Troy	71
Port Ewen	49	U. S. Military Academy	38
Port Henry	115	Vergennes	103
Port Kent	118	Verplanck's Point	33
Prattsville	59	Waterford	70
Rhinebeck	48	Weehawken	20
Riverdale	24	West Hurley	55
Riverside	86	West Kill	58
Rondout	49	West Point	37
Round Lake Station	74	Westport	116
Rouse's Point	125	West Rupert	92
Rupert	93	West Rutland	90
Rutland	90	West Troy	69
RUTLAND R.R.	99	Whitehall	89
RUTLAND AND WASHINGTON DIV. D. & H. C. C. R. R.	91	ADDISON R. R.	103b
		Whiting	103b
Salem	92	Windham	59
		Yonkers	25

THE HUDSON RIVER.

AMONG the thousand streams which drain the great Atlantic slope of North America, none is more attractive than the noble river at whose mouth stands the Empire City of the Western World. The European visiting America can have no better introduction to the Western Continent than that which is afforded by a voyage up the Hudson; and travelers generally will find that the river forms naturally the first stage of any extended pleasure-tour through the Northern and Eastern States.

SCENERY so charming as that of this beautiful river affords a delightful change from the glaring walls and pavements of New York. Before the limits of the metropolis are passed the eye is charmed by the green wooded hills of Westchester County on the one hand, and by the frowning precipices of the Palisades on the other—a contrast the like of which cannot be found so near any other of the world's great capitals. For twenty miles this mighty dyke of basaltic trap-rock shuts off the western sky, then suddenly disappears, and the view opens upon the rolling hills of Rockland County and the blue outline of the distant Ramapo Mountains; while on the east bank are thriving towns and elegant country-seats in almost continuous succession. Here, too, the river widens to the dimensions of a lake, which stretches its beautiful expanse nearly to the magnificent southern portal of the Highlands; when it suddenly contracts to a channel half a mile in width, overhung by the scarred and rugged crags of the Donderberg and Anthony's Nose. For a score of miles above, the river winds amid the grand and rugged mountains of "The Highlands," at whose northern limit another portal opens, through which the swift steamer glides to new scenes of beauty beyond. Above the Highlands the banks continue high and in some places precipitous, opening now and then as if to afford glimpses of the charming country on either side, until some thirty miles more have been passed when the banks become still less abrupt, and the lofty range of the Catskill Mountains is seen to the westward.

THE REMOTE SOURCES of the Hudson are among the highest peaks of the Adirondack Mountains, 4,000 feet above tide-water. Its numerous upper branches unite in the neighborhood of Fort Edward, 180 miles from the ocean, and thence follow a southerly course, broken by numerous falls and rapids, to Troy, where it meets tide-water. The remaining 150 miles are navigable by large steamers and coasting craft. Ships can ascend to Hudson. The principal tributaries are the Mohawk and Hoosick rivers, the former rising in the central part of New York, and the latter in Southern Vermont, both joining the Hudson near Troy, below which city the tributaries, though numerous, are small, none of them being navigable for more than two miles.

The mountain-ranges through or near which the Hudson passes are part of the Appalachian system. The Highlands are a continuation of the Blue Ridge, which, after crossing Pennsylvania and New York, ends in the Green Mountains of Vermont and New Hampshire. The Catsbergs and Hilderbergs are continuations of the westward ranges of the Alleghanies. The mean rise and fall of the tide at New York is about five feet, and at Albany two and a half feet.

THE COMMERCE of the Hudson River, during the season when it is not obstructed by ice, is extensive and constantly increasing. It is the natural outlet for lumber from the vast forests of the North. This is floated down the main stream and its branches during the high water of early spring, and several millions of feet are every year brought to market in this manner. The Delaware and Hudson Canal brings vast quantities of coal from Pennsylvania, and keeps numerous barges constantly plying between its junction with the river at Rondout and the various cities reached by water from that point. The Erie Canal, connecting the Great Lakes with the ocean, through the Hudson River, affords means of transportation for Western produce and for the manufactured goods of the East. The immense "tows" of canal boats ascending and descending the river form an important and interesting feature of its commercial life. Quarries of various kinds of stone, valuable for building, paving, flagging, etc., are found at various points on and near the river; and in Ulster County water limestone, making the best cement, is found in inexhaustible quantities. In the vicinity of Haverstraw, are extensive beds of clay which give employment to thousands of brick makers, whose kilns are seen for miles along the river bank. Manufactories, foundries, machine-shops, ship yards, and agricultural products unite to swell the numbers of every sort of vessel suitable for navigating these waters, and the fisheries afford employment and support to many men. During the winter, many thousand tons of ice are stored for domestic use and for exportation.

IN HISTORY the river assumes a prominent place in the annals of the country. In September, 1609, when Hendrick Hudson sailed through the Narrows, and anchored his vessel, the "Half-Moon," in New York Bay, the shores were covered with a magnificent forest, unbroken save by natural meadows, or by the villages of Indians. The beautiful bay and river, now one of the busiest scenes of commercial activity in the world, were without signs of human life, except the few canoes of the natives; and Manhattan Island with its dense population of a million souls, its splendid streets and buildings, and its proud commercial position as the Metropolis of the Western Continent, was a hilly, thickly-wooded island, inhabited by a fierce and warlike race of savages. Hendrick Hudson was sent out by the Dutch East India Company to search for a northwest passage to India, a problem which tempts explorers even in our own day; and when he looked up the long line of the Palisades and noted the strong ebb and flow of the tidal currents at the mouth of the river, he thought his object gained. Accordingly, he sailed up the river, viewing, with wonder and delight, the magnificent scenery, and observing the natural wealth of the country, until, on September 21, having reached the present site of Albany, he became convinced that he was following a river, and not a strait. He was everywhere received with great friendliness by the Indians; but when returning to the ocean, Hudson's mate shot an Indian for stealing, which caused an immediate collision, and several natives were killed. Hudson returned to Europe, and in consequence of his reports, trading vessels were soon sent out, and after a few years of traffic in furs, a settlement was made in 1614, on the southern point of Manhattan Island. During the Revolutionary War, the Hudson was the scene of constant activity on the part of both armies. Washington early perceived the strategic importance of the river and its dependencies, and used every means to retain possession. The British, however, in 1776, wrested Manhattan Island from our then inexperienced troops, and retained it during the war. They were unable to effect a permanent lodgment above the island, although they made several successful raids up the river, once as far as Kingston. Fortifications were erected at various commanding points along the river.

The connections by rail from points on the Hudson River are of great importance to the Northern tourist. From New York, the New York Central, Harlem, and New York & New Haven Railroads, and numerous steamboats run to the north and east, connecting with the principal routes all over Northern New York, New England and Canada. Jersey City is the terminus of the Pennsylvania, Erie, Morris & Essex, and Delaware & Lackawanna roads, besides numerous shorter roads running to the suburbs. At Nyack, the Northern Railroad of New Jersey affords a quick means of transit to Jersey City, via the Hackensack Valley. At Haverstraw is the terminus of the New York & New Jersey Railroad. At Newburg a branch of the Erie Railway touches the river, and nearly opposite, at Dutchess Junction, the Dutchess & Columbia road has its terminus. This connects with the Connecticut Western. At Rondout, the Kingston & Syracuse, and the Wallkill Valley roads run westward through the beautiful mountain region and afford convenient access to the Catskills. At Rhinebeck, nearly opposite, is the Rhinebeck & Connecticut Railroad. At Hudson, is the Hudson & Chatham branch of the Boston & Albany Railroad, which has its western terminus at Greenbush, and from Albany to the west, southwest, and north, diverge the New York Central, the Delaware & Hudson Canal Co.'s Railroads, leading, with their connections, to every point of the Empire State.

LINES OF TRAVEL ON THE HUDSON.
THE DAY LINE OF STEAMERS

Plying between New York and Albany possesses attractions and advantages which are seldom combined in one route of equal length. The whole distance is most remarkable for the beauty of its scenery, and for the evidences of commercial prosperity which greet the eye on every hand.

The boats of this line—the Albany and the well-known C. Vibbard—are probably the swiftest steamboats in the world. Built especially to meet the requirements of summer travelers on the Hudson River, these boats combine qualities of speed and comfort with facilities for viewing the glorious scenery of this world-renowned river. Ample retiring-rooms are provided for ladies or invalids, and the decks are usually broad and open, so that an unobstructed view of the scenery may be obtained from almost any part of the boat. Spacious and well ventilated dining-saloons enable the traveler to dine in comfort and luxury.

The Albany is a departure from the conventional Hudson River steamer in essential particulars, but most radically so in the fact that her long, gracefully curving hull is constructed wholly of iron, and is as fine a piece of work as ever left ship-yard. It was built by Harlan & Hollingsworth, of Wilmington, Delaware. The largest steamer thus far built for day service, her length is 295 feet, and her width 40 feet, or 75 feet at the widest point, including the wheel-houses. The engine—a ponderous one, with a 73-inch cylinder and a 12-foot stroke—works almost noiselessly, and the vessel moves without the least perceptible tremor. The three boilers are 33 feet long and 8 feet 10 inches diameter. They are placed athwartship, below deck, and each has its own smoke stack. This new feature of three smoke stacks gives the boat a peculiar appearance that distinguishes these day line steamers from all others on the river. The walls are of combined mahogany, ash and maple, with an abundance of carved work; and there are eight large private parlors for the use of parties, families, bridal excursions, or persons traveling with invalids. The dining-room is on the main deck, thus affording the tourist an opportunity of dining while enjoying the beautiful scenery of the river. The only gangway is amidships, so that passengers need not be confused as "which end the boat will land at." It is so divided that the baggage can be handled while the passengers are landing. The hurricane deck is arranged with seats and affords ample room for promenades. There will be ample accommodation on the three floors, including the upper deck, for at least 2,000 passengers, but, in a crisis, the Albany can carry all the passengers that can be crowded on board. Her draught of water is nearly a foot less than that of a wooden hull of equal dimensions. The Albany is probably the fastest steamboat afloat. On her trial trip she ran from Yonkers to New York, 16 miles, in 37 minutes and 30 seconds. She can easily run 25 miles an hour. The Chauncey Vibbard, so long a favorite on the Hudson River, has been remodeled after the pattern of the Albany, of which she is an exact counterpart, except in dimensions. On both these steamers the traveler will find everything for his convenience, and he could not be any more comfortable in his own home than on one of these beautiful steamers.

These steamers leave Pier 39, North River, foot of Vestry Street, New York, at 8:35 o'clock A. M., touching 15 minutes later at 24th Street, and reaching Albany at 6 o'clock P. M., landing at the foot of Hamilton Street, whence they start on their return trips at 8:30 o'clock A. M., reaching New York at 6 o'clock P. M. To reach the foot of Vestry Street, New York, by horse-cars, take any of the up and down lines, and request the conductor to let you off when he crosses the Grand Street crosstown line, which will land you at foot of Desbrosses Street, one block North of the Pier. To reach the foot of 24th Street, North River, take any north and south line of horse-cars and get off at 23d Street, whence the 23d Street line will take you to foot of West 23d Street, one block from the landing.

At Rondout passengers for the Overlook Mountain House and the Catskills take the Ulster & Delaware Railroad. Those wishing to reach Lake Mohonk take the Wallkill Valley Railroad.

At Albany connections for Saratoga, Lake George and points on New York Central and Delaware and Hudson Canal Co.'s R. R.

THE PEOPLE'S LINE OF STEAMERS

Runs from Pier 41, North River, foot of Canal Street, New York, to Albany, leaving New York at 6 P. M., except in winter, and arriving in Albany at about 6 A. M. the next morning. It makes no landings between the two cities. The steamers of this line, the Drew, St. John and Dean Richmond, are palatial in character, and are furnished with 200 elegant State Rooms and with ample berth accommodations for the immense travel which patronize this popular line. This route affords opportunity to view the Hudson at sunset and evening, and the scenery of this charming river on a clear moonlight night is entrancingly beautiful.

THE CITIZENS' LINE OF STEAMERS

Plies between New York and Troy, leaving Pier 49, at the foot of Le Roy Street, Hudson River, daily at 6 P. M., during the season of river navigation, and reaching Troy at about 6 A. M. the following morning, connecting with the morning trains for all points North, East and West. The boats of this line are the City of Troy and Saratoga, both new and palatial steamers supplied with an abundance of elegant State Rooms, and ample berth accommodations. It is a very popular route to Troy, Saratoga and points north, affording sunset and moonlight views of the charming Hudson, and a beautiful sail in the cool, evening hour—a delightful contrast to the heat of the midsummer day.

THE MARY POWELL

Runs from New York to Rondout, stopping at Cozzen's, West Point, Cornwall, Newburg, New Hamburgh, Milton and Poughkeepsie. She leaves New York, Pier 39, North River, every afternoon in summer, except Sunday, at 3:10, stopping at foot of West 24th Street for passengers from the upper part of the city, from which landing she departs at 3:30 P. M.; and returning, leaves Rondout at 5:30 A.M., reaching New York at 10 A.M. She is a very swift and popular steamer, and has become such a favorite as to be justly called the "Pride of the Hudson."

STEAMER DREW OF THE PEOPLE'S EVENING LINE,
Plying between New York and Albany.

PANORAMA OF THE HUDSON.

PROMINENT OBJECTS OF INTEREST THAT MAY BE SEEN FROM THE STEAMERS OF THE "DAY LINE," ON THE TRIP OF THE HUDSON FROM NEW YORK TO ALBANY.

As the steamer leaves the dock, a fine view of New York Harbor is opened to the south. Beyond the lower end of the city is Governor's Island, fortified by General Putnam prior to the battle of Long Island in 1777. The circular fort is Castle William. Beyond this may be seen The Narrows and Staten Island, and beyond these, on a clear day, the Navesink Highlands. Of the two small fortified islands farther to the westward, the nearer is Ellis Island and the farther Bedloe's Island.

In the following arrangement the objects of interest on the west bank are described in the left-hand column and those on the east bank in the right-hand column.

WEST BANK.

Jersey City, pop. 100,000; terminus of Pennsylvania R.R., Central N. J., Midland, Erie, and Northern N. J. Railroads. Cunard Steamers' docks. Opposite dock of Day Line is Erie Depot.

Bergen Heights in distance.

Hoboken, a little north, pop. 30,000; terminus of Delaware and Lackawanna R.R., Morris and Essex R. R., and Hamburg Line of Steamers.

EAST BANK.

New York City. Of the prominent church spires, the southernmost is Trinity.

North of this, in succession, and conspicuous for their height, are the Boreel Building, the Equitable Life Insurance Building, the Mutual Life Insurance Building, the Western Union Telegraph Building, the Evening Post Building, the Post Office, which may be distinguished by its large dome, the Tribune Building, recognized by its lofty, pointed clock-tower, and beyond all these the piers and cables of the East River Bridge.

NEW YORK TO TARRYTOWN.

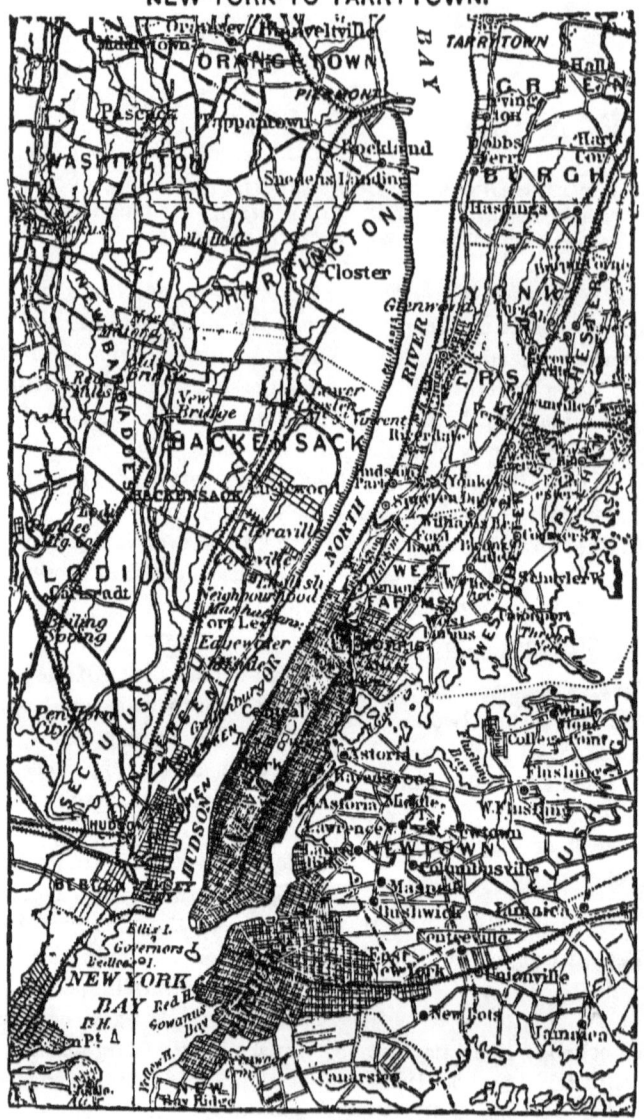

WEST BANK.

Castle Hill, just above and north of Hoboken, is the site of the Stevens' Mansion; near by, fronting on a fine public square, is the Stevens' Institute of Technology. The famous Stevens' Ironclad was constructed a few hundred yards south of this square. At this writing she still occupies her berth, but is not visible from the river.

Monastery of the Passionist Fathers on the summit of the ridge, marked by a lofty dome.

Weehawken, scene of Hamilton and Burr duel in 1804. The spot is but a few yards from the shore; a plateau, on whose edge is an old cedar where Hamilton stood on the morning of the duel.

Guttenburg, seven-story white building above Weehawken, is a brewery.

Pleasant Valley, opposite Carmansville.

. Fort Lee, ten miles from New York, opposite Deaf and Dumb Asylum. The site of the old fort is marked by a flagstaff on the bluff. Large summer hotels. Large house, residence of Capt. Bradbury of Pacific Mail S. S. line.

EAST BANK.

Other prominent buildings may be seen further up town, but to describe all of them, so that they can be recognized by a stranger, is impracticable.

Manhattan Market (34th St.), is conspicuous on the river front, a huge building with an arched roof.

St. Thomas' Church spire, 5th Ave. and 53d St.

Roosevelt Hospital, 59th St., a brick structure with many-pointed finials.

Sixty-Fifth St., New York, N. Y. Orphan Asylum.

Grain elevator of N. Y. Central Railroad.

Bloomingdale Lunatic Asylum, bet. 115th and 120th Sts.

Manhattanville, 132d St.

Iron works, Audubon Park.

Carmansville, home of Audubon the naturalist.

Old Claremont Hotel, near river.

Trinity Cemetery—above hotel.

New York Institute for Deaf and Dumb.

Jeffrey's Hook, a point jutting into the river—site of old fort. Here Washington landed, but recrossed to Fort Lee just before the heights were captured by the British in 1778.

NEW YORK TO TARRYTOWN.

WEST BANK.

The Palisades begin at Fort Lee and extend 15 miles to the north, from 200 to 500 feet in height.

Palisade Mountain Hotel, opposite Inwood. Below the hotel is a wharf, from which, by an easy grade, a fine carriage-road leads over the Palisades to Englewood, N. J.

The Palisades stretch along an unbroken wall of columnar traprock, for nearly 15 miles, varying in height from 200 to 500 feet above the river.

Indian Head, the highest point of the Palisades, 550 feet above the river.

Tappan Bay, or Tappan Zee, extending north 15 miles to Croton Point, nearly four miles wide.

Piermont, twenty-four miles from New York; formerly terminus of Erie Railway. Pier one mile long, extending into river. Palisade formation terminates here. Boundary between New York and N. J. just at end of Palisades.

Nyack. Pop. 4,000. Ramapo Mountains in distance.

EAST BANK.

Washington Heights, 185th St.

Fort Washington, 10 miles from New York. Site near James Gordon Bennett's residence, with gilded dome.

Inwood, once known as Tubby Hook.

Spuyten Duyvil Creek, or Harlem River. Main line of Hudson River R. R. diverges from river through cut to Grand Central Depot, 42d St., New York. Pump tower at High Bridge visible over the hills.

Westchester Heights, site of old Ft. Independence.

Riverdale, 14 miles from N. Y.

Convent and Academy of Mount St. Vincent, with Font Hill in front, built by Edwin Forrest.

Yonkers, 17 miles from New York. Pop. 20,000. Site of old Phillipse mansion.

Spring Hill Grove.

Dudley's Grove above.

Hastings-on-the-Hudson, 21 miles from New York. Sugar refinery near river.

Dobbs' Ferry, 22 miles from New York.

Irvington, 24 miles from N. Y.

WEST BANK.

Upper Nyack, one mile above Nyack.

Rockland Lake, among the hills, opposite Sing Sing. Source of Hackensack River, and great ice-quarry in winter. It is 150 feet above the river. Hook Mt. which separates it from the river is 610 feet high. The point which abuts on the river is Verdritege Hook, or, as the river men call it, "Point no Point."

Haverstraw Bay, five miles wide—the widest part of the Hudson, extending from Croton Point on the south to Verplanck's Point on the north.

High Torn Mountain—a peak below Haverstraw (820 ft. high).

Haverstraw Village, with two miles of brick-yards.

Treason Hill, north of Haverstraw, where Arnold met André at Joshua Hett Smith's.

Grassy Point, two miles north of Haverstraw.

Stony Point, one mile north of Grassy Point. Stormed by the Americans under Gen. Antony Wayne, July 15, 1779.

Tompkins Cove—with lime-kilns and quarry.

Kidd's Point, now Caldwell's Landing.

EAST BANK.

Sunnyside, home of Washington Irving, half a mile north of R.R. Station, scarcely visible through the trees, near the river. Residence of Bierstadt, the artist, on the heights above.

Tarrytown, 29 miles from N. Y. Pop. 5,000. Steamer stops beside ferryboat in middle of the river, transferring passengers for both Tarrytown and Nyack.

Sing Sing, 30 miles from New York. Pop. 3,000.

State Prison, near the river, south of the village, built of white marble.

Croton River empties into Hudson one mile north of Sing Sing.

Croton Point, just above Croton River—junction of Tappan Bay and Haverstraw Bay.

Teller's Point. Off this point the Vulture anchored when she brought André to meet Arnold.

Croton Village above.

Montrasse's Point.

Verplanck's Point.

King's Ferry before Revolution—between these two points half a mile.

Manito Mountain.

Peekskill. Pop. 6,000. 43 miles from New York.

TARRYTOWN TO NEWBURCH.

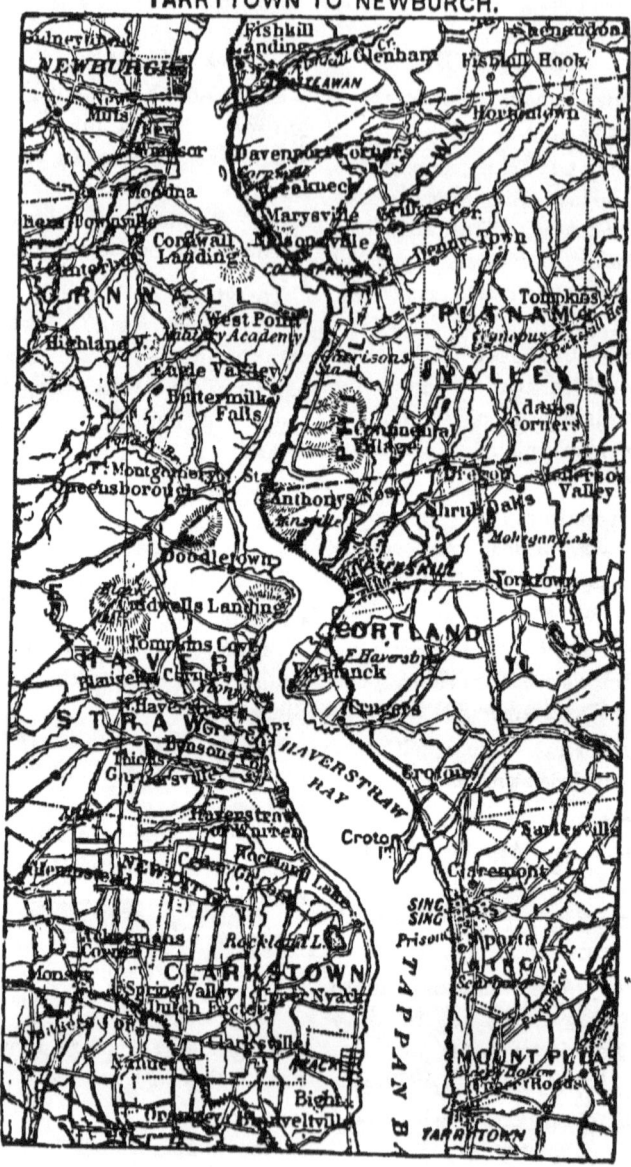

WEST BANK.

Donderberg Mountain, 1,098 feet high.

Iona Island—with hotel and picnic grounds.

Fort Montgomery Creek, opposite Anthony's Nose.

Fort Clinton south side creek.

Fort Montgomery on north side.

Parry House—with ruins of old mill in front.

Benny Haven's cottage at waterside.

Buttermilk Falls, cascade above.

Cozzen's Hotel, 250 ft. above river, the most fashionable resort on the river.

Highland Falls—village behind bluff. Population, 1,500.

Cozzen's Landing.

West Point, one mile above Cozzen's, U. S. Military Academy, Parade Ground, and Barracks. The most commanding strategic point of the Hudson during the Revolution.

Old Fort Putnam—ruins of the Revolution—596 feet above river.

Kosciusko's Monument, above West Point Landing, on the point.

West Point Lighthouse.

West Point Hotel on the bluff.

West Point Village.

EAST BANK.

Nameless Highland.

The Race, between Iona Island and the east bank of river.

Anthony's Nose, 1,220 feet high, with R. R. tunnel near river.

Sugar Loaf Mountain toward north-east.

Beverly Dock, close by river.

Robinson House.

Hon. Hamilton Fish's residence, brick house on the bluff.

Garrison's, 50 miles from New York, opposite West Point.

Highland House, half a mile from river, splendid site.

Constitution Island, opposite point.

Miss Warner's home, White Cottage, near the river. Author of "Queechy" and "Wide, Wide World."

The Two Brothers—rocks.

Cold Spring, 54 miles from New York, with extensive iron foundries.

Undercliff, home of George P. Morris, just north of Cold Spring.

Mount Taurus, 1,486 ft. high.

Little Stony Point, promontory at foot of Bull Hill.

NEWBURG AND FISHKILL TO RHINEBECK.

WEST BANK.

Old Cro' Nest, 1,418 ft. high.

Kidd's Plug Cliff—the precipice on bank of river.

Butter Hill.

Storm King, 1,529 feet high—northernmost point of the Highlands.

Cornwall Village, 56 miles from N. Y.

Idlewild, home of N. P. Willis, just north of Cornwall Village.

Shawangunk Mountains west.

New Windsor, four miles north of Cornwall. Hendrick Hudson anchored here Sept. 15, 1609.

Newburg Bay.

Washington's Headquarters—a flagstaff marks the location.

Newburg City, pop. 15,000, 60 miles from New York.

Duyvels Dans Kamer—flat rock covered with cedars—scene of the traditionary Indian pow-wow which Hendrick Hudson and his comrades witnessed at night, with all its Indian accessories of fire and paint.

Hampton Point—with fine white cedars—64 miles from New York.

Marlborough, 66 miles from New York. The Arbor Vitæ grows in great perfection here.

EAST BANK.

Breakneck Mountain, 1,187 feet high.

South Beacon Hill, 1,685 feet high.

North Beacon Hill, 1,471 feet high.

Pollipel's Island, at the north entrance of the Highlands.

Dutchess and Columbia R.R. Junction.

Fishkill Mountains to the east.

Fishkill Landing, 60 miles from New York.

Clinton Point.

Low Point, or Carthage, 64 miles from New York.

New Hamburg, 66 miles from New York, at the mouth of Wappinger's Creek.

Locust Point, country seat of the late Prof. S. F. B. Morse, inventor of electric telegraph.

Poughkeepsie Cemetery.

Ruins of Old Livingston Place just above.

City of Poughkeepsie, population 20,000, 75 miles from New York—Queen City of the Hudson, 200 feet above river.

River View Military Academy—brick building, on commanding site.

Vassar Female College is a mile and a half east of Poughkeepsie.

NEWBURG AND FISHKILL TO RHINEBECK.

HUDSON RIVER ROUTE.

WEST BANK.

Milton Ferry, or Barnegat, 71 miles from New York. Famous for the great quantity of raspberries raised in the vicinity.

New Paltz Landing, opposite Poughkeepsie, 75 miles from New York.

Large Ice Houses on the river bank.

John Astor's summer residence.

Mr. Pell's great apple orchard, with 25,000 fruit-bearing trees.

Port Ewen, or Deserted Village.

Rondout, pop. 20,000. Now City of Kingston. Point of departure from Hudson River for Southern Catskills. Terminus of Ulster & Delaware R. R., Walkill Valley R.R., and Delaware & Hudson Canal. Extensive cement works here.

Glasgo.

Saugerties, pop. 5,000, at mouth of Esopus Creek.

Malden — with "Plattekill Clove" west.

Evesport, above Malden.

West Camp Island.

EAST BANK.

College Hill, north-east of city.

Poughkeepsie Water Works, in north part of the city, near river.

Hyde Park, 80 miles from New York. Named in honor of Gen. Edward F. Hyde, one of the early British Governors of New York.

Placentia, former home of the late James K. Paulding, one mile north of Hyde Park.

Dr. Hussack's estate, with Corinthian pillars.

Esopus Island, 2 miles north of Hyde Park.

Staatsburg, 85 miles from New York.

"Wildercliff," built by Rev. Freeborn Garrettson.

Rhine Cliff, 90 miles from New York—with

Rhinebeck Village two miles east.

Barrytown, 96 miles from New York.

Rokeby, residence of William B. Astor.

Montgomery Place, one mile north of Barrytown, built by the widow of Gen. Richard Montgomery, who was killed at the storming of Quebec in 1775.

Cruger's Island, two miles north of Barrytown, with ruins brought from Italy.

RHINEBECK TO HUDSON.

WEST BANK.

"Four-County Island," junction of Dutchess, Columbia, Greene, and Ulster counties.

Catskill Mountains, 4,000 feet above the sea. Indian name, "Onti Ora," or "Mountains of the Sky."

Round Top, the highest peak of the Catskills, 4,000 feet above the river.

Catskill Mountain House, white building on the mountain, 3,000 feet above the river.

Catskill Village, 111 miles from New York. Pop. 4,000. Steam ferry connects with Catskill Station, three minutes in crossing.

Prospect Park Hotel, on bluff near the landing, 250 feet above the river.

Residence of John Breasted, Esq., second house north of hotel.

Athens, opp. Hudson. N. Y. Central R.R. Depot for freight near river, north of village.

Four-Mile Point, 125 feet high.

Coxsackie, pop. 2,500, 123 miles from New York.

EAST BANK.

Tivoli, 100 miles from N. Y.

Place where first steamboat, the Claremont, was built by R. Fulton.

"Claremont," original Livingston Manor.

Germantown, 105 miles from New York.

Livingston, 109 miles from New York.

Catskill Station.

Church, the artist, has a fine residence on the high point opposite Catskill.

Residence of John E. Gillette, Esq., nearer the river.

Roger's Island, behind which the shipping of the New York merchants was concealed during the Revolution.

Mount Merino, two miles above, just south of the

City of Hudson, 115 miles from New York, pop. 10,000. Extensive Iron Works near river. The Hudson & Chatham R.R. terminates here.

Stockport, four miles north of Hudson.

HUDSON TO ALBANY.

WEST BANK.

New Baltimore—here begins the government dykes.

Beeren, or Bear Island—meeting-point of the four counties of Albany, Rensselaer, Columbia, and Greene—site of the "Castle of Rensselaerstein," from whose wall Nicholas Kroon, the agent of Killian Van Rensselaer, the Patroon, compelled passing vessels to dip their colors and pay tribute, or take the chances of being sunk by the ordnance of the fort.

Coeyman's, Helderberg Mountains to the west.

Shad Island, north of Coeyman's, three miles long—old Indian fishing ground.

Albany, 144 miles from New York. Pop. 70,000. Toward the south we see the buildings of the Convent of the Sacred Heart, Almshouse, and further north the Cathedral, State House, City Hall, etc. Two extensive railroad bridges cross the river at this place. Both are over 4,000 feet in length.

Principal hotels are the Delevan and Stanwix Hall.

EAST BANK.

Newtown Hook and Prospect Grove.

Stuyvesant, formerly Kinderhook Landing.

Schodac Island, 8 miles long.

Schodac Village, opposite Coeyman's.

Nine-Mile Tree.

Castleton, 135 miles from New York.

Overslaugh, or Castleton Bar, extends about two miles up the river.

Campbell's Island, with light on the south end.

Greenbush, or East Albany, connected with Albany by two fine railroad bridges.

Troy, six miles above Greenbush, 150 miles from New York. Population, 50,000. Extensive iron works just south of the city.

Seat of Rensselaer Polytechnic Institute.

Large building on the hill, with four pointed towers, is a Roman Catholic institution.

At Albany we leave the steamer and take the Rensselaer and Saratoga R. R. for Saratoga Springs. An omnibus conveys passengers to the railroad depot.

ALBANY AND TROY TO SARATOGA.

THE HUDSON RIVER ROUTE.

JERSEY CITY AND HOBOKEN.

As the steamer leaves her wharf and turns her head to the north, Jersey City and Hoboken are seen to the westward. The limit of the latter place is marked by a rocky promontory known as Castle Hill, on which stands the mansion of the Stevens family. In the vicinity of Hoboken are many elegant residences of wealthy New Yorkers, but the rapid increase of population is fast depriving them of the almost rural seclusion which they have until recently enjoyed, and the ornamental grounds which for a long time beautified the ridge back of the town are cut up into city lots. On the east side of the river is New York, with its apparently interminable line of wharves and rows of warehouses, stretching northward as far as the eye can reach, and ending in a forest of masts toward the south, beyond which are the gray walls of Castle William on Governor's Island, and still further the waters of New York Bay, the Narrows, and Staten Island. The scene is always full of life and variety, and at certain times when wind and tide are favorable, the waters are alive with craft of all sizes, making for their various destinations all over the world, and seemingly in constant danger of collision.

WEEHAWKEN.

North Bergen, Bergen Co., N. J.

Between Hoboken and Weehawken are the Elysian Fields, formerly a beautiful park, but now retaining few traces of the rural walks which once made it a favorite resort of New Yorkers. It continues to be visited by large numbers of pleasure-seekers, but the attractions are mainly such as are afforded by base-ball matches, boat races, and other athletic sports. The Indian name was Weehawk, but custom has added the termination now invariably affixed. The scene of the duel between Alexander Hamilton and Aaron Burr is in Weehawken. The spot was formerly marked by a monument, but some reckless person destroyed it. It is a green plateau raised a few feet above the river just below the precipitous cliff that marks the southern end of the Palisades, or "Great Chip-Rock" as it was called by the Dutch. It is a short distance above the point where a steep bank approaches the shore of the river. The fatal quarrel between these two prominent men was a political one, and was marked by great malignity on the part of Burr, who took deadly aim, notwithstanding Hamilton's avowed purpose—which he carried out—of not returning his fire. Hamilton received a wound which proved fatal in a few days, and Burr was from that time almost ostracized, owing to the indignation of the public at what was esteemed a cold-blooded murder.

MANHATTANVILLE

is a part of New York. The name is applied to the neighborhood of 132d Street. The conspicuous building on high ground, a little south of Manhattanville, is the Lunatic Asylum. It is surrounded by about forty acres of ornamental grounds, which are devoted to the use of the inmates of the Asylum. Nearer the river is the Claremont Hotel, where in former years lived Viscount Courtenay, afterward Earl of Devon. Joseph Bonaparte occupied the house during the first year of his exile in this country. It is now a popular resort for frequenters of the Bloomingdale Road.

CARMANSVILLE.

At 152d Street is another suburb of New York, and, being further from the city, contains more of the elements of a rural district. The distinguished naturalist Audubon lived here for many years, and is buried in Trinity Cemetery near by. The large building surmounted by a dome a little above Carmansville is the New York Institution for the Deaf and Dumb. It stands on the southern slope of Washington Heights, commanding a wide view, and surrounded by spacious and cultivated grounds. The buildings are in the form of a quadrangle, and are capable of accommodating 450 pupils. The institution is the oldest of its kind in the country, excepting that at Hartford, Conn. It was incorporated April 15, 1817.

FORT WASHINGTON.

10 miles from New York.

That portion of Manhattan Island known by the name of Washington Heights is the only part which retains, to any great degree, the natural attractions which formerly rendered the whole island so beautiful. The grading and leveling of city engineers has not yet reached this charming region, although it is penetrated by streets in every direction, and contains elegant residences throughout its whole extent. The fortification after which this place is named was an extensive earthwork occupying the crown of Washington Heights, and commanding the river above and below, as well as the neighboring country. It formed the end and citadel of an irregular line of works extending along the northern part of the island. The point extending into the river under Washington Heights is Jeffrey's Hook, and among its cedars are mounds which mark the site of a redoubt built at the same time with the neighboring fortifications. These works, with their garrison of 2,700 men, were captured by the British after a sharp resistance, on Nov. 15, 1776. This was the second defeat of the Americans in New York, and was a severe blow to the friends of the republic in this vicinity.

FORT LEE.

Hackensack, Bergen Co., N. J., 10 m. fr. New York.

The traveler is now opposite the lower end of the Palisades, which stretch in an unbroken wall of columnar trap rock for 15 miles along the river. These rocks vary in height from 300 to 500 feet above the water, and are crowned by a heavy growth of timber. Houses are already beginning to be erected along the edge of this cliff, which commands a wide and beautiful view of the river and its shores, including Manhattan Island and the East River to Long Island Sound. Doubtless before many years a continuous line of villas will crown the top of this remarkable ridge. Fort Lee stood on the summit of the ridge at its southern extremity. A little village now occupies its site, and large hotels for the entertainment of excursion parties rise one above another on the slope of the declivity. The remains of the fort are scarcely discernible, and cannot be seen at all from the river. This fort was occupied by the Americans until after the British had captured Fort Washington in 1776, when it also was abandoned, and the Americans retreated across the State of New Jersey.

The large white building with two towers, standing in the gorge at the beginning of the Palisades, is the Fort Lee Park Hotel. The large octagon building at the base of hill is a Pavilion. The building on dock is a large waiting-room for the accommodation of daily excursionists who frequent the popular resort by a line of boats running from Canal, 24th, and 34th Streets, New York, and ferry from Manhattanville, 125th Street. The hotels, steamboats, and Manhattanville ferry are all owned and managed under the head of the Fort Lee Park and Steamboat Company, with George L. Huggins, of the Cosmopolitan of New York, as proprietor of the hotel.

SPUYTEN DUYVIL.
New York City and Co., 12 m. fr. New York.

The cluster of houses on the upper side of the creek whose mouth is here seen, is known as Spuyten Duyvil, but the name was originally applied only to the creek itself, which connects Harlem River with the Hudson, thereby forming Manhattan Island. Through this estuary tide-water flows, the currents meeting at or near Kingsbridge, about a mile from the Hudson. Here the main line of the Hudson River Railroad strikes the shore of the river, curving sharply through a deep rock-cutting, just north of the bridge. The branch which crosses the bridge is used mostly for freight, but has also a passenger station at 31st Street. The main passenger terminus is at the Grand Central Depot at 42d Street and Fourth Avenue. The name Spuyten Duyvil is ascribed by the veracious Diedrich Knickerbocker (Washington Irving), to Anthony Van Corlear, the redoubtable Dutch trumpeter, who, being bound on an important mission to the mainland, and finding himself unable to procure a boat, swore that "en spuyt den duyvil" he would swim the creek. He plunged in, and when midway across was observed to struggle violently, until no longer able to resist the Duyvil, who was doubtless tugging at his legs, he raised his trumpet to his lips, gave a loud blast, and sank forever to the bottom. However it obtained its name, the vicinity is interesting. The creek formed the southern boundary of the famous neutral ground of revolutionary times, where the regular troops of the American and British armies were continually making raids. At Kingsbridge, redoubts were thrown up on both

THE PALISADES.

sides of the creek, and on December 19, 1780, an encounter took place between the Americans and a large detachment of British and Hessians, which led to no decisive result. Another skirmish occurred here in 1776, between a party of American stragglers and a Hessian guard, in which the former gained the advantage. Prior to these events, Hendrick Hudson and the Manhattan Indians had a long sustained fight just at the mouth of the creek, where Hudson anchored the "Half-Moon," in October, 1609. The Indians tried to board the yacht from their canoes, but were repulsed.

PALISADES MOUNTAIN HOUSE.
Englewood, Bergen Co., N. J.

Opposite Spuyten Duyvil is Lydecker Peak, one of the highest points of the Palisades, which projects somewhat into the river. Upon this peak stands the magnificent Palisades Mountain House, in full view from the railroad and river. It is one of the finest summer hotels on the Hudson, and owing to the charming scenery it commands, the beautiful drives about it, its nearness to New York, its ease of access, and the superb style in which it is kept, it is a very popular resort for New Yorkers. It is reached by steamboats from Harrison Street, New York, to the dock at the foot of the Palisades, or from 30th Street depot to Inwood, on the Hudson River Railroad, whence a steam ferry crosses the river, or by Northern N. J. R.R., from Chambers Street and W. 23d Street, to Englewood, N. J.

RIVERDALE.
New York City and Co., 14 m. fr. City Hall.

This village is composed almost entirely of the country residences of gentlemen doing business in New York. About a mile and a half above Riverdale is Mt. St. Vincent, a Roman Catholic educational institution, under the immediate control of the Sisters of Charity, who purchased Font Hill, as the place was called, from the celebrated tragedian, Edwin Forrest. The castellated structure of dark stone, built by Forrest as a private residence, is now part of the Mt. St. Vincent Academy, though, unfortunately, the two buildings are architecturally inharmonious.

PALISADES MOUNTAIN HOUSE, ENGLEWOOD, N. J.
On the Hudson River opposite Spuyten Duyvil.

YONKERS.

Westchester Co., N. Y., 17 *m. fr. New York.*

Yonkers is a flourishing town at the mouth of the Neperah or Saw-Mill River. The former name was given by the Indians, and signifies "rapid-water village," aptly describing the series of falls and rapids with which the stream joins the Hudson. The town is largely composed of the residences of city business men. Hendrick Hudson anchored off Yonkers when ascending the river in September, 1609, and was visited by large numbers of Indians with whom he traded. In the evening the tide set strongly up stream, which confirmed Hudson in the belief that he was in a passage between two oceans. The name Yonkers is derived from the Dutch "Yonk-heer," signifying the heir of a family. The greater part of this region was purchased from the Van der Donck family, to whom it was originally granted by Frederick Philipse.

The old "Philipse Manor" still exists, and is a most attractive object for those interested in relics of the olden time. The manor stands within the town of Yonkers. The older portion was built in 1682, and the more modern portion in 1745. It is probably the finest specimen of an old-fashioned mansion in the country. The interior decorations have been scrupulously preserved, and are very quaint and curious. In this old Hall was born Mary Philipse, the belle of her day and the early love of Washington. She chose to marry another, Roger Morris; but it is said that Washington always cherished the memory of the beautiful heiress of Philipse Manor.

HASTINGS.

Greenburg, Westchester Co., N. Y., 21 *m. fr. New York.*

About midway between Yonkers and Hastings, on the opposite side of the River, is the highest point of the Palisades, nearly 500 feet above the river. It is known as "Indian Head," and from it may be obtained a wide view over the neighboring country. Hastings is similar in its characteristics to Yonkers, and contains many beautiful country-seats. It is said to have been a favorite resort of Garibaldi's when the Liberator of Italy kept a soap and candle factory on Staten Island. The country in the vicinity is diversified, and intersected by excellent roads, which render the rides and drives in every direction most attractive. A British force, under Cornwallis, crossed the river at this place in 1776, joined another force in capturing Fort Lee, and then pursued the Americans to the Delaware River.

DOBBS' FERRY.

Greenburg, Westchester Co., N. Y., 22 m. fr. New York.

A village of considerable size, containing villas and cottages of tasteful and elegant appearance. The village is named after a ferry which was kept in olden times between this place and Piermont, opposite, by one Dobbs, a Swede. An attempt was made some years since to have this name changed to "Paulding," as being both more euphonious and appropriate. The proposition led to quite a controversy in the newspapers; but public opinion decided, for the time at least, in favor of the old Swedish ferryman. The river here widens into Tappan Bay, or as it was called by the Dutch, Tappan Zee. This bay extends to Croton Point, having an average width of nearly four miles. Dobbs' Ferry is well known in Revolutionary annals. The British concentrated their forces here after their dearly-bought victory at White Plains, five miles east. This battle took place in October, 1776. In 1777 a division of the American army, under General Lincoln, was encamped here for several months. The Commission sent by Sir Henry Clinton to intercede for the life of the unfortunate spy, Major André, landed here and held a long but unsuccessful consultation with General Greene, the president of the court which condemned him to death. Greene met the Chief of the Commission by permission of General Washington, only in the character of a private gentleman; but although both friend and foe desired to save André's life, the conference proved unavailing. Dobbs' Ferry was the first place appointed for a meeting between André and Arnold. The plan, however, was not successfully carried out.

PIERMONT.

Orangetown, Rockland Co., N. Y., 24 m. fr. New York.

A short distance below Piermont is the line between New York and New Jersey, near which the Palisades recede from the shore and lose their precipitous character. The ridge continues, however, in a series of hills reaching, in some places, a height of nearly 700 feet, but nowhere resuming the peculiar palisade formation. The long pier which projects into the river from this place is the terminus of a branch of the Erie Railway, which connects with the main line at Suffern, 18 miles west. Two miles back of Piermont is Tappan, where, on October 2, 1780, Major André was tried, condemned, and executed. (See page 29.) We may here call attention to the beautiful "Arbor Vitæ" (Thuja Occidentalis), which is frequently seen, singly or in groves, along the banks. It is, in fact, the common white cedar, which in this vicinity assumes a beautiful pencil-like habit of growth, and forms a distinctive feature of the landscape.

IRVINGTON.
Greenburg, Westchester County, N. Y., 24 m. fr. New York.

Is a village of comparatively recent growth, inhabited, in great part, by the families of gentlemen whose place of business is in New York. The river is here about three miles wide, and the sloping hills that look over this tranquil bay are literally covered with beautiful villas and charming grounds. At no point on the Hudson are there more evidences of wealth and refinement, and this locality around Irvington is noted as one of the most aristocratic suburbs of the great metropolis. Many of these palatial structures are furnished with the choicest that art and wealth can produce, and are the abodes of luxury, culture, and the most exquisite taste. The village is named in honor of Washington Irving, the genial author whose pen has done so much to preserve whatever is interesting in the traditional history of the Hudson River. "Sunnyside," the home of Irving during the last years of his life, is a little north of the village, and glimpses of the picturesque house and grounds may be caught from the steamer as it passes. This house, with its quaint Dutch gables, includes the original building known to readers of Irving's works as "Wolfert's Roost," where Ichabod Crane courted the lovely Katrina Van Tassel, as related in the "Legend of Sleepy Hollow." Irving died November 28, 1859, and was buried in the cemetery near Tarrytown, in that very "Sleepy Hollow" which his graceful pen has made forever famous.

TARRYTOWN.

Greenburg and Mt. Pleasant, Westchester Co., N. Y., 29 m. fr. New York.

Tarrytown is delightfully situated on a hillside overlooking the river and the Palisades to the southward, and commanding a distant view of the Ramapo Mountains and the Hudson Highlands to the west and north. The whole town is thickly studded with dwellings of every size and every style of beauty. Prominent among these is the white marble edifice known as Paulding Manor, which stands just below the town. It was built by descendants of Commodore Paulding, and is one of the finest specimens of the Elizabethan style of architecture in this country. It has passed out of the possession of the Paulding family. A little above Tarrytown is the Pocantico, a small stream flowing through the valley, called by the Dutch "Slaeperigh Haven," and translated into English as "Sleepy Hollow." About half a mile from the mouth of this stream is an old Dutch church, which is a curiosity in its way. It is the oldest church edifice in the State of New York, having been built in 1699. Its walls contain bricks which were imported from Holland when the church was erected. The old bell hangs in the belfry, on whose pointed roof an iron vane still turns, bearing the monogram of the founder of the church, Frederick Philipse, whose mansion, known as "Philipse Castle," stands on the banks of the stream not far distant. This is the dwelling whence the Philipse family moved when the mansion at Yonkers was built. To the eastward of the church is the valley of Sleepy Hollow, and the identical bridge, or at least its successor, over which the Headless Hessian pursued Ichabod Crane, as related by Irving in the "Legend of Sleepy Hollow." Between this bridge and Tarrytown the road crosses "André's Brook," and near by stands a monument marking the spot where he was captured. A suitable inscription gives the leading facts connected with that event.

ANDRÉ AND ARNOLD.

The story of Arnold's treason and of André's capture and execution is one of the most interesting and at the same time one of the saddest in our history. Benedict Arnold was a major-general in the American army, having won his position by distinguished gallantry and zeal. It is not necessary here to trace the successive steps which led to his fall. Suffice it to say that certain acts of his while in command at Philadelphia led to his trial by court-martial. He was sentenced to be reprimanded, but the sentence, mild as it was, embittered him toward his country, and he began to take steps toward opening a correspondence with the enemy. Assigned to the command of West Point and vicinity, he soon began negotiations for surrender to Sir Henry Clinton. Finally arrangements were made for a meeting with Major John André, Adjutant-General of the British army. The British sloop of war "Vulture" was sent up to Teller's Point with André on board. On the second night he landed on the west side of the river, just below Stony Point, and meeting Arnold consulted with him until daylight. Their plans were incomplete when day broke, and Arnold persuaded his companion to go with him to a tory house near by. Horses were at hand, provided, and the two rode together through the dark woods. Presently they were challenged by a sentry, and then André perceived that he was within the enemy's line. They went on, however, and entered the house. As soon as daylight was sufficiently clear, an American gun opened fire on the "Vulture" from Teller's Point, and the vessel weighed anchor and dropped down the river. André was in uniform, but in order to provide against discovery he put on a plain coat, and by this act assumed the disguise which deprived him of his official character, and rendered him open to conviction as a spy. In the course of the day plans for the surrender of the garrisons about West Point were completed, and André became anxious to regain the British lines. Being unable to get a boat to take him down to the "Vulture," he was forced to take the land route. Accordingly he crossed King's Ferry, and on the strength of Arnold's passes passed all the regular American outposts. On this particular morning, however, three volunteers had agreed to watch the road at Tarrytown, and on André's appearance halted him, and made him dismount, and discovered inside his stockings the evidences of his mission. André offered bribes to a large amount if they would let him go, but the stern patriots refused, and marched him off to the nearest American post. The commanding officer, Colonel Jamieson, was very near sending prisoner, papers, and all to Arnold, but Major Tallmadge persuaded him to send only a letter detailing the circumstances of the arrest. This Arnold received while at breakfast. He immediately left the table, ordered his horse, saying that he was wanted down the river, rode to Beverly Dock (see page 37), and leaping into a boat went down the river to the "Vulture."

André at once wrote to Washington, frankly telling the whole truth, and closing with the words "Thus was I betrayed (being Adjutant-General of the B. army) into the vile condition of an enemy in disguise within your posts." Washington convened a court, which tried André at Tappan. The accused so freely admitted all the charges and specifications, that it was not necessary to examine a single witness, and the court, after long deliberation, reluctantly sentenced him to death. Much sympathy was felt for André throughout the American camp, but every one acknowledged that under the circumstances no leniency should be shown. An informal proposition was made to exchange him for Arnold, but neither Washington nor Sir Henry Clinton would officially consider this plan, and on October 2, 1780, André was hung. In 1832 his remains were removed to England, and a monument stands in Westminster Abbey on which the sad story is inscribed. Arnold was made a Major-General in the British army, and received £10,000, the price of his treason, but was despised even by his brother officers, and died with hardly a friend to mourn his loss. Monuments have been erected to the memory of Paulding and Van Wart, two of the men engaged in André's capture at Peekskill and Tarrytown. In 1878 the Rev. Arthur Penrhyn Stanley, Dean of Westminster, visited this country, and secured permission to have a stone, bearing a suitable inscription, raised to André's memory on the place of his execution.

NYACK.

Orangetown, Rockland Co., N. Y., 27 m. fr. New York.

Nearly opposite Tarrytown, at the foot of a precipitous hill. On the western side of the Tappan Zee the mountains sweep back from Piermont in the form of a semicircle, and meet the river again at the northern extremity of the Zee, in a series of bluffs familiarly known as the Hook, almost as imposing as the Rock of Gibraltar, which it strongly resembles in outline and general appearance. Within this semicircle—one of the loveliest spots on the river—nestles the village of Nyack, which is rapidly growing into a large suburban town. The Rip Van Winkle sleep which seems to have possessed this part of the western shore of the river from time immemorial, has been very properly disturbed by the extension of the Northern Railway to Nyack, and now all is bustle and activity. Looking out from the promontory which extends into the "Zee," on a point nearly central between Piermont and the Hook, is the Tappan Zee Hotel.

SING SING.

Ossining, Westchester Co., N. Y., 32 m. fr. New York.

This town is on the east bank, and a large part of its houses command an extensive view down the river. Sing Sing is generally known as the site of the State Prison, to which most of the convicts of New York City are sent. The white prison buildings will be readily recognized at the lower end of the town. The marble of which these buildings are constructed is the kind known as dolomite. It is quarried near by, and the prisons have been built by the convicts themselves. The main building was ready for occupation in 1829, but has received improvements and additions since. In connection with the prison, the name of Capt. Elam Lynds should not be forgotten. This officer took charge of a party of one hundred convicts at Auburn, brought them to Sing Sing (there were no railroads in those days), and set them to work to wall themselves in, which in due time was accomplished, and thus Sing Sing prison was begun. Capt. Lynds was a natural disciplinarian, and is said to have brought the hundred men from Auburn with the aid of only a few guards. Opposite

Sing Sing is a high hill, projecting somewhat into the river. This is known by its old Dutch name of "Verdritege Hook." The name signifies "grievous," and was given in consequence of the frequent squalls which beset the sailor in this neighborhood. "Rockland Lake" lies on one of the shoulders of this mountain. This lake is about half a mile from the river, and 300 feet above it. Large quantities of ice are cut from its surface every winter. The slide by which the ice is sent down to be loaded on barges may be seen near the landing, leading straight up the hillside to the lake shore. The peculiar sharp pointed peak near by is known as the "High Torn."

TELLER'S AND CROTON POINTS.

Cortland, Westchester Co., N. Y., 36 m. fr. New York.

The extremity of this tongue of land, projecting far into the river from its eastern bank, is known as "Teller's Point." "Croton Point" is that portion nearer the shore of the river. It separates Tappan Bay from Haverstraw Bay. Off this point the "Vulture" anchored when she brought André to meet Arnold, and from thence the gun was brought to bear which drove that vessel down the river. Croton Point is now occupied by the vineyards of Dr. Underhill, whose pure wines are much used for medicinal purposes. Just below Teller's Point is the mouth of Croton River, which supplies New York with water. This stream has a wide mouth, sometimes called Croton Bay, which was partly filled up in 1841 by the washing away of the Croton Reservoir dam. The work was, however, pressed forward, and in 1842 water was supplied to the city through the Croton pipes. The aqueduct is built of solid masonry, and follows the course of the Hudson at an average distance of about a mile from its shore. This aqueduct is capable of discharging 60,000,000 gallons per day into the receiving reservoir in the Central Park, New York. The entire cost of the Croton works at their completion was about $14,000,-000. Since that time great improvements and additions have been made, to meet the demands of the growing city. It is estimated that the Croton River will supply water enough for New York even if the city should reach five times its present size.

HAVERSTRAW.

Haverstraw, Rockland Co., N. Y., 36 *m. fr. New York.*

For a few miles below Haverstraw, the summits of the Highlands are distinctly in sight, up the river, although their bases are hidden by intervening hills. The long ridge-like elevation, toward which the boat heads, is the "Donderberg," near 1,000 feet in height. Haverstraw is the village seen on a high bank, or plateau, on the west side of the river, which above Croton Point spreads out into the wide and beautiful expanse known as "Haverstraw Bay." Extensive brick kilns line the river bank.

VERPLANCK'S POINT AND STONY POINT.
38 *m. fr. New York.*

These two points mark the upper end of Haverstraw Bay. "Stony Point" is on the west side of the river, a bold rocky eminence, having a lighthouse on its summit. Opposite, on the east side of the river, is "Verplanck's Point," which may be recognized by several large brick-making establishments, with their kilns and drying-houses. Just below Stony Point is "Grassy Point," and opposite to it "Montrasse's Point." Between Stony and Verplanck's Point the river is only half a mile wide, which fact, together with the commanding positions afforded by the neighboring hills, rendered this an important pass during the Revolutionary War. Long previous to that war a ferry was established here known as "King's Ferry," forming an important avenue of communication between the Eastern and Middle States. The importance of the Hudson River as a base of operations and as a natural boundary was early recognized by Washington, and here, as at Washington Heights, fortifications were erected commanding the river. A short distance southwest of Stony Point is Treason Hill, whereon stands Smith's house, in which André and Arnold completed their scheme for the surrender of West Point, and whence André started to cross King's Ferry, on his fatal journey toward New York. North of Stony Point a high limestone cliff rises from near the water's edge. At its foot are the "Tompkins Lime Kilns," looking like a stone fortress with arched casemates. These quarries have been worked for many years, and vast quantities of slaked lime are annually shipped to market. Besides the lime, between 30,000 and 40,000 tons of gravel, too coarse for slaking, are used for roads in the Central Park, New York, and other public highways in the vicinity.

THE CAPTURE OF STONY POINT.

The forts located at Stony Point were held by the Americans until June 1, 1779, when they were simultaneously invested by a British force commanded by Sir Henry Clinton. No direct attack was made on Fort Lafayette, the work on Verplanck's Point, until after the evacuation of Stony Point. The garrison at the latter place numbered only 40 men, and abandoned the work on the approach of an overwhelming force of the British, who quietly took possession, ran up the cross of St. George on the flagstaff, and opened fire on Fort Lafayette with the captured guns. At the same time Gen. Vaughan attacked on the east side of the river, and the weak garrison of 70 men was soon forced to surrender. The loss of this position was a severe blow to the Americans, compelling them to make a wide détour in order to keep up their communications. General Anthony Wayne at once requested and obtained permission to storm Stony Point, and at midnight on the 15th of July, 1779, led two columns of picked men to the assault. They advanced undiscovered until they were close upon the British picket, which of course gave the alarm, and the garrison turned out. The parapet was manned, and a scathing fire of grape and musketry swept the hillside; but "Mad Anthony" was at the head of his column, and, within half an hour after the first shot, carried the works at the bayonet's point, capturing the entire garrison with its stores. Wayne was knocked over, but not seriously injured, by a musket ball. The next morning a cannonade was opened on the works at Verplanck's Point, and continued through the day. Re-enforcements were sent to the British, and it soon became evident that sufficient force to hold Stony Point could not be spared by the Americans. They therefore dismantled and abandoned the fort, and it passed again into British hands. They, however, in turn abandoned the position in October, and from that time the Americans retained possession. On the one hundredth anniversary of the capture of Stony Point, commemorative exercises were held on the spot and the battle was fought over again, the cadet battalion from West Point participating.

PEEKSKILL.

Cortland, Westchester Co., N. Y., 43 m. fr. New York.

Soon after rounding Verplanck's Point, Peekskill may be seen near the Highlands, on the east bank of the river. At this point, in ascending the river, a stranger naturally infers that the stream follows the base of the high hills stretching to the eastward. This delusion is aided by the wide creek or inlet which opens in that direction. It will not therefore be thought strange that in early times Jan Peek, a Dutch skipper, steered his craft up this creek and in due time ran her hard and fast aground. Jan looked about him, and seeing that the land was good, concluded to remain, which he accordingly did, and the place is called Peekskill unto this day. The village is a pleasant one, and within easy reach of all interesting parts of the Highlands. The Rev. Henry Ward Beecher has a country residence a little east of the village. Fort Independence stood, during Revolutionary times, on the point above Peekskill, where its ruins may still be seen. And on the point below is the Franciscan Convent Academy of "Our Lady of Angels." The village on the point opposite Peekskill is Caldwell's Landing. Above it rise the rocky and weather-beaten crags of the Donderberg, or Thunder Mountain, around which, at the close of a sultry summer day, black clouds are wont to gather, casting a deep inky blackness over mountain and river, while mutterings of thunder are echoed from peak to peak, with such strange and confused rumblings that we can hardly wonder at the superstitions which, according to Irving, peopled the hills with a crowd of little imps in sugar-loaf hats and short doublets, who were seen at various times "tumbling head over heels in the rack and mist," and bringing down frightful squalls on such craft as failed to drop the peaks of their mainsails in salute to the Dutch goblin who kept the Donderberg. As the boat passes Peekskill the view up stream becomes truly magnificent. On the east shore opposite, and a little above the Donderberg, is Anthony's Nose, over 1,200 feet high. In the "History of New York," Irving gives an amusing account, too long to quote here, of the origin of this name. Another, and perhaps more trustworthy account, says that it was once jocularly compared to

THE STEAMER MARY POWELL ENTERING THE HIGHLANDS OF THE HUDSON RIVER.

the nose of one Anthony Hogans, the captain of a sloop, who possessed an unusually large nose, and thus the name obtained a local currency which eventually became fixed as the title of this majestic hill. On the west side of the river is Iona Island, on which were formerly extensive vineyards, and which now has a hotel and is a well-known place of resort. This island is the northernmost point which is reached by the sea-breeze. The effect upon vegetation is very noticeable in the spring of the year. The stream which may be seen falling into the river below Anthony's Nose is known as "Brocken Kill." It is full of romantic cascades, almost from its mouth to its sources.

FORTS CLINTON AND MONTGOMERY.
Cornwall, Orange Co., N. Y., 47 m. fr. New York.

On the west side of the river, nearly opposite to Anthony's Nose, may be seen the mouth of Montgomery Creek. On the rocky heights above and below the creek stood Forts Clinton and Montgomery, which were in 1777 the principal defences of the Hudson. They were considered impregnable to an assault from the land side, and with the ordnance of the day they had little to fear from a naval attack. A heavy boom, made of a huge iron chain on timber floats, stretched across the river, and was made fast to the rocks at Anthony's Nose. This, it was thought, would effectually prevent the ascent of a hostile fleet. On October 6, 1777, Sir Henry Clinton sent a strong detachment around and over the Donderberg to attack these forts in the rear. A demonstration on the east side of the river had led General Putnam to anticipate an attack on Fort Independence, near Peekskill, and a portion of the garrison at Fort Montgomery was temporarily withdrawn to strengthen that post. The British had a sharp skirmish with an American detachment at Lake Sinnipink, which is still known among the inhabitants as "Bloody Pond." This attack was the first warning which aroused the garrison at the forts. In the course of the afternoon the forts were attacked, and the garrisons defended themselves gallantly until evening, when, it having become evident that they could not hold out, they took to the mountains, an orderly retreat being impossible, and so the greater part escaped. An American flotilla, consisting of two sloops and some smaller craft, which lay above the boom, had to be abandoned and burned to prevent its falling into the enemy's hands. The next morning the boom, which had cost the Americans so much labor and money, was destroyed, and the British fleet, with a detachment of troops, proceeded up the river. A short time afterward the British received the news of Burgoyne's surrender, and abandoned the forts.

WEST POINT (Landing).

Cornwall, Orange Co., N. Y., 51 m. fr. New York.

Soon after passing the former site of Fort Montgomery, the gray ruins of Fort Putnam appear crowning the heights above West Point. A little cove may now be seen in the east bank of the river, where is a stone wharf, and two or three small buildings. This is "Beverly Dock," from which Arnold started in his hasty flight to the "Vulture," which lay in Tappan Bay. On the hill, not far distant, is Robinson's house, where Arnold was breakfasting when he received the news of André's capture. Nearly opposite, and a little above Beverly Dock, Buttermilk Falls may be seen breaking in snow-white foam over a black sloping rock. A considerable village stands on the stream above the fall, called Highland Falls. Cozzen's Landing is about one mile below the regular Government Landing at West Point. Several of the Steamboats that run on the Hudson make both landings, but the Steamers of the Day Line make but the one stop at the Government Dock at West Point. Stages for Cozzen's Hotel and Highland Falls await the arrival of the Steamers at the West Point Landing, and at Cozzen's. The carriage road from Cozzen's to West Point runs along the side of the mountain, and affords very delightful views of the river, and the picturesque mountain region on the east side of the Hudson. The region is the most charming of any portion of the Hudson River. Cozzen's Hotel, a favorite and fashionable resort during the summer months, is on a commanding height near the falls. This hotel is surrounded on all sides by the most charming walks and pleasure grounds.

COZZENS' HOTEL.—*Cozzens' Landing. West Point, N. Y.*
GOODSELL BROTHERS, *Proprietors.*

This elegant and favorite summer resort stands on a commanding eminence on the west side of the Hudson, 250 feet above the river, and about one mile and a half south of the Military Academy of West Point. It commands one of the finest views on the Hudson, embracing the very heart of the Highlands, and the wildest and most picturesque scenery on this famous river. Its location is remarkably healthful; no cases of sickness having originated at this resort in twenty-five years. West Point was selected as the site of the Military Academy partly because of the healthfulness of the locality. Its location is particularly convenient for New York families, as it is but fifty miles distant, and gentlemen are enabled to visit New York daily, returning to Cozzens' at night if they desire. Among the many places of interest around Cozzens' are the U. S. Military Academy, where daily military exercises of interest occur, old Fort Putnam, Beverly Dock, Robinson House, Buttermilk Falls, etc. The drives among the historic Highlands are celebrated for their enchanting beauty, and one or two, including the five-mile drive to Crystal Lake, have recently been laid out. Distinguished visitors, including our national officials and celebrities, annually visit West Point Academy during the examinations, which begin on the 1st of June.

The hotel is built of brick, and is so constructed that all its rooms command delightful views of the river and mountain scenery. It will accommodate about 400 guests, who are the most refined and respected classes of our metropolitan society. The house is kept in a style to suit such patronage, and Cozzens' Hotel stands unrivaled among our summer resorts in its quiet elegance and comfort.

The table is not surpassed by any hotel in America in luxuries or style, and excellent music daily enlivens the enjoyments of this elegant and unexceptional resort. It can be reached by the Hudson River Railway to Garrison's Station, whence a steam-ferry conveys passengers to Cozzens' Dock; or by Day Line Steamers to West Point, with omnibus to Cozzens' Hotel, or the Mary Powell, James W. Baldwin, or Tho's. Cornell to Cozzens'. Carriages await at Cozzens' Dock and West Point all boats and trains. Daily excursions may be made from New York, stopping for dinner and spending three or four hours at the hotel, returning to the city the same day. Passengers should not mistake the West Point or Government Hotel for Cozzens', but drive to *Cozzens' Hotel*, kept by *Goodsell Bros.*

HUDSON RIVER AT WEST POINT, LOOKING SOUTH.
COZZEN'S HOTEL IN THE DISTANCE.

THE UNITED STATES MILITARY ACADEMY.

West Point is best known as the site of the United States Military Academy. Before the commencement of the present century, Washington suggested this place as well adapted for the establishment of such an institution, but no formal steps were taken by Congress until 1802. Ten years later, in 1812, the school was fairly established, and has ever since continued to increase in importance and excellence. Few of the academy buildings can be seen from a passing boat, the buildings being situated on an elevated plateau, about 180 feet above the river. This plateau is occupied by the various barracks, schools, arsenals, etc., connected with the institution bordering a broad parade open for military evolutions, parades, etc., and overlooked by the grand summits of the surrounding hills. There is no institution in the land better calculated to make a favorable impression on the visitor than this academy. The good order and strict discipline which prevail, however irksome they may be to the cadets, have the effect of imparting to them a mental and physical training which they never forget. The most accomplished officers of the army are detailed as instructors, with a special professional staff appointed from civil life. Visitors properly introduced may be present at recitations and indeed observe all the elaborate organization that gives this famous military school its well-deserved fame. The life of a cadet is by no means an easy one. His physique must be perfect and his mental capacity of no mean order to enable him to pass successfully through the four years of study and military training. The average number of cadets is about 250. Candidates for admission are nominated by members of Congress and by the President, a certain number being fixed for each congressional district. These candidates report for examination in June of each year, and, if they are mentally and physically qualified, are admitted as cadets, which is, in military rank, a grade below second lieutenant. The course of instruction is very thorough and complete, especially in mathematics; military tactics and operations bearing an important place. The best time to visit West Point is during the months of July and August when the cadets go into camp. Drills, parades, and guard-mountings are the order of the day, all being done in the best manner known to military science. West Point was the scene of no actual fighting during the Revolution, although it was fortified. A boom similar to that which was prepared at Fort Montgomery was stretched across the river to Constitution Island which was also heavily fortified toward the latter part of the war, and remains of the old batteries may still be seen. This island is now owned by, and is the residence of Miss Warner, author of " The Wide, Wide World," etc. Of the fortifications on the west side of the river Fort Putnam is the most interesting. It is 596 feet above the river, and the view from its crumbling walls is exceedingly fine.

INDIAN FALLS, GARRISON, N. Y.

GARRISON.

Philipstown, Putnam Co., N. Y., 50 m. fr. New York.
HOTEL—*Highland House.*

This station, named in honor of a distinguished family of Revolutionary fame, is on the east bank of the Hudson, opposite

West Point. It is surrounded by the most sublime and picturesque scenery of the Hudson, and is associated with some of the eventful scenes of Revolutionary times. On the east bank of the river, about one mile south of the depot is, the Robinson House, where Benedict Arnold received the letter from Colonel Jamieson, informing him of the arrest of André.

COLD SPRING.

Philipstown, Putnam Co., N. Y., 54 m. fr. New York.

Cold Spring is noted for its iron foundry. Here, under the superintendence of Major Parrot, were cast the celebrated Parrot guns, which did such good service in the war of the Rebellion. On an elevated plateau near the village is "Undercliff," the country-seat of the late George P. Morris. The mountain immediately above "Cold Spring" is "Bull Hill," or, to give its more classic name, "Mt. Taurus." It is 1,586 feet in height. Just above this elevation, and separated from it by a valley, is "Breakneck Hill," 1,187 feet high. It is stated that the former of these hills was once the abode of a wild bull, which became such a source of dread to the inhabitants that they organized a hunt, and drove the animal from his accustomed haunts across the valley to the neighboring hill, where he dashed over the rocks and broke his neck. The two hills were named in honor of this adventure. "Breakneck Hill" was formerly distinguished by a huge mass of rock, bearing a marked resemblance to a human face. This singular formation was for many years one of the sights to be looked at by every passenger up or down the river. In 1846 a party of workmen was blasting near by, under the charge of a Captain Ayers, and an unfortunate blast loosened the rock, so that "St. Anthony's Face," as it was called, was forever destroyed. Mr. Blake accuses Ayers of intentionally causing this mutilation of the mountain, but we are loth to believe that such could have been the case. The face was on the southwestern angle of the mountain, and the wreck of fallen rocks may still be seen from the passing boat. The promontory at the foot of Bull Hill is known as "Little Stony Point." On the west side of the river are "Cro' Nest" and "Butter Hill." The former is the one next above West Point. It is 1,418 feet high, and sepa-

PACIFIC HOTEL,
Cold Spring, N. Y.
S. B. TRUESDELL, Proprietor.

A pleasant homelike country hotel, newly furnished throughout. Running water with baths; good mattresses and cheerful rooms; plenty of food well cooked, and an abundance of rich milk. A good dinner for fifty cents. Board by day or week at reasonable rates. The house is situated near R.R. Station and Steamboat dock. The steam yacht "Cadet," conveys passengers to Cold Spring from Cozzens' Landing, Upper West Point docks, Cornwall and Newburg.

COLLEGE SONGS.

CARMINA YALENSIA:
A New Collection of Yale and other College Songs, with Music and Piano-Forte Accompaniments, and Engraving of Yale College Buildings. Extra cloth, $1.75. Extra cloth, full gilt, $2.25.

SONGS OF COLUMBIA:
A New Collection of Columbia College Songs, with Music and Piano-Forte Accompaniments. Bound in extra cloth, showing the Columbia College colors, blue and white. Price, $1.75.

HAPPY HOURS: a New Song-Book for Schools, Academies, and the Home Circle. 188 pp. 12mo. Price, board covers, 50 cents. Cloth, 75 cents.

Any of above books sent by mail, post-paid, on receipt of price.

TAINTOR BROTHERS, MERRILL & CO., Publishers,
758 Broadway, New York.

POUGHKEEPSIE HOTEL

MAIN ST., opposite MARKET ST.,
POUGHKEEPSIE, N. Y.

The most centrally located hotel in the city, being within one block of all the principal places of business, and within half a block of the Post Office, American Express Office, Western Union, Atlantic and Pacific, and American Union Telegraph Offices. Street cars from depot and steamboat landing pass the door. Favorite commercial house. First-class in every respect.

H. N. BAIN,
PROPRIETOR.

rated from Butter Hill by a wild and picturesque valley. The name "Cro' Nest" probably was at first applied to a deep rocky depression which exists near the summit, but it is now understood to mean the mountain itself. The name will recall Joseph Rodman Drake's beautiful poem, "The Culprit Fay," the scene of which is laid among these hills.

The precipice which forms the river-face of "Cro' Nest" is known as "Kidd's Plug Cliff." It owes its name to a singular projecting mass of rock which may be seen near its summit. The neighboring mountain named "Klinkersberg" by the Dutch, has of late come to be called the Storm King, and as the old name is neither beautiful nor appropriate, it will soon be forgotten. Its summit is 1,529 feet high. To the late N. P. Willis is due the credit of rechristening this grand peak, as well as giving appropriate names to other objects of interest in the vicinity.

CORNWALL LANDING.

Cornwall, Orange Co., N. Y., 56 m. fr. New York.

The village of Cornwall is a short distance west of the river. The beauty of its situation renders it a fashionable resort during the summer, when its many beautiful residences are the scene of a constant round of gayety. Entertaining summer visitors has become the characteristic business of the town. About 5,000 persons annually take their summer abode in this town, and the permanent population has increased within a few years to about 8,000 souls. The hotels and boarding-houses do not reach the magnificent proportions of some of the Saratoga hotels, but are neat and convenient, and from its nearness to New York, and facilities of access, the town has reached a great popularity for summer residence. There are several schools and churches, a savings bank, public library and reading-room in the village. "Idlewild," the former residence of N. P. Willis, and where he passed the last fifteen years of his life, is on the road leading from Cornwall to Newburg. It is scarcely visible from the river. Several other handsome country-seats are scattered along on the west bank of the river. After passing Breakneck Hill, "Beacon Hill" may be seen to the eastward. This elevation is 1,471 feet in height, and commands a prospect which has given it considerable celebrity. It was used during the Revolution as a signal station. Looking to the westward as soon as the Storm King ceases to obstruct the view, the summits of the *Shawangunk* (pronounced Shonggum) *Mts.* may be seen trending away to the northward and almost joining the blue outline of the distant *Catskills*. Just at the upper entrance to the Highlands is *Pollipel's Island*, a rocky bit of ground, to which a supernatural origin was ascribed by the Indians. In 1777 a *chevaux de frise*, made of logs with pointed iron heads, was sunk between the island and the mainland to prevent British ships from ascending the river; but it seems to have proved ineffectual. This island and the neighboring hills have from time to time been searched for deposits of treasure supposed to have been concealed by the almost mythical Captain Kidd. The view down stream from above Breakneck Hill is one of the finest on the river, including several of the grandest peaks of the Highlands, with the noble river flowing at their feet.

There are numerous hotels and boarding-houses at Cornwall, offering good accommodations at very reasonable prices. One of the best of these is the Linden Park House, situated about fifteen minutes' drive from the steamboat landing. It has a lawn of seventeen acres. and near it a beautiful lake of pure spring water, well stocked with fish and supplied with row-boats. Linden Park is the centre of several charming drives, among which is the new *West Point* drive, recently opened.

FISHKILL LANDING.

Fishkill, Dutchess Co., N. Y., 60 *m. fr. New York.*

This landing is the port, so to term it, of *Fishkill*, five miles inland. The Matteawan Creek falls into the Hudson at this point. At Fishkill this stream furnishes water-power for several mills and factories of large size. The situation of this town is extremely romantic, being surrounded on all sides by high and rocky hills, which are full of wild and picturesque ravines.

The *Dutchess and Columbia Railway* has its western terminus at Dutchess Junction, just below Fishkill Landing, connecting, through the *Connecticut Western Railway*, with all parts of the New England States, and forming, through the Newburgh branch of the Erie Railway, a continuous route between Boston and the West. A steam ferry connects Fishkill Landing and Newburgh.

NEWBURGH.

Newburgh, Orange Co., N. Y., 60 *m. fr. New York. Pop.* 20,000.
Hotel—*United States.*

This is one of the largest and most thriving cities on the Hudson. It stands on an elevation on the west bank of the river, commanding a noble view of the Highlands and of the Matteawan Mountains. It is the eastern terminus of the *Newburgh Branch* of the *Erie Railway,* which joins the main line at Greycourt, nineteen miles west. This branch is largely used in transporting coal from the Pennsylvania coal-fields. Over a million tons are delivered annually at this point, and shipped by water to various destinations. The city rises from the river in a succession of terraces, the first plateau being about 130 feet above the water, the second 190 feet, and still further west it reaches an elevation of 300 feet above the Hudson. It has several charitable and educational institutions, among which are the Newburgh Alms-House, about two miles west of the center of the city, the Home for the Friendless, on Montgomery Street, and the Theological Seminary of the Associate Reformed (United Presbyterian) Church. This seminary stands on a commanding height, overlooking the city and river. In this institution is a library of over 5,000 volumes, some of which are very rare and valuable. The Public Schools are excellent, and are attended by about 5,000 children. The Public Library is a beautiful building in the central part of the city, and contains about 10,000 volumes of well-selected books, etc., controlled by the school officers of the city. Newburgh is one of the handsomest cities on the Hudson, and is celebrated as the residence of a wealthy and cultured class of people, some of whom are famous for their literary productions. N. P. Willis, J. T. Headley, and many other celebrities, had their country-seats in or near Newburgh.

Its highly cultured society, historic associations, beautiful shaded streets, and high location, have made it a popular summer resort city, and many houses in town and in the suburbs are thrown open to summer boarders.

The hotels of Newburgh are few, the principal one being the favorite United States, situated near the steamboat landing in the central part of the city, commanding a full view of the Hudson

River, Fishkill Village, and the mountains on the East. It is only six blocks from Washington's Headquarters, and near the principal churches, Court House, and other public buildings and places of interest in the city. It is the only first-class hotel in Newburgh,

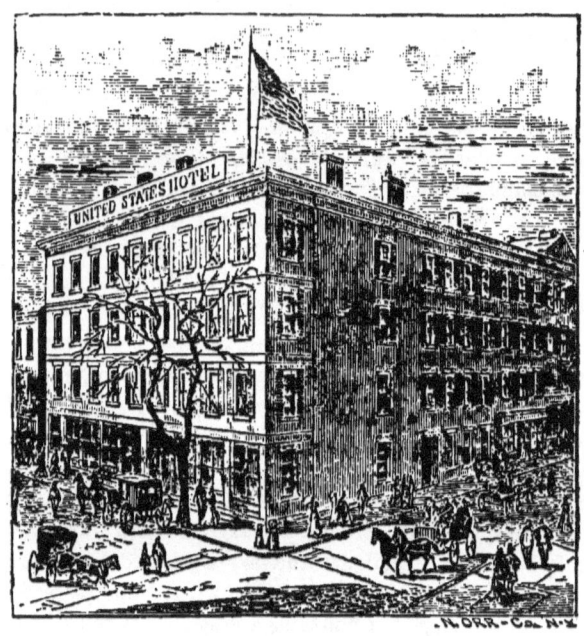

and is excellently kept at popular prices by its proprietor, Mr. J. C. Griggs. Excursionists from New York and along the Hudson River have time at Newburgh for dinner and to enjoy the Hudson Highlands and Newburgh Bay before returning, as dinner is served on the arrival of the day line and excursion steamers.

A flag-staff, standing in the southern part of the town, may be seen from the steamer. Near this is an old stone house now owned and kept in order by the State, which was occupied by Washington as his headquarters when the army lay at New Windsor, two miles south. This house contains many interesting relics of the Revolutionary War. At the foot of the flag-staff before mentioned, the last surviving member of Washington's Life Guard was buried in 1856, and a monument, with an appropriate inscription, stands over his grave. A short distance south of Newburgh is the site of the American camp, where, during the winter of 1783, the troops suffered so severely from small-pox:

The Newburgh Institute, or Mr. Siglar's School, is an excellent and well-established boarding-school for boys. The building is a large stone structure, overlooking the city, and commanding a view of some of the finest scenery of the Hudson. The school is one of the best in New York State.

LOW POINT.

Fishkill, Dutchess Co., N. Y., 64 m. fr. New York.

This is a small village on the east bank of the Hudson. Opposite, on the west bank, is a flat rock, now crowned with cedars, which Hendrick Hudson and his comrades named the *Duyvels Dans Kamer*, in consequence of an Indian pow-wow which they witnessed at night, with all its hideous accessories of fire and war-paint. The rock is still known by this name.

NEW HAMBURG,

Poughkeepsie, Dutchess Co., N. Y., 66 m. fr. New York,

stands at the mouth of *Wappinger's Creek*, which falls into the Hudson on the east side. This stream is crossed at its mouth by a long trestle bridge, with a draw in the middle. Wappinger's Falls is on Wappinger's Creek, 2 miles from New Hamburg village. A ferry plies between New Hamburg and Hampton, opposite. On the heights above the landing are charming views of the Hudson and its surrounding scenery.

MARLBOROUGH,

Marlborough, Ulster Co., N. Y., 66 m. fr. New York,

is pleasantly situated on the west bank of the Hudson, overlooking the river and the country beyond. Back of the village are the Shawangunk Mountains, and intervening is a hilly country of great beauty. In this vicinity the *Arbor Vita* is found in great perfection. This tree is also known as the white cedar. Its scientific name is *Thurja Occidentalis*. A beautiful grove of these trees will be noticed on the west bank, above Marlborough, where an entire hillside is covered with the delicate, pencil-like forms of this symmetrical and graceful tree, giving a very picturesque effect to the scenery of this region.

MILTON FERRY OR BARNEGAT.

Poughkeepsie, Dutchess Co., N. Y., 71 m. fr. New York.

The village, or part of it, may be seen crowning the steep bank which rises from the western shore of the river. Large quantities of raspberries are raised in this vicinity for the New York market, the soil and climate being peculiarly adapted to the cultivation of that fruit. Just before reaching Poughkeepsie, which city may be seen on the bluff beyond, we pass Locust Grove, the country-seat of the late Prof. S. F. B. Morse. It can hardly be necessary to remind any civilized being that Prof. Morse is the inventor of the Morse alphabet, which made the electric telegraph, of which he was also one of the original discoverers, indispensable to every nation of Christendom. The professor made other useful inventions, and had in his earlier life a reputation as an artist. His fame, however, rests on the discovery of the electric telegraph and its handmaid the alphabet, and for this he has received many testimonials from European sovereigns, and from scientific associations all over the world.

POUGHKEEPSIE.

Poughkeepsie, Dutchess Co., N. Y., 75 m. fr. New York.

The city of Poughkeepsie is built on a table-land, at a considerable height, so that its spires and buildings may be seen from a long distance up and down the river. The name is a corruption of the Indian name given to the cove which once existed at the mouth of Fall Kill. Two peculiar elevations will be noticed at the river-side, the southern of which bears the name of "Call Rock," from the fact that the inhabitants used to hail passing vessels from its summit. The place was settled by the Dutch about 1698, and incorporated as a city in 1854. The principal object of interest to the antiquary is the Van Kleck house, a stone structure with loop-holes in its walls. It was built in 1705. The State Legislature met in it in 1777 and 1778, when the British held New York, and had burned their former meeting place at Esopus. There also the State Convention for the ratification of the Federal Constitution met, in 1788. 57 members were

POUGHKEEPSIE, N. Y.—THE CITY OF SCHOOLS AND BEAUTIFUL RESIDENCES.
The Location of Eastman Business College.

present, and after a long debate, in which such men as Governor Clinton, John Jay, and Alexander Hamilton took part, the Constitution was ratified by a majority of three. Poughkeepsie is the shire town of Dutchess County, and contains the usual court and jail buildings. Its streets are beautifully shaded, its situation is very healthful, and everything combines to make it most attractive as a residence. The Vassar Female College is the largest and most important of the many excellent educational institutions of Poughkeepsie. The late Matthew Vassar, a wealthy citizen of Poughkeepsie, founded and endowed this extensive college. It is intended for the education of women only, and is the most complete establishment of its kind in the world.

NEW PALTZ.

Lloyd, Ulster Co., N. Y., 75 m. fr. New York.

This village is the shipping point for the farm produce of the rich agricultural region to the westward. Ice is cut from the Hudson in considerable quantities, and stored for use in the large buildings on the river-bank.

HYDE PARK.

Hyde Park, Dutchess Co., N. Y., 80 m. fr. New York.

Named in honor of Sir Edward Hyde, one of the early British Governors of New York. The village is half a mile east of the river-bank, on a beautiful and fertile table-land. The bend in the river between rocky bluffs is known to river men as "Crom Elbow," a combination of the original Dutch name and its English equivalent. A creek of the same name falls into the river. The point on the east shore is "De Vroos Point." A light iron foot-bridge will be noticed crossing a deep cutting of the Hudson River Railroad. The house beyond is that of Joseph Boorman, first President of the Hudson River Railroad. Between Hyde Park and Oak Hill, 30 miles above, there are many extensive and ancient country-seats, some of them antedating the Revolution. The beauty of the country seems to have attracted men of taste and wealth in those days to make their homes along this fertile bluff, and in many cases their descendants still occupy the old mansions of their fathers—a state of things

THE MEMORIAL FOUNTAIN, POUGHKEEPSIE, N. Y.
Erected by the Hon. H. G. Eastman.

so rare in America as to deserve especial notice. About a mile above Hyde Park landing is "Placentia," the former home of the late James K. Paulding, one of the pioneers of American literature, and the friend of Washington Irving. Opposite, on the west bank, but scarcely in sight from the river, is the famous apple farm of R. L. Pell, Esq. On this farm there are said to be 25,000 bearing apple-trees. The fruit of these trees is packed with the greatest care, and much of it is shipped to Europe.

STAATSBURG.
Hyde Park, Dutchess Co., N. Y., 85 m. fr. New York.

The banks of the river from this place northward lose the precipitous character which has marked them thus far, and slope less abruptly from the river. Two miles above Hyde Park "Esopus Island" will be noticed near the east bank. Just below, on the west side of the river, is the residence of John Astor, Esq. Opposite are two fine estates, the lower owned by Dr. Hussack, and the upper by Mrs. M. Livingston. The village of Staatsburg is on the east bank.

RHINEBECK.
Rhinebeck, Dutchess Co., N. Y., 90 m. fr. New York.

Not far above Staatsburg, on the east side of the river, is the country-seat known as Wildercliff. It is by no means so elegant as many of the neighboring estates; but to members of the Methodist Church in America it is interesting as having been built by Freeborn Garrettson, the eminent preacher, who married a sister of Chancellor Livingston, and to whose energy is due much of the prosperity of that branch of the Christian Church. The place may be recognized by the broad lawn which lies in front of the house. Next above this place is Ellerslie, the residence of the Hon. William Kelly, long prominent in political life. His estate contains about 600 acres, much of which is devoted to gardens and ornamental grounds, and the rest is highly cultivated as a farm. The quaint stone house on a hill near Rhinebeck Landing is the Beekman House, built prior to 1700. It served as a church and as a fort during early times, when the Indians were hostile and powerful. The village of Rhinebeck is 2 miles from the river, and cannot be seen from the steamer. Within the

VIEW IN THE GROUNDS OF EASTMAN PARK, POUGHKEEPSIE, N. Y.

limits of the town there is an extensive vein of gold-bearing quartz, which yields the precious metal in paying quantities. The principal lode is on the property of R. W. Millbank, but it probably extends to and beyond the river. This quartz is found between well-defined walls of the ordinary talco-argillaceous slate characteristic of the region.

This is one of the principal points of entry to the Catskill Mountain region.

RONDOUT.
Kingston, Ulster County, N. Y., 90 m. fr. New York.
HOTEL.—*Mansion House.*

Rondout Creek enters the Hudson from the westward. Its mouth is the eastern end of the Delaware and Hudson Canal, which joins the creek 2½ miles above. This canal, finished in 1828, extends to the vicinity of the Pennsylvania coal-fields; and every provision is made at Rondout for the trans-shipment of vast quantities of coal. Rondout is now a part of the city of Kingston, with which it was incorporated in 1878. From it the Ulster and Delaware R.R. runs in a northwesterly direction into the Catskill Mountain Regions. It is the point of departure from the Hudson River to the southern part of the Catskill range, including the Overlook Mountain. Passengers going to this region, land at Rhinebeck, and cross the river by steam ferry to Rondout, thence by rail to the Catskills and Delaware County. The Wallkill Valley R.R. runs southwest from Rondout, connecting with Erie R.R. for New York or the West.

PORT EWEN
is a comparatively new village, below the mouth of the creek. Nearly all the inhabitants of these villages are engaged in one way or another in the coal business, and in the extensive Rosendale cement quarries, whose products are highly valued, and largely used all over the country.

KINGSTON,
formerly Esopus, is on Esopus Creek, which at that point approaches within about 2 miles of Rondout, and then curves to the northward, entering the Hudson 12 miles above. Kingston was settled in 1614, and was thrice destroyed by Indians before a

The SIDEWALK APPROACH to and MARBLE WALL fronting EASTMAN PLACE, the Residence of the Hon. H. G. Eastman, Poughkeepsie, N. Y.

permanent footing was obtained by the Europeans. In 1777 the State Legislature met and formed a constitution. In the autumn of the same year, soon after the capture of Forts Montgomery and Clinton by the British, General Vaughan, with 3,000 troops, landed at Rondout, marched to Kingston (then Esopus), and sacked and burned the town, remaining until he received the news of Burgoyne's surrender, when he at once retired to New York, abandoning all that he had gained. While Esopus (Kingston) was burning, the inhabitants fled to Hurley, a neighboring village, where the small force of American troops tried and hung a messenger who was caught carrying dispatches from Clinton to Burgoyne. When first caught, this man swallowed a silver ball, which an emetic brought again to light, and which was found to contain the fatal dispatch.

BARRYTOWN.

Red Hook, Dutchess County, N. Y., 96 *m. fr. New York.*

Formerly known as Lower Red Hook Landing. A little above Rhinebeck is the residence of William B. Astor. It may be recognized by its tower and pointed roof. This estate is named "Rokeby," and is one of the finest on the river. Next above is the estate known as Montgomery Place, surpassing in beauty, if possible, the last one mentioned. The house was built by the wife of General Montgomery, who fell in the assault on Quebec in 1775. Her brother, Edward Livingston, succeeded her in the ownership of the place, and his family still occupies it. Near the eastern shore, 2 miles above Barrytown, is Cruger's Island, a spot made beautiful by nature and art. In a grove near the southern end stands a ruin which was imported from Italy by the former proprietor of the island. Its broken arches may be seen among the trees as the boat passes, forming a singular contrast with the modern architecture of the neighboring house. The latter, however, is not in sight from the boat at the same time with the ruin. A glimpse of it may be caught in passing, a short distance above.

TIVOLI.

Red Hook, Dutchess Co., N. Y., 100 *m. fr. New York.*

This is a small village around the railway station. It is connected with Saugerties on the west bank of the river by a steam ferry. It is one of the stations at which passengers depart from the railroad trains who desire to go to the famous Overlook Mountain House—one of the finest mountain hotels in the Catskills. Passengers from the steamers leave the boat at the Saugerties landing, and go thence by stage 12 miles to the "Overlook." Near the village is an old mansion, now owned by Col. De Peyster, which was built before the Revolution by one of the Livingston family. The British, on their way to burn Claremont, a little above, in 1777, stopped here under the impression that this was the house to be destroyed. The proprietor, however, aided by his well-stocked wine-cellar, convinced them of their mistake, and they left him unmolested.

SAUGERTIES.

Saugerties, Ulster Co., N. Y., 101 *m. fr. New York.*

It is an important village of about 4,000 inhabitants, and the market town for a wide region of country on the west side of the Hudson. The village is about 1 mile from the steamboat landing, with which it is connected by stages that meet all passenger boats and trains. Saugerties is near the mouth of Esopus Creek, which is navigable to the village. There are extensive iron works and paper mills at this place, and large quantities of flagging-stone are quarried in the vicinity. The Bigelow Blue Stone Co. employ in their various quarries in Ulster County 3,500 men, and quarry 200,000 tons of stone annually. "Plattekill Clove," which lies back of this place, in the mountains, is a remarkably wild and rugged chasm, affording scenery of varied grandeur and beauty. A road winds through this gorge up to the Catskill Mountain House region beyond.

GERMANTOWN.

Germantown, Columbia Co., N. Y., 105 *m. fr. New York.*

The view of the Catskill Mountains is here very fine. The entire range can be seen. Germantown is not directly upon the river bank, and cannot be seen from the boat. The large white building on a hill near the landing is the "Riverside Seminary," established by Philip Rockafellow. A few miles above Germantown is the mouth of "Roeleff Jansen Kill," where the original Livingston Manor House stood. Robert R. Livingston, Chancel-

PROSPECT PARK HOTEL,
CATSKILL, N. Y.
FIRST-CLASS SUMMER HOTEL,
Of Easy Access on the Banks of the Hudson River,

WITH ALL THE LATEST IMPROVEMENTS.
Accommodation for 400.

The grounds, walks, avenues and shubbery are adapted to the chief design: which is, to produce such an establishment, on a liberal and appropriate scale, as can offer to those who with their families annually seek in the country, during the Summer months, health and grateful change from the heat and confinement of the city. No malaria, hay fever or mosquitoes. Croquet, Lawn Tennis, Billiards, Bowling Alley, Fishing, Boating, Bathing, good Music.

THE VIEWS FROM THE HOTEL ARE UNSURPASSED IN EXTENT AND BEAUTY.

The annually increasing tide of visitors to this region—drawn hither by the pursuit of health and pleasure—has already vindicated its right to the title of "The Switzerland of America."

With a commanding view of the River in front, and for miles North and South, and the grand old Mountains in the background, with a climate of great salubrity, healthy mountain air, and the accessories of field and river sports and pleasure drives, it is unsurpassed in all the borders of the Hudson in its attractions and advantages.

CARRIAGES WILL BE IN ATTENDANCE AT THE CARS AND BOATS.

Accessible by trains on the Hudson River Railroad, and by the Day Boats CHAUNCEY VIBBARD and ALBANY. Also by Night Steamers every evening from foot of Harrison street, New York, for Catskill.

☞ First-class Livery connected with the Hotel, with good stabling for horses in new brick stables.

☞ Telegraph in the Hotel.

Transient Rates $3.00 per Day.

Liberal arrangements made by the week or month, prices acoording to Rooms, Location, &c.

Address, **PROSPECT PARK HOTEL CO., Catskill, N. Y.**

L. F. BOGARDUS, Manager.

Open June 15th.

PROSPECT PARK HOTEL, CATSKILL, N. Y. L. F. BOARDUS, *Manager.*

lor of New York, built an elegant house, a little south of the old one, where his mother continued to reside. Chancellor Livingston's active sympathy with the cause of the Republic during the Revolution made him so obnoxious to the British, that when General Vaughan burned Esopus he sent an expedition up the river to burn Claremont—the name of the Livingston estate. They burned both the houses, but new and more elegant ones were at once erected near the ruins, and Claremont is still one of the finest country-seats on the river. Chancellor Livingston's name will always be associated with that of Robert Fulton. The experiments of Fulton would probably have been delayed for years had it not been for the generous aid of Chancellor Livingston. After a series of discouraging failures in Paris and New York, their efforts were crowned with success, and in September, 1807, the "Claremont" made her first trip from New York to Albany, bearing Fulton, the Chancellor, and others.

CATSKILL.

Catskill, Greene Co., N. Y., 111 m. fr. New York. Pop. 4,000.
HOTELS—*Prospect Park Hotel; Irving House.*

Catskill Landing is at the end of a long causeway, reaching across the shallows, on the western shore. But little of the town can be seen from the river. Cats Kill enters the Hudson near by, winding through rocky bluffs, with a deep channel, which is navigable for large vessels a mile from its mouth. Travelers intending to visit the Catskill Mountains can reach their destination most easily from this point, as lines of stages run regularly to the Mountain and Laurel Houses, 12 miles distant. The village of Catskill has become the most popular summer resort on the Hudson, and with the mountains, is one of the most famous and extensive in the country. The Prospect Park Hotel, on the high bluff overlooking the river and village, is the leading resort hotel of the town, and its commanding position and excellent management have made it a popular summer resort hotel. From the Prospect Park Hotel the views of the mountains on either side of the river are really sublime, and the combination of mountain, river, and intervale scenery is marvelously beautiful and charming. The rapidly-passing commerce of the Hudson adds a panoramio effect, enlivening the scene and delighting the spectator with ever-varying views. The Prospect Park Hotel opens about the middle of June for the season. The Irving House is a new, commodious hotel in the center of the village of Catskill, affording excellent accommodations for very moderate prices. It is kept open throughout the year. Hendrick Hudson anchored the "Half-Moon" at the mouth of Cats Kill, on the 20th of September, 1609, and was visited by large numbers of friendly Indians, who brought provisions of all sorts, in return for which, as is stated by Juet, the historian of Hudson's voyage, some of them were made drunk. Thomas Cole, one of the pioneers of American Landscape Art, had his studio in this vicinity, where he could study nature in her most beautiful forms. Here he painted the celebrated allegorical series of pictures known as "The Voyage of Life." Church, the great landscape painter, has a beautiful country-seat on the summit on the east side of the Hudson, opposite Catskill. It commands some of the sublimest river views.

IRVING HOUSE, CATSKILL, N. Y.

Is a large, new and commodious brick building in the centre of the village, with first-class accommodations for travelers and tourists. Board by the day or week. Free Omnibus attends all Trains and Boats. An authorized Agent will be on hand to give information, accommodate and attend to the wants of the guests of this House. Parties desiring Country Board furnished with information regarding the different localities and prices. **H. A. PERSON, Proprietor.**

CATSKILL MOUNTAIN HOUSE.

THE CATSKILLS.

The Catskill mountains have probably been seen and admired, if not visited, by more travelers than any other mountain group on the American continent. The mountains of this region belong to the great Appalachian range, which traverses the eastern portion of the United States from the States bordering on the Gulf of Mexico to the basin of the St. Lawrence River. Approaching within ten miles of a great natural highway, they have, since the earliest days of the settlement of the country, commanded the attention of all voyagers on the Hudson River, and, since the enormous increase of travel induced by modern multiplication of railroads and steamboats, they are annually seen by millions and visited by thousands. Moreover, they have been celebrated in song and story, and one of the most popular and successful actors of our time has made Irving's character of Rip Van Winkle, with the mountain region where he lived and slept, familiar to the English speaking world. The group of summits known under this name lies within the counties of Greene, Ulster, and Delaware, in New York. They are a part of the great mountain system which follows the Atlantic seaboard from the Arctic regions almost to the Gulf of Mexico, and known at different parts of its course as the White Mountains, the Green Mountains, the Blue Ridge, etc., etc.

In ascending the Hudson the first point of divergence for mountain travel is Rondout (City of Kingston). The landing made by the Day Line of Steamers is at Rhinebeck, on the east side of the river, whence a steam ferry conveys passengers across the river to Rondout. Here is the terminus of the Ulster & Delaware Railroad, following up the valley of the Esopus which skirts and penetrates the southern and western portion of the mountains. The opening of this road rendered access to this portion of the mountains so easy that numerous and excellent hotels have been built in localities which the traveler could formerly reach only by a long and tedious stage route.

The track rises by a steep gradient 184 feet above the river, and almost immediately comes in sight of Overlook Mountain. In the nine miles which are passed before reaching West Hurley, the train climbs 530 feet above the river. Before reaching the station the

OVERLOOK MOUNTAIN HOUSE

may be seen perched upon the shoulder of the mountain, and seeming much nearer than the railway will seem when viewed from above. The profile of the range is exceedingly fine from this point of view, and there are many who derive more enjoyment from looking *at* a mountain range than in looking *from* it. The stage road tends in a northerly direction after leaving the station, leaves the outlying range with its three summits, "Tonche Hook," "Ticetenyck," and "Little Tonche" on the left, and soon begins the long ascent of Overlook Mountain. The hotel stands on a plateau 3,000 feet above tide water, and a little below the highest point of the mountain, and commands views toward all points of the compass, that toward the south embracing a large portion of the Hudson Valley, and those in other directions commanding mountain and valley scenery in great variety and picturesqueness. Built in 1878, well furnished, and fitted with all the modern conveniences, the Overlook has few rivals among mountain resorts. The thermometer averages 15 to 20 degrees lower than in New York. "Hay fever" and its attendant ills are never known at this elevation. In Plattekill Clove, three miles north of the hotel, is a succession of waterfalls, and in every direction there are charming walks to many points of interest. The Overlook may be reached, as we have seen, from Rondout by the Ulster & Delaware Railroad. Rondout is reached from New York by the Albany Dayline (see page 49), by the steamers "J. W. Baldwin" and "Thomas Cornell," daily, at 4 P.M., during the season, from the foot of Harrison Street. By the "Mary Powell" at 3.10 P.M., from foot of Desbrosses Street, and by the "Ansonia," which leaves for Saugerties Tuesdays, Thursdays, and Saturdays from the foot of Franklin Street. At Saugerties private carriages may be procured for the hotel. Rondout may be reached by rail via Hudson River Railroad from New York, or via the Erie & Wallkill Valley Railroad from Jersey City.

FROM WEST HURLEY the railroad follows a westerly course passing Brodhead's Bridge where there are fine falls on the Esopus and an attractive view from the bluffs above the creek.

SHOKAN is picturesquely situated at a mountain gateway through which the Esopus rushes in rapids. "High Point

OVERLOOK MOUNTAIN HOUSE,
Woodstock, Ulster County, New York.
JAMES SMITH, *Proprietor.*

Mountain," 3,100 feet high, is seen to the southward. The valley here takes a more northerly course, and on the west side of the track is seen a group of fine summits. The northernmost is the Wittenberg, and the next Mt. Cornell. The walk to the summit of these peaks is a favorite one with mountain climbers.

AT BOICEVILLE the road reaches an elevation of 615 feet above tide-water.

MT. PLEASANT, 24 miles from Rondout, and 700 feet above the river, is the opening of the "Shandaken Valley," a mountain depression full of the most enchanting natural scenery.

PHŒNICIA, 27 miles from Rondout, and nearly 800 feet above the Hudson, is a place of considerable resort, and the point of departure for Hunter and Tannersville, through Stony Clove, a remarkable ravine, where it is said snow and ice can be found the year through.

THE TREMPER HOUSE

is a fine new hotel just at the entrance to Stony Clove. It is on a terrace 300 feet broad and 1,500 long, and almost between Slide Mountain and Hunter Mountain, two of the highest peaks in the Catskills. The hotel will accommodate 200 guests, and has every modern convenience, with pure water direct from a mountain spring carried to every floor. A carriage road ascends to the summit of Mt. Tremper, affording a superb view of Shandaken Valley, the Lake Mohonk Gap, Wittenberg, Cross Mountain and an assembly of mountains too many for enumeration here.

AT FOX HOLLOW the elevation is 990 feet. Before reaching the station a bridge is crossed at the entrance of Woodland Valley. On the northern side of the road are Mts. Sheridan and North Dome.

SHANDAKEN is 33 miles from the river, and 1,060 feet above it. Here passengers for West Kill, Lexington, and Jewett Heights leave the cars and take stages for their destinations.

BIG INDIAN (36 miles) is 1,202 feet above the river. A bridge here crosses the Esopus, from which a fine view is obtained up Big Indian Valley. This station is nearest to Slide Mountain, and thence parties usually start for the ascent of that peak. Carriages can go without especial difficulty within five miles of the summit, and here parties sometimes remain overnight. Dutch-

THE FAWN'S LEAP.

ers is the name of the place, but it does not pretend to be more than a mountain farm house. The view from Slide Mountain is among the finest in the Catskills.

PINE HILL is 39 miles from Rondout. The railroad is here 1,660 feet above the sea-level. For five miles south of the station this grade is 145 feet to the mile. Half a mile from the station is the

GUIGOU HOUSE,

a well-known resort, which has recently been refitted and put in complete order. Walks and drives of the most romantic description abound in all directions, and the trout-fishing is exceptionally good.

SUMMIT STATION, 1,886 feet above the river at Rondout, the highest point on the railroad. Before reaching the station a grand curve known as the "Horse Shoe," will be noticed. From Summit the grade is downward, and all save the outlying ranges of the Catskills are left behind. There are, however, pleasant resorts, with comfortable hotels and boarding houses all through this region which is more retired, and for that reason more attractive to many than the fashionable resorts among the higher hills.

THE CATSKILL MOUNTAIN HOUSE.

This is the oldest of the mountain resorts, and was for many years without a rival in the mountains among which it occupies a central position. The hotel is reached by stage from Catskill, where are fine hotels, if the traveler desires to rest overnight before undertaking the long ride up the mountain. The ride is, however, a most enjoyable one, for the road is firm and the ascent so gradual that a good team can trot almost the entire distance. The natural curiosities in the vicinity of the Mountain House are almost infinite in number, and unequalled in variety. Chief among them are the Kaaterskill Falls, and here has been erected the

LAUREL HOUSE, J. L. Schutt, Proprietor,

a spacious hotel commanding magnificent views down the Clove and within easy reach of all the points of interest which have for so many years made this region one of the most popular of our mountain resorts. The great beauty of this locality is so well

LAUREL-HOUSE, KAATERSKILL FALLS

In the finest scenery of the Catskill Mountains. J. L. Schutt, Proprietor.

known, that a description is unnecessary. To the lovers of quiet, its secluded walks afford delightful retreats; while the drives in the vicinity—especially through the Cloves—challenge comparison with any similar place in the United States. There is also good trout-fishing in the neighborhood. Carriages and an authorized agent are in attendance at the cars and boats, Catskill.

PALENVILLE is at the lower entrance of Kaaterskill Clove. It is 10 miles by road from Catskill village, 3 miles below the falls, and has a number of excellent hotels and boarding houses.

TANNERSVILLE is 15 miles from Catskill Village, high up in the Kaaterskill Clove, on the way to Hunter. It is a very central location, commanding no very extended views, but surrounded on all sides by towering summits and wild ravines. Stony Clove is near by, and through this is a road leading to Phœnicia on the Ulster & Delaware Railroad.

HUNTER is about 4 miles west of Tannersville, and while it is a village of a somewhat more prominent character, possesses, in the main, similar natural advantages. The Hunter House, Breeze Lawn, and Central House may be mentioned as among the most prominent abiding places for summer visitors.

LEXINGTON is 9 miles from Hunter, and 10 miles from railway connections on the Ulster & Delaware Railroad. The O'Hara House and the Douglass House will be found comfortable stopping places.

WEST KILL, 4 miles from Lexington, is near Deep Hollow Gorge, in some parts of which the sun never shines.

CAIRO is 10 miles from Catskill, near Round Top Mountain, and facing the Hudson Valley. Merritt's Grand View House and the Webster House are among the principal hotels. The surroundings are highly picturesque and attractive.

FREEHOLD is a resort of considerable popularity. It is reached by stage from Catskill or Athens, and commands a very fine view of the mountain range. Black Head, 3,965 feet high, being the nearest and most conspicuous.

ACRA is on the road from Catskill northward. Mott's Sunside Farm is one of the resorts of the vicinity.

EAST WINDHAM is reached by a good road from Catskill. Lamoreau's Summit House is the principal hotel. From here it is

CAUTERSKILL FALLS, CATSKILL MOUNTAINS,
Near Laurel House.   J. L. Schutt, Proprietor.

HUDSON RIVER ROUTE.

said that the Adirondacks and White Mountains can at times be seen.

WINDHAM, a delightful village 25 miles from Catskill, is beautifully situated amid lovely mountain scenery. Reasonably good roads lead in all directions. The Windham House is one mile from the village.

JEWETT HEIGHTS is a small village in full sight of the Catskill range, and commanding a wide view of the Hudson. The Jewett Heights House is available for boarders.

PRATTSVILLE on Schoharie Hill, with well-shaded streets and the purest of mountain air. There is a daily line of stages from Catskill and from Stratton's Falls on the Ulster & Delaware Railroad. The village contains several excellent hotels and boarding houses.

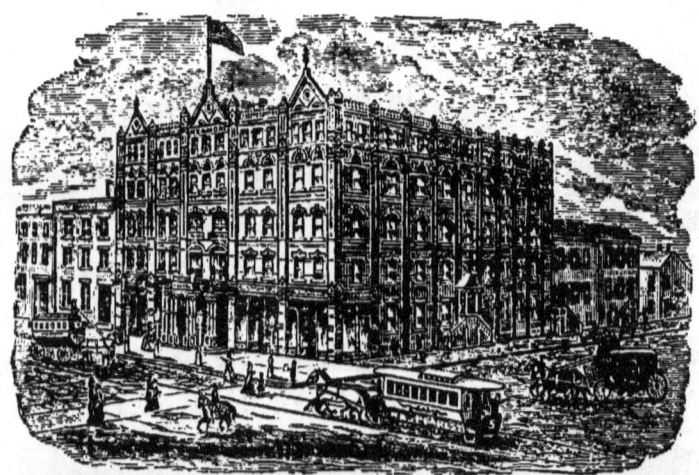

HOTEL KENMORE, - - - - Albany, N. Y.
This HOTEL is located on North Pearl Street, convenient to Post Office, Capitol, and Depots. With Elevator, and all modern appliances for Elegance and Comfort. Hot and Cold Water, Steam Heaters, and Telephone, connecting with office, in each room. This Hotel, both as to Building and Furnishing, is entirely new, and will be conducted as a first-class house in every respect.
ADAM BLAKE, Proprietor, - Albany, N. Y.

CASCADE IN PLATTEKILL CLOVE.

HUDSON.

Hudson, Columbia Co., N. Y., 115 *m. fr. New York.*
HOTELS— *Worth House ; Mansion House.*

The City of Hudson is the capital of Columbia County, and occupies a site of great beauty, being built upon a promontory jutting into the Hudson River, and commanding the most extensive and charming views in every direction. The city extends up the slope of "Prospect Hill," which rises to a height of 200 feet. The elevation just below Hudson landing is Mount Merino. It is cultivated over almost its whole surface of 600 acres. Hudson, being at the head of ship navigat'on, was of great importance in the early commerce of the river, and it rapidly grew to be a place of considerable size and wealth. The "Claverack Creek," a romantic stream, is a little east of Hudson, and running northward, joins other streams, forming Columbiaville Creek.

The Hudson & Chatham Railway, leased by the Boston & Albany R.R. Co., has its western terminus here, and connects at Chatham with the Boston & Albany and Harlem Railways.

ATHENS.

Athens, Greene Co., N. Y., 115 *m. fr. New York.*

This village, directly opposite Hudson, was originally fixed upon as the eastern terminus of the Erie Canal, but the project was abandoned. The inhabitants are largely engaged in ship-building and brick-making. A branch of the New York Central Railway connects Athens with Schenectady, and has added much to its prosperity. Above Athens and Hudson, on the east side of the river, is Roger's Island, behind which the shipping of New York merchants was concealed during the Revolutionary War. At that time the island was densely wooded, and formed an effectual screen.

COLUMBIAVILLE.

Stockport, Columbia Co., N. Y., 119 *m. fr. New York.*

On the west side of the river is a promontory, with a lighthouse tower, which old river pilots call "Chaney Tinker," but which is now known as Four-mile Point. Directly opposite to this is the mouth of Columbiaville Creek, on which, a short distance from the river, are large flannel mills.

CASCADE OF HIGH ROCKS.

COXSACKIE.
Coxsackie, Greene Co., N. Y., 123 m. fr. New York.
This village is on the west side of the river. Its name is derived from an Indian word signifying "cut banks." The chief occupations of the inhabitants are ship-building, farming, and fishing. The headland nearly opposite is Newtown Hook. A mile below Coxsackie are the extensive vineyards of Mr. Ezra Fitch.

STUYVESANT.
Stuyvesant, Columbia Co., N. Y., 125 m. fr. New York.
Formerly Kinderhook Landing. The village of Kinderhook is 4 miles inland. Ex-President Martin Van Buren lived there for many years before his death.

NEW BALTIMORE.
New Baltimore, Albany Co., N. Y., 127 m. fr. New York.
The chief business of this place is ship-building. There are several yards with complete sets of ways, etc. Schooners, sloops, and barges are the craft which are built.

SCHODAC.
Schodac, Rensselaer Co., N. Y., 132 m. fr. New York.
A small village on the east bank of the river. Good farming lands lie along the river, and the surrounding region is a pleasant rolling country. The name is of Indian origin, signifying "a meadow."

COEYMAN'S.
Coeyman's, Albany Co., N. Y., 132 m. fr. New York.
This village is on the west bank of the river. Its name (pronounced Que-mans) is that of one of its early settlers. The range of mountains seen to the westward are the "Helderbergs."

A little below Coeyman's, near the west shore, is a high rocky island on which the boundaries of four counties meet, namely, Albany, Greene, Columbia, and Rensselaer. This island was named by the Dutch "Beeren," or "Bear Island," and on its summit once stood the "Castle" of "Rensselaerstein," from whose wall Nicholas Kroon, the agent of Killian Van Rensselaer, the Patroon, compelled passing vessels to dip their colors and pay tribute, or take the chances of being sunk by the ordinance of the fort. An amusing account of the whole difficulty between Governor Kieft of New Amsterdam, and the Patroon, is given in "Knickerbocker's History of New York."

CASTLETON.
Schodac, Rensselaer Co., N. Y., 135 *m. fr. New York.*

A small and compact village, built upon a steep hillside on the eastern bank of the river. The domes and spires of Albany, 9 miles distant, may be seen from this point.

Castleton Bar, formerly known as the "Overslaugh," has always been a serious impediment to navigation at this point. As early as 1790 State appropriations were made for the purpose of improving the channel, but all efforts were unavailing until the present system of dykes was commenced. A. Van Santvoord, Esq., of Albany, President of the Day Line of New York and Albany steamers, and other prominent citizens of Albany and Troy, had the subject brought before the State Legislature, and work was begun in 1863. In 1868 the United States Government assumed the work of completing the dykes, and they may now be seen stretching for several miles along the river, effectually accomplishing the purpose for which they were intended.

GREENBUSH.
Greenbush, Rensselaer Co., N. Y., 144 *m. fr. New York.*

Is situated on the east side of the river opposite to Albany. Its population is largely made up of employés on the great railway lines which meet here from all parts of the Eastern States and from New York. Along the river bank, both above and below the village proper, handsome houses, and many pleasant-looking villas and cottages may be seen on the high bluff which rises beyond the alluvial flats that border the river. Greenbush is a translation of the old Dutch name, which was doubtless appropriate in its day. During the French War, in 1755, Greenbush was a military rendezvous, and again in 1812 the United States Government established extensive barracks whence troops were forwarded to the Canadian frontier.

STANWIX HALL,
ALBANY, N. Y.

This Hotel contains all the MODERN IMPROVEMENTS, and every convenience that Health and Comfort can suggest, such as HOT AND COLD WATER IN ROOMS.

ROOMS EN SUITE, with PARLORS, BEDROOMS and BATH, ETC., PASSENGER ELEVATOR, ELECTRIC BELLS, TELEPHONE, TELEGRAPH OFFICE.

UNDER NEW MANAGEMENT.

The STANWIX is located directly opposite the New York Central and Hudson River and Boston and Albany Passenger Station, and is only one block from the Rensselaer and Saratoga, Boston, Hoosac Tunnel and Western, Delaware and Hudson Canal Co's Railway lines Station, and less than ten minutes' walk to People's Line and Day Line Steamboats.

Connecting by Horse Cars every ten minutes and Omnibuses on arrival of boats.

Its central location, being the nearest first-class Hotel to Railroads and Steamboats and the mercantile interests, makes it the most convenient and accessible Hotel in the City.

Rooms with or without board.
Rates—$1.00 per day and upward, for Rooms.
Rates for Board and Rooms—$2.50 and $3.00 per day.
Special rates will be made for large parties and permanent guests.

CEBRA QUACKENBUSH,
Manager.

ALBANY.

Albany Co., N. Y., 144 *m. fr. New York. Pop.* 80,000.

HOTELS—*Delavan House Kenmore and Stanwix Hall.*

This city lies upon the west bank of the Hudson River, near the middle of the county, and embraces a strip of land about one and one half miles wide, extending thirteen and a half miles in a northwest direction, to the northern boundary of the county. Before incorporation it was known under the names of "Beverwyck," "William Stadt," and "New Orange." The seat of the State Government, originally fixed at New York City, was removed to this place in 1798. The early growth of the city was exceedingly slow; its population numbering less than 10,000 at the end of a century from its incorporation, which was in 1686. In 1714, when a century old, it contained only 3,329 inhabitants, nearly 500 of whom were slaves. Steam navigation, originated by Fulton on the Hudson in 1807, and the completion of the Erie Canal in 1825, each gave powerful impulses to its growth, and in less than half a century it added more than 50,000 to its population. In 1875 the census report shows about 80,000. The whole city, comprised within the limits of Pearl, Steuben, and Beaver Streets, in 1676, was surrounded by wooden walls, with openings for musketry. There were six gates to the city, and the maintenance of these fragile defenses was the source of unceasing contention between the authorities and the inhabitants. A portion of these walls were remaining so late as 1812. They were thirteen feet in height, and made of timber about a foot square. The city has many handsome avenues, and the walks and drives about the city are exceedingly beautiful. A walk of half a mile from the city brings to view the verdure-clad mountains of Vermont and the towering Catskills. The first railroad in the State of New York, and the second in the United States, was opened from Albany to Schenectady in 1831. The commerce of Albany is considerable.

Besides the great natural means of communication which the river affords, in *Day Line* and *People's Line* of steamers, the city is connected with New York by two lines of railroad, the *New York Central and Hudson River* and the *Harlem*. The *New York*

Central and Hudson River Railroad and the *Erie Canal* connect it with the Great Lakes. It communicates with Northern New York, Vermont, and Canada by the *Delaware and Hudson Canal Co.'s* and by way of Troy by the *Troy & Boston* railways, and by the Champlain Canal. By the *Boston and Albany Railway*, it communicates with the New England States, and by the *Albany and Susquehanna* division of the *Delaware and Hudson Canal Co.'s R. R.* with Binghamton on the *Erie Railway*, and the coal regions of Pennsylvania. The Hudson River at Albany is crossed by two railroad drawbridges, each over 4,000 feet in length, one at the northern part of the city, now used entirely for freight trains, and the magnificent new iron bridge at the central part of the city, at the west end of which is the passenger depot for the city of Albany, and at the east end is the station for East Albany. The bridge cost nearly $2,000,000.

The manufactures are extensive and varied. Its numerous *stove founderies* and *breweries* are on an immense scale. Seventy thousand barrels of ale are made annually at one brewery. The *workshops* of the N. Y. C. & H. R. Railroad, at West Albany, give employment to more than two thousand persons. Its other manufactures are varied and extensive. The sales of barley amount to more than 2,000,000 bushels per annum, most of which is consumed by the brewers. *Lumber* is another very important article of trade. Albany is also one of the leading *cattle marts* of the country. The markets at Bull's Head, in New York, and at Brighton, near Boston, receive many of their supplies from here.

The *State buildings* include the new Capitol, a magnificent structure at the head of State Street, State Hall, State Library, Geological and Agricultural Hall, Normal School, and State Arsenal and Armory. The *City Hall* is an elegant structure, faced with Sing Sing marble, and surmounted by a gilded dome. The new post-office is being built on Broadway, at the foot of State Street, and when completed will be one of the finest post-offices in the State. The Albany County Almshouse is the magnificent brick building observed on the west bank of the Hudson just before reaching Albany. The Penitentiary in west part of the city.

Besides Public Schools, the Educational Institutions are the *Albany Academy, Albany Female Academy, Albany Female Semi-*

nary, Albany Institute, and the *Albany Industrial School*. The public schools afford instruction to 20,000 children of both sexes, and are conducted at an annual expense of $100,000. There are two *Christian Associations, Protestant* and *Catholic*, the former being the oldest institution of the kind in the United States. The *Dudley Observatory*, on an eminence in the northern border of the city, was incorporated April 2, 1852; it was founded through the munificence of Mrs. Blandina Dudley, who gave $90,000 for its construction and endowment. The building, constructed in the form of a cross, is admirably arranged, and is furnished with some of the largest and finest instruments ever constructed. It has an extensive library attached. The *Albany Medical College* and the *Law School of the University of Albany* are on Eagle Street, and have all the facilities for teaching the respective sciences. The *Albany Almshouse, Insane Asylum*, and a *Fever Hospital* are located upon a farm of 116 acres, one and a half miles southwest of the city, and are under the management of the city authorities. The *Industrial School* building is located on the same farm. The *Albany City Hospital*, on Eagle Street, was incorporated in 1849. The *Albany Orphan Asylum*, on Washington Street, at the junction of the Western Turnpike, was incorporated in 1831; it was erected, as was the City Hospital, by private subscription; it is now aided by State funds. The *St. Vincent Orphan Asylum*, incorporated in 1849, is under the charge of the Sisters of Mercy. The male department, two miles west of the Capitol, is under the charge of the Christian Brothers.

The first church (Ref. Prot. D.) was formed in 1640. A Lutheran Church existed in 1680. The first Protestant Episcopal Church (St. Peter's) was erected in 1715; it stood in the centre of State Street, opposite Chapel Street. The communion plate of this church was presented to the Onondagas by Queen Anne. The most costly edifices are the Catholic Cathedral of the Immaculate Conception, corner of Eagle and Lydius Streets, and the St. Joseph's (R. C.) Church.

Water is supplied to the city from Rensselaer Lake, about five miles west of the City Hall, and 225 feet above the level of the water of the Hudson. This lake covers thirty-nine acres, and its capacity is 180,000,000 gallons. A brick conduit conveys the water to Bleecker Reservoir, on Patroon Street, whence it is distributed through the city. This reservoir has a capacity of 30,000,000 gallons. The cost of the construction of these works was upwards of $1,000,000.

The Delavan House, on Broadway, adjoining the New York Central and Hudson River R. R. Depot, is one of the finest hotels in the country. It has long been celebrated for its excellent cuisine

and fine furnishings. It is kept by Charles E. Leland & Co., and its management is very efficient and remarkably popular.

Stanwix Hall is on Broadway, corner of Maiden Lane, less than one block from the New York Central and Hudson River and Delaware and Hudson Canal Co.'s R. R. Depot, and but a few steps from the steamboat landings of the Day and People's Lines, and the centre of the business part of the city.

The Hotel Kenmore is a new house, kept by Mr. Adam Blake, and is situated on North Pearl Street, two blocks from the N. Y. Central R. R. Depot, and a short distance from the Capitol. It is fitted up in modern style, with elevator, hot and cold running water, and steam heaters; telephone connected with the office in each room. It is strictly first class in all respects.

DELAWARE & HUDSON CANAL COMPANY:

Rensselaer & Saratoga Department.

Albany to Rouse's Point, 208 miles. Albany to Rutland, via Saratoga Springs, 101 miles. Schenectady to Rutland, 85 miles. Troy to Rutland, via Eagle Bridge, 85 miles.

The Rensselaer and Saratoga Department of the Delaware and Hudson Canal Co. now embraces the original Rensselaer and Saratoga Railroad, extending from Troy to Ballston, 25 miles; the Saratoga and Schenectady Railroad, from Schenectady to Saratoga, 22 miles; the Albany and Vermont Railroad, from Albany to Albany Junction, 12 miles; the Saratoga and Whitehall and the Rutland and Whitehall Railroads, from Saratoga to Castleton, 54 miles; and the Troy, Salem, and Rutland Railroad, from Eagle Bridge to Rutland, 62 miles. It will be seen, by reference to the map, that these associated roads form portions of the great direct through routes from New York to Montreal, by the way of the valleys of the Hudson River and Lake Champlain. This route also forms the avenue to the popular watering-places of Ballston, Saratoga, and Lake George, and is the great thoroughfare of summer pleasure travel. In going North from Albany and Troy the road affords two routes—one by way of Saratoga Springs, and one by way of Eagle Bridge; and passengers wishing to go to Rutland or, all the way by rail to Burlington, can take either route to suit their convenience or choice; but travelers for Lake George, Whitehall, or Ticonderoga, and Lake Champlain, should go *via* Saratoga Springs.

For *Lake George*, passengers may change cars at Fort Edward, and at Glen's Falls take stages for Caldwell, at the head of Lake George, from whence steamers run down the Lake to Baldwin and connect by a branch R. R. of four miles with the Lake Champlain steamers and the Champlain Division of the R. R. at Fort Ticonderoga; or take the cars to Fort Ticonderoga and

Baldwin, whence the Lake George steamers convey passengers to Fort William Henry Hotel, Lake House, and the various landings on Lake George.

Travelers not wishing to go *via* Lake George can make the connection direct with the Lake Champlain steamers at Fort Ticonderoga, and avoid the stage ride and changes at Glen's Falls, Caldwell, and Baldwin.

For Montreal, passengers go direct from Albany to Whitehall and over the new route on the west side of Lake Champlain, *via* Plattsburg, Rouse's Point, St. John's and Victoria Bridge, to Montreal, without change of cars.

By continuing through to Rutland, the route to Burlington and Montreal is made all the way by rail, with a change of cars at Rutland.

Connections.

At Albany the Rensselaer and Saratoga Railroad, besides its connections with the various lines of Hudson River steamers, connects also with the New York Central and Hudson River Railways for New York; with the Boston and Albany Railway for Boston; with the Albany and Susquehanna Railway for Binghamton, and with the New York Central Railway for Niagara and the West.

At Troy connections are made with steamers on the river, with the New York Central and Hudson River Railways, and the Troy and Boston Railway.

At Schenectady the Schenectady branch from Saratoga and Ballston connects with the New York Central Railway. The connection at this point is the most convenient one for travelers going West or coming from the West.

At Saratoga Springs the Adirondack Railroad connects for Luzerne, Thurman, North Creek, and the Adirondack Mt. Region.

At Fort Edward the Glen's Falls Branch connects with Glen's Falls, forming a part of the Lake George route above mentioned, a route much patronized in the season of summer travel.

At Whitehall direct connection is made with the Champlain Division of the Delaware & Hudson Canal Co.'s R. R. for Fort Ticonderoga, where passengers can take the Lake Champlain steamers, or pursue the route to Montreal by rail. No change of cars is required between Albany and Montreal, and this forms the shortest and most direct route from New York to Montreal.

At Rutland both branches of this road intersect the Central Vermont Railroad for Burlington and all points north, and for Bellows Falls and the White Mountains and points east. The Harlem Extension R. R. also connects at this point—running South to Manchester, Bennington and Troy.

These numerous connections give to the Rensselaer and Saratoga R. R. the character of a great trunk route, and make it perhaps the most important of the Northern routes. Having connections with steamer lines, both north and south, it derives therefrom important advantages both for freight and passenger traffic not possessed by any other route between New York and Montreal.

ALBANY RURAL CEMETERY.

Watervliet, Albany Co., N. Y., 148 *Miles from New York.*

One of the most beautiful rural cemeteries in the country, abounding in romantic dells, shaded ravines, cascades, miniature lakes, rustic bridges over forest streams, &c. It is a place of rare picturesque beauty.

WEST TROY.

Watervliet, Albany Co., N. Y., 150 *Miles from New York.*

This place has important manufactories of woolen goods, bells, carriages, and various other articles. An extensive United States Arsenal, consisting of more than thirty buildings of brick and stone, is located here. Its grounds occupy about one hundred acres. It is the principal government manufactory of gun-carriages, machinery, equipments, ammunition, and military supplies.

COHOES.

Watervliet, Albany Co., N. Y., 153 *Miles from New York.*

An important manufacturing city on the Mohawk River. An extensive dam creates an immense water-power here, comprising the whole body of the Mohawk River, with a total descent of 103 feet. The railroad bridge across the Mohawk is 900 feet in length, and is in full view of the Cohoes Falls, about three-fourths of a mile above. The river here flows over a rocky declivity 78 feet in height, of which 40 feet is a perpendicular fall. The main fall is 900 feet wide, and the banks above and below are wild and precipitous. The Erie Canal rises by a series of 18 locks from the Hudson River, through the village of Cohoes. to the northerly part of the town of Watervliet, three miles above, at which point it crosses the river in a stone aqueduct, 1,137 feet long, 26 feet high, and resting on 26 piers. The products of the knitting and cotton mills, axe and edge tool, and other factories, amount to over $2,000,000 per annum. In recent excavations made in the rocky bank of the Mohawk, for the foundation of a new mill, the fossil remains of a gigantic mastodon were discovered. The Harmony Mills Co. of Cohoes have liberally donated this interesting relic of the earth's ancient history to the State collection at Albany. It is considered as the most perfect skeleton of the mastodon ever discovered.

WATERFORD.

Waterford, Saratoga Co., N. Y., 154 Miles from New York. Hotel, Morgan House.

This township was formed from that of Half Moon in 1816. It occupies the angle formed by the confluence of the Hudson and Mohawk rivers, the village itself being near the point where the two unite. An almost perpendicular range of slate cliffs extends along the Mohawk for some distance from its mouth. Falls in both rivers furnish an excellent water-power.

The Hudson River was bridged at this point in 1804. The original bridge, however, was removed in 1812, and the present structure erected in its place.

ALBANY JUNCTION.

Waterford, Saratoga Co., N. Y., 155 Miles from New York.

At this place the Albany division unites with the main road from Troy. The railroad now runs along between the Champlain Canal and the Hudson River, on an interval about half a mile in width for several miles.

TROY.

Population, 50,000.

Rensselaer County, N. Y., 150 *miles from New York.*

HOTELS.—*Troy, American, Revere, and Mansion.*

This city is principally located upon an alluvial flat, three fourths of a mile wide, between the Hudson River and the high bluffs which bound it on the east. The bluff directly east of the city is known as Mount Ida, and that on the northeast as Mount Olympus. Mount Ida is principally composed of clay, and has been the scene of several destructive land-slides. Poesten Kil and Wynant's Kil, breaking through these hills in narrow ravines, form a series of cascades which afford an excellent water-power. The city charter was granted April 12, 1816. A terrible fire in 1862 destroyed forty acres of its dwellings, which, with the other property destroyed, amounted to not less than $3,000,000, half being covered by insurance.

The city contains a very handsome court-house of Sing-Sing marble, wide and well-paved streets, planted with shade-trees, extensive water-works, gas-works, and other improvements usual in a prosperous modern city. The *Troy water-works* were built by the city in 1833–1834, and have since been extended. The water is drawn from the Piscawin Creek, and the reservoir is sufficiently high to raise it to the top of most of the houses.

There are twenty-two factories operated by water-power, a part of which is afforded by a dam thrown across the Hudson, which also renders the river above navigable for canal-boats. Numerous iron-foundries and machine-shops afford employment to large numbers of the inhabitants. Some of these are of great magnitude, and in the aggregate employ 3,000 men. The establishment of Messrs. Winslow, Griswold & Holley, where the Bessemer cast-steel is manufactured, is the largest of the kind in the United States. The famous original "Monitor" was constructed by these gentlemen; they also had a contract subsequently to build six other iron-clad vessels. The Troy horseshoe, railroad-spike, and nail manufactory is one of the largest in the

State. The manufacture of cotton and woolen goods is also conducted on a large scale. The railway-car manufactory here is the largest in the State. Paper, hosiery, carriages, clothing, shirts, collars, mathematical instruments, etc., are largely manufactured. Breweries, distilleries, flour and grist-mills, are many in number.

The educational institutions, besides the public schools, are the *Troy Academy*, incorporated in 1834; the *Troy Female Seminary*, first established at Middlebury, Vt., in 1813, removed to Waterford in 1819, and thence to this place in 1821, incorporated in 1837. This institution gained a national reputation under the charge of Mrs. Emma Willard. Upwards of 7,000 pupils have been educated here. The *Rensselaer Polytechnic Institute*, organized in 1824, was endowed by Stephen Van Rensselaer. It was formed for the purpose of teaching the application of mathematics to civil engineering and the natural sciences. Next to West Point this institute has the best reputation in its special departments of any school in America. The *Troy Lyceum of Natural History* was incorporated in 1820. *St. Peter's College* is built on Mount St. Vincent. The college building, in process of erection, was destroyed by a land-slide in 1859: has since been rebuilt. *St. Joseph's Academy* was founded in 1842.

The charitable institutions are many. The *Troy Hospital*, in the care of the Sisters of Charity, was incorporated in 1851. The *Marshall Infirmary*, incorporated in 1851, was built at an expense of $35,000, which was donated by Benj. Marshall, Esq. The *Troy Orphan Asylum*, incorporated in 1835, situated on Grand Division street, is built of brick, and supported by private donations and State appropriations. Children between three and nine years are received, and dismissed at ten, when suitable situations can be obtained. *St. Mary's Orphan Asylum*, connected with St. Mary's Church (R. C.), is under the care of the Christian Brothers and Sisters of Charity. The *Warren Free Institute*, a school for indigent female children, was incorporated in 1846. It was endowed by the Warren family. A free church for the pupils and their parents is connected with the Institute.

Troy being at the head of tidal waters, steamers run to it daily. Besides the Hudson River, the Erie Canal, and the Champlain, giving water communication of vast extent, railroads connect the city with every part of the country. The Union Railway Depot is a magnificent building, and was built for the joint accommodation of the four great railroads that center here, viz. : the Hudson River, the New York Central (uniting at Schenectady with the other branch from Albany), the Rensselaer and Saratoga, and the Troy and Boston Railways, the two latter running northerly through Eastern New York and Western Vermont and connecting with roads to Plattsburgh, Burlington, Montreal, etc. The Troy and Boston Railway forms a direct route to Boston *via* Hoosac Tunnel, the longest tunnel in the world. To people arriving at the Union Depot in Troy, the Revere House—immediately opposite the Depot—offers an excellent means for obtaining a good night's rest and excellent meals. The House has been entirely refitted, and its proximity to the Depot makes it a very desirable place for those persons who are to remain but a short time in the city.

GREEN ISLAND.

Watervliet, Albany Co., N. Y., 151 *miles from New York.*

This island is about one mile long and half a mile wide; it lies in the Hudson River, its upper end being opposite to the mouth of the Mohawk River. The surface of the island is generally level. Most of the buildings which stand upon it are railroad machine-shops or factories of some kind. The lower end of the island is opposite the city of Troy, with which it is connected by bridges. The track of the Rensselaer and Saratoga Railway runs from end to end of the island. It was occupied as a camp during the revolution by the Americans under General Gates.

MECHANICSVILLE.

Stillwater, Saratoga Co., N. Y., 162 *miles from New York.*

An incorporated village, lying partly in Half Moon, but principally in Stillwater. It has an extensive linen thread manufactory. Population 1,500. The township of Stillwater contains the battle-grounds of "Bemis Heights," where the engagements were fought which resulted in the surrender of Gen. Burgoyne to Gen. Gates in 1777.

ROUND LAKE.

Malta, Saratoga Co., N. Y., 168 *m. fr. New York.*

HOTEL—*Round Lake.*

This station takes its name from the lake situated about a quarter of a mile East. In the large and beautiful grove near the depot is located the celebrated camp-meeting ground of the Methodist Church. Meetings are held here annually, and the attendance at times exceeds 25,000 people. The grounds contain about two hundred acres of land, mostly gravel loam, entirely free from malaria. The magnificent grove contains over forty varieties of stately trees; while the hemlocks, pines, and cedars give the atmosphere a peculiar and invigorating "Adirondack odor."

The lake is less than five minutes' walk from the grove, and is one of the most lovely among the many for which New York is so justly famous. It is well stocked with fish, and affords the best of facilities for fishing, boating, and bathing. There is a small steamer and an abundant supply of row-boats for the accommodation of visitors.

There are about two hundred and sixty cottages on the ground, and the number is rapidly increasing. All of them are neat, commodious structures, and many of them are models of elegance and beauty. In addition to these permanent summer structures, any required number of tents are supplied for the more transient guests. Besides the cottages, there are a great number of other buildings on the ground, used for the post-office, book and news store, telegraph office, and other purposes. Beside these, it has the most convenient and beautiful *preaching stand* to be found, surrounded by well-arranged, comfortable seats, for thousands of hearers. This beautiful stand is located in the very center of this "*city among the trees.*"

A subject of vital importance, second only to that of pure air, especially in the heated days of summer, is that of the water we drink. The water at Round Lake is brought to the grounds from a pure spring, and supplied, in the greatest abundance, both for ordinary use and fountain adornments.

ROUND LAKE HOTEL, Round Lake, N. Y. GEORGE L. PEABODY, Proprietor.

The greatest interest and value are added to the other attractions of this summer resort by its MINERAL WELL. After sinking a shaft about fourteen hundred feet an abundance of water, of the most valuable quality, was obtained. A scientific analysis shows it to be composed of chloride of sodium, chloride of potassium, bicarbonate of LITHIA, bicarbonate of soda, bicarbonate of magnesia, bicarbonate of lime, and carbonic acid. Numerous and most unequivocal testimonials of striking cures, effected by this water, have been given. In pleasantness of taste and medicinal qualities it is said to be unsurpassed by any of the famous waters of *Saratoga*.

"A Palestine Park," showing the cities, rivers, and sacred mountains of the Holy Land, has been constructed near the lake. It was built by Rev. Dr. W. W. Whythe, whose experience in building the Chautauqua Park has enabled him to make improvements, thus giving Round Lake the largest representation of Palestine ever made.

The absence of good hotel accommodations has heretofore discouraged transient travel and summer boarders. The Round Lake Hotel, just completed, will now obviate this objection. It is a beautiful and substantial structure, as may be judged from the accompanying representation.

It is first class in all of its appointments, every room being furnished in the latest style and supplied with spring water. The ventilation and drainage are as thorough as science and labor can make them. The terms are moderate, and here one can enjoy the comforts of home, and the attractions of social and public life. Messrs. E. H. Armstong & Co., are gentlemen of established reputation in catering to a traveling public, and visitors to Round Lake desiring good hotel accommodations may reasonably **expect to be entertained to their entire satisfaction.**

This new and pleasantly located hotel will be opened for the reception of guests, for the season of 1880, on June 1st, under the management of Mr. George L. Peabody, (late of the United States Hotel, N. Y., also for the season of 1877, of the United States Hotel, Long Branch,) where he will be pleased to see any of his old friends and patrons.

BALLSTON SPA. Milton, Saratoga Co., N. Y.
175 *Miles from New York.*

HOTELS—*Sans Souci and Medbury's.*

BALLSTON SPA is the shire town of Saratoga County, and contains the County Court-House, Jail, and other public buildings. The village has a population of 4,000, is incorporated, and has several fine churches and good schools. The general appearance is very pleasant, and it possesses many attractions as a summer resort. It has long been celebrated for its mineral springs The principal ones already developed are the Artesian Lithia, Sans Souci Boiling, Washington, Franklin, and New Corporation. The waters are quite similar in chemical properties to those of Saratoga, and are, doubtless, drawn from the same natural medicinal reservoir; but the comparative value of the Ballston Waters with those of Saratoga, as medicinal agents, is said to be greater, as their mineral properties are greater in quantity.

Mineral springs have long been known at this place, and as far back as 1792, Benj. Douglas, father of Hon. Stephen A. Douglas, built a log-house near the *"Old Spring,"* for the accommodation of invalids and visitors.

The Artesian Lithia Spring.

The water of this remarkable spring is shown to be richer in valuable Remedial agents than any other water found in Saratoga County, and to surpass in excellence all the Waters found in other parts of the United States. Flowing from a depth of six hundred and fifty feet, through a tube bored into the solid rock, it is not diluted or contaminated by surface water, as is generally the case with shallow springs.

Its medical properties partake of the most celebrated Springs of the world, and in fact combine the ingredients of all the principal ones in Europe and America. It is very strongly impregnated with *that valuable mineral, Lithia, which is so effectual in dissolving the Chalk, or Limestone and Urate* deposits in RHEUMATISM, GOUT, and GRAVEL, and has been successfully used by hundreds in these diseases, with quick and telling effect; as also in KIDNEY DISEASE, LIVER COMPLAINT, CATARRH, DYSPEPSIA, BILIOUSNESS, ACIDITY OF THE STOMACH, CONSTIPATION and PILES, and has proved itself a perfect panacea for these difficulties.

The large quantities of Lithia, Bromine, and Iodine which it contains, specially recommend it to the attention of every Physician.

ANALYSIS BY PROF. C. F. CHANDLER, Ph.D.
School of Mines, Columbia College, N. Y. April 21, 1868.

Chloride of Sodium	750.030 gr.	Sulphate of Potassa	0.520	gr.
Chloride of Potassium	33.276 "	Phosphate of Soda	0.050	"
Bromide of Sodium	3.613 "	Biborate of Soda	trace.	
Iodide of Sodium	0.124 "	Alumina	0.077	"
Fluoride of Calcium	trace.	Silica	0.761	"
Bicarbonate of Lithia	7.750 "	Organic Matter	trace.	
Bicarbonate of Soda	11.928 "			
Bicarbonate of Magnesia	180.602 "	Total per gal. (231 cub. in.).	1233.246	
Bicarbonate of Lime	238.156 "			
Bicarbonate of Strontia	0.867 "	Carbonic Acid Gas	426.114 cub. in.	
Bicarbonate of Baryta	3.881 "	Density	1.0159	"
Bicarbonate of Iron	1.581 "	Temperature	52 deg. F.	

The Water is carefully and securely bottled, and packed in boxes of four-dozen Pints, and will bear transportation to any part of the world. To prevent imposition, the corks are marked thus: ARTESIAN SPRING CO., BALLSTON, N. Y.

The Sans Souci Hotel

Is a very large hotel situated in the center of the village, on its main street, and will accommodate about 300 guests. It is open only in summer, from June 1st to October, of each year. It has been leased by Mr. R. F. Cole for a term of years and thoroughly repaired. A billiard room, new bowling alley and bar-room have been added, and three handsomely decorated private dining-rooms where supper and dinner parties can be served, and spacious and comfortable apartments. It affords the advantages of the new

Sans Souci Spouting Spring,

which is situated in the hotel grounds. It was opened up from the old original Ballston Spring vein, and by a careful analysis its waters prove superior to *any* of the renowned springs of Saratoga. It presents the double aspect of a boiling and spouting spring. The shaft was sunk, in 1872, to a depth of 693 feet, through a solid limestone rock, when it penetrated a cavern, supposed to be about four or five feet deep, from which the water is forced up by a pressure of carbonic acid gas about twenty-four pounds to the square inch at the surface. This gas thoroughly charges the water, giving it a pleasant acid taste; and, though the water is rich in salts, it is not at all disagreeable. It is particuarly valuable on account of the Lithia Salts, Bromine, and Iodine, which it contains, and which are highly beneficial in cases of *Gout, Rheumatism*, and kindred diseases.

ANALYSIS BY MAURICE PERKINS, A.M., M.D.
Union College, Schenectady, N. Y.

Chloride of Sodium	572.306 gr.	Silica	1.140
Chloride of Potassium	5.680 "	Bicarbonate of Baryta	1.790 "
Bromide of Sodium	1.055 "	Bicarbonate of Strontia	trace.
Iodide of Sodium	.620 "	Chloride of Rubidium	trace.
Bicarbonate of Soda	4.757 "		
Bicarbonate of Lithia	11.793 "	Total	986.345
Phosphate of Lime	3.175 "	in a U. S. gallon of 231 cubic inches.	
Bicarbonate of Lime	193.179 "		
Bicarbonate of Magnesia	181.106 "	Carbonic Acid Gas	538.074 cubic inch.
Bicarbonate of Iron	9.239 "	Density	1.015 "
Alumina	trace.	Temperature	50° Fahr.

The gas shows a pressure at the opening of twenty-four (24) pounds to the square inch. The waters are bottled, and sent to the principal markets throughout the United States. Another attractive feature is the beautiful lawn connected with the Hotel, comprising two acres, which has been arranged and laid out with great care and attention, so as to provide amusement, pleasure and comfort for the guests. We append a few words from the *Ballston Journal* of May, 1875, which alludes to this hotel, its Improvements, and reminiscences of its past glories:

"THE SANS SOUCI.—The work of improvement and embellishment is still going forward as rapidly as is consistent with the aim of making this famous hotel one of the most charming resorts for summer pleasure-seekers. What has already been done displays an elegance seldom surpassed, seldom even equalled. Mr. Robinson the artist, who planned and supervised the decorations, has shown remarkable taste and skill, and has done honor to himself by adorning the parlors of the Sans Souci in a superb manner.

"The Sans Souci has a history. When first opened in 1804, it was the largest and best appointed hotel in the country. It immediately became the resort of health-seekers, tourists, fashionables, politicians, statesmen, jurists, and merchant princes. Year after year, Martin Van Buren, Silas Wright, William M. Marcy, Edwin Crosswell, Ambrose L. Jordan, Enos T. Throop, Wm. C. Bouck, Daniel Cady, Ambrose L. Spencer, Azariah C. Flagg, John C. Spencer, Aaron Hackley, Michael Hoffman, and hundreds more of eminent men and high officials in every State of the Union, came here and booked themselves, not for a week, but for two or three months, their families sharing with them the recreations and pleasures of the season.

"Those were golden years in the glorious olden time, when our village offered not half the inducements which now make it attractive. It had then the best mineral waters in the country; it has them now. It had then rural scenery unrivaled in variety and beauty; it has that scenery now, only of wider expanse, and more diversified by forest and glen, hill and plain, lake and stream. It had then the usual facilities of a country village; it has now all the modern advantages of a city. It had the most famous hotel in the country for summer visitants; it has now, in the remodeled Sans Souci, an edifice altogether superior to its former glory, whose proprietor is determined to recover its former popularity, and who will spare no means to make it a most desirable resort to those who wish to avoid extremes of fashion and extravagance of expenditure."

Around Ballston are many beautiful drives, as the country is diversified with hills, lakes and beautiful streams. Three miles to the east, is Saratoga Lake, a beautiful sheet of water; and to the south, Lake Ballston, about the same distance from the village. A little south of Lake Ballston is Round Lake, about which are the grounds of the National Camp Meeting Association of the Methodist Church. Along the banks of the Kayaderosseras River as it winds through its beautifully shaded valley, with sharply cut bank on either side, is a delightful drive. A new avenue, 80 feet wide, has recently been opened between Ballston and Saratoga Springs, six miles distant, running through the region of the group of pulsating springs, including the celebrated Geyser and Glacier Spouting Springs. This is one of the most popular drives, as it connects these two celebrated watering places.

Ballston and Saratoga are also connected by almost hourly trains of the Rensselaer & Saratoga R. R. during the fashionable season, thus enabling visitors to enjoy the gayety of Saratoga, without being subject to the inconvenience of crowded hotels.

SCHENECTADY BRANCH OF RENSSELAER AND SARATOGA R. R.
SCHENECTADY.

Schenectady County, N. Y., 17 *Miles from Albany.* 22 *Miles from Saratoga Springs. From Buffalo,* 281. *Hotels.—Givens', Carley (late Eagle).*

THE site of this city is a tract purchased from the Indians by the agent of the Rensselaer estate. The settlement was commenced in 1661. It is situated on the Mohawk, and on the borders of one of the finest intervales in the State. In 1690 it contained eighty houses. On the 8th of February in that year, about three hundred French and Indians entered the Palisades which surrounded the city at the unguarded portals, and fired the dwellings, and attacked the slumbering inmates. Most of the dwellings were destroyed; and the inhabitants who were not carried off, rushing from their beds to escape the savages, perished in the snow. Only a few reached Albany, the nearest shelter In 1795 Schenectady was made the head-quarters of the " Western Navigation Company," organized to navigate the Mohawk River to Oneida Lake. It was incorporated as a city in 1786. Besides a considerable amount of trade, which is now carried on here by means of the canal and the railways which center here, the people are largely engaged in various manufactures, among which are included machinery, cotton, carriages, agricultural implements, and various utensils, implements, etc. The engine-houses and repair-shops of the N. Y. Central Railroad Co. are very extensive, and one of the largest locomotive manufactories in the country is located here. This is a great market for broom corn, a staple product of the valley.

Union College, incorporated in 1795, was first erected in the city, but now graces an eminence on its eastern boundary, and commands a fine view for many miles up and down the Mohawk valley. The first college building was erected in 1814. It is largely endowed by grants from the State, and by private contributions. The college has attained a high reputation under the presidency of Dr

Nott, Dr. Hickok, and its present president, Dr. Potter. Aid is furnished to students of limited means from the State fund, without reference to what profession they propose to follow. Through the liberality of E. C. Delavan, Esq., the "Wheatley Collection" of minerals and shells was secured for the college at a cost of $10,000. A department of civil engineering and analytical chemistry has been organized, affording ample facilities in this direction. Union College is the *alma mater* of the Hon. W. H. Seward, and many other distinguished statesmen, and men of science and letters. The public schools are well conducted.

The *Vale Cemetery Association* was organized in 1858. The cemetery contains fifty acres, and is located in a beautiful vale on the border of the city. It is covered with native pines, and is tastefully laid out and ornamented.

Passengers from Schenectady to Saratoga are now conveyed without change of cars at Ballston Spa, as formerly, and travelers going west from Saratoga will find this the most direct route connecting with the New York Central R. R. at Schenectady.

81

AMERICAN HOUSE,
TROY, N. Y.

Corner Third and Fulton Streets,

ONE BLOCK TO THE LEFT OF STEAMBOAT LANDING.

H. J. ROCKWELL, - - Proprietor.

FORMERLY OF

ROCKWELL'S HOTEL, LUZERNE, N. Y.
ROCKWELL HOUSE, GLEN'S FALLS, N. Y.
LAKE HOUSE, LAKE GEORGE, N. Y.
AND SUMMER OF '78, FORT WILLIAM HENRY HOTEL, LAKE GEORGE, N.Y.

GEORGE A. ROSS,
CHARLES R. KELLEY, } CLERKS.

TERMS: $2.00 and $2.50 per Day, According to Rooms.

SARATOGA SPRINGS.

Saratoga Springs, Saratoga Co., N. Y.
182 Miles from New York.

The village of *Saratoga Springs* is approached by rail from the south-west, and but little of the village can be seen from the railroad It is somewhat irregularly laid out, and many of its streets are pleasantly shaded. The land on which the village proper stands is sufficiently level to render all parts of the place of easy access on foot or in a carriage, and yet is broken into low, rolling hills, so that the monotony of a dead level is pleasantly relieved. The population is about 9,000 during the winter, and rather more than double that number at almost any given time during the summer. Saratoga County, near the center of which are the Springs, is bounded on the south and east by the Mohawk and Hudson rivers, along whose banks are a variety of picturesque drives leading through scenery, interesting from its intrinsic beauty as well as for its historic associations.

Near the central part of the village, and overlooked by many of the principal buildings and hotels, is a shallow valley, beneath which, deep in the bowels of the earth, is one of the most wonderful of Nature's laboratories. There she prepares solutions of various medicinal and mineral substances with a subtle power of combination which no chemistry has been able successfully to imitate, and sends the different solutions to the surface of the earth by channels which reach the light within a few rods of one another, yet discharge waters distinct in constituents, various in medicinal effects, and uniform in temperature.

We cannot wonder that, in an age which believed in a plurality of gods, mineral springs were regarded with mingled fear and veneration. We have very ancient accounts of such springs, which were valued for their natural and worshipped for their supernatural properties. Greek and Roman, and even Hebrew and Chaldaic writers, mention charmed fountains whose waters cured disease and almost restored the dead to life. The fabled fountain of eternal youth doubtless had its origin in the bubbling waters of some mineral spring, as well as in the fancy of the poet who first gave it a name. Even in the time of our Saviour, the Pool of Bethesda was famous and was visited by invalids from all Palestine.

Congress Spring.

This spring is located in Congress Spring Park, opposite the southern end of Congress Hall. There is an artistic and very beautiful pavilion built over it to protect visitors from sun and rain. The principal entrance to the spring-house is at the grand entrance to the Park, near Broadway. On entering the Park, turn to the left, pass along the arbor-like colonnade to the pavilion about the spring, where seats are provided, and the spring water, drawn by a novel process, is served upon small tables by the attendants. Visitors will find this method of obtaining the waters far more agreeable than the old way followed at the other springs, as they can partake leisurely while seated, without being jostled by the crowd, and enjoy the beautiful view of the Park and the delightful music by the Park Band. By descending a few steps to the east, along the colonnade to the *café*, hot coffee and other refreshments may be obtained at moderate prices. Admission to the Park is regulated by tickets, for which a merely nominal charge is made; but access to the spring can be obtained on Congress Street, without entering the Park, and the waters are served free of charge.

Congress Spring is more generally known and used than any of the other Saratoga springs, and has probably effected more cures of the diseases for which its waters are a specific, than any other mineral spring in America. It was discovered in 1792. The waters were first bottled for exportation in 1823, by Dr. John Clarke, of New York, who purchased the spring from the Livingston family, who held it under an ancient grant. The property was purchased of Dr. Clarke's executors in 1865, by the "Congress and Empire Spring Company," the present proprietors.

The medicinal effects of Congress water have been tested for nearly a century, and its use is prescribed by physicians, with the utmost confidence, after long knowledge of its great efficacy, and the entire comfort and safety with which it may be used. To professional men and others whose occupations are sedentary, and to all sufferers from the various forms of bilious disorders, it is invaluable. It contains of the laxative salts (chloride of sodium and bicarbonate of magnesia) enough to render its effects certain

CONGRESS SPRING PAVILION.
ERECTED, 1876.

without the addition or use of cathartic drugs; and it produces free and copious evacuations without in any manner debilitating the alimentary canal or impairing the digestive powers of the stomach. At the same time it does not contain an excess of those salts, the presence of which in the cruder mineral waters, native and foreign, often renders them drastic and irritating, producing very serious disorders.

In connection with a recent analysis of Congress Spring, Prof. C. F. Chandler remarks, that "the superior excellence of this water is due to the fact that it contains, in the most desirable proportions, those substances which produce its agreeable flavor and satisfactory medicinal effects—neither holding them in excess nor lacking any constituent to be desired in this class of waters. As a *cathartic* water, its almost entire freedom from iron should recommend it above all others, many of which contain so much of this ingredient as to seriously impair their usefulness." Prof. Chandler also remarks, that a comparison of his analysis with that by Dr. John H. Steel, in 1832, proves that the Congress water still retains its original strength, and all the virtues which established its well-merited reputation.

ANALYSIS OF CONGRESS SPRING WATER,

BY PROF. C. F. CHANDLER.

One United States gallon of 231 cubic inches contains:

Chloride of Sodium	400.444 grains.	Bromide of Sodium	8.559 grains.
Chloride of Potassium	8.049 "	Iodide of Sodium	0.138 "
Bicarbonate of Magnesia	121.757 "	Sulphate of Potassa	0.889 "
Bicarbonate of Lime	143.399 "	Phosphate of Soda	0.016 "
Bicarbonate of Lithia	4.761 "	Silica	0.840 "
Bicarbonate of Soda	10.775 "	Fluoride of Calcium,	
Bicarbonate of Baryta	0.928 "	Biborate of Soda,	each a trace.
Bicarbonate of Iron	0.340 "	Alumina,	
Bicarbonate of Strontia, a trace.		Total	700.895 grains.
Carbonic Acid Gas			392.289 cubic inches.

It should be remembered that this water is never sold in barrels. Genuine Congress water is sold only in bottles. In this form it is sent to almost every part of the world, and its name is a household word.

Columbian Spring.

This spring is located in Congress Spring Park, just west of the park entrance and a little nearer Broadway. It is covered by the beautiful and artistic pavilion, and is approached through the park entrance to the right, or down a few steps from Broadway opposite Columbian Hotel. The spring is owned by the Congress and Empire Spring Company. It is a fine chalybeate mineral water, and possesses singularly active properties in certain diseases.

It is said to be especially valuable in liver complaints, dyspepsia, erysipelas, and all cutaneous disorders. As a tonic water for frequent use, no spring in Saratoga is so popular as the Columbian.

The water is recommended to be drank in small quantities frequently during the day, generally *preceded* by the use of the cathartic waters taken before breakfast. Only from one-half to one glass should be taken at a time. When taken in large quantities, or before breakfast, a peculiar headache is experienced.

The proper use of this water will strengthen the tone of the stomach, and tend to increase the red particles of the blood which, according to Liebeg, perform an important part in respiration. Though containing but 5.58 grains of iron in each gallon, this water has a perceptible iron taste in every drop. Is it much to be wondered at, then, that a mineral which has so great a power of affecting the palate should possess equally potent influence upon the whole system? The happy medicinal effects of these iron waters seem to consist, to some extent, in the minute division of the mineral properties, so that they are readily taken into the system. The water is exported largely, and descriptive pamphlets, containing full directions for drinking the water, may be obtained at the Company's office opposite Congress Spring.

ANALYSIS OF COLUMBIAN WATERS, BY PROF. E. EMMONS.

Specific gravity 1007.3. Solid and gaseous contents as follows:

Chloride of Sodium......	267.00 grains.	Carbonate of Lime.......	68.00 grains.
Bicarbonate of Soda.....	15.40 "	Carbonate of Iron.......	5.58 "
Bicarbonate of Magnesia.	46.71 "	Silex	2.05 "
Hydriodate of Soda......	2.06 "	Hy'o-Bro'ate of Potash scarcely a trace.	

Solid contents in a gallon.. 407.80 grains.
Carbonic Acid Gas.. 272.06 inches.
Atmospheric Air... 4.50 "
                                                                        ─────────────
                                                                        276.56 inches.

The Empire Spring.

This spring, one of the best in Saratoga, is located in the north part of the shallow valley that runs through the village. To reach it from Congress Hall, follow Broadway north to the first street north of Town Hall; then to the right, then left, through Front Street, down the hill, to the large bottling-house at the foot of the hill. This spring is in a pavilion before the building. For full information concerning this spring, call at the office of the Congress and Empire Spring Company, near Congress Hall.

Although the existence of mineral water in this locality was known for a long time, it was not until 1846 that any one thought it worth the necessary expense of excavation and tubing. The rock was struck twelve feet below the surface of the earth, and so copious was the flow of water that the tubing proved to be a work of unusual difficulty. When once accomplished, the water flowed in great abundance and purity. It soon attracted the attention of medical men, and was found to possess curative properties which rendered it available in diseases which had not before been affected by Saratoga waters. It has proved itself adapted to a wide range of cases, especially of a chronic nature, and its peculiar value is recognized by eminent medical men. Its general properties closely resemble the Congress, although from the presence of a larger quantity of magnesia in the Congress water, the operation of the latter is perhaps somewhat more pungent.

The Empire Spring water is a great favorite with many people, being preferred for its mild but positive medicinal effects.

ANALYSIS OF EMPIRE SPRING WATER,
BY PROF. C. F. CHANDLER.

One United States gallon of 231 cubic inches contains:

Chloride of Sodium	506.630 grains.	Bromide of Sodium	0.266	grains.
Chloride of Potassium	4.292 "	Iodide of Sodium	0.006	"
Bicarbonate of Magnesia	42.953 "	Sulphate of Potassa	2.769	"
Bicarbonate of Lime	109.656 "	Phosphate of Soda	0.023	"
Bicarbonate of Lithia	2.080 "	Silica	1.145	"
Bicarbonate of Soda	9.022 "	Alumina	0.418	"
Bicarbonate of Baryta	0.075 "	Fluoride of Calcium,		
Bicarbonate of Iron	0.793 "	Biborate of Soda,	each a trace.	
Bicarbonate of Strontia, a trace.		Organic Matter,		

Total.. 680.436 grains.
Carbonic Acid.. 344.699 cubic in.

EMPIRE SPRING.

Excelsior Spring,

Is found in a beautiful valley, amid picturesque scenery, about a mile east of the town hall, and near the centre of Excelsior Park. The principal park entrance is on Lake Avenue, half a mile from Circular street, or we may approach it by Spring Avenue, which will lead us past most of the principal springs, and the Loughberry Water Works with its famous Holly Machinery, by which the village is supplied with an abundance of the purest water from the Excelsior Lake. Leaving the Water Works, we see just before us, as the avenue bends towards the Excelsior Spring, the fine summer hotel known as the Mansion House. Surrounded by its grand old trees and beautiful lawn, it offers an inviting retreat from the heat and dust of our crowded cities.

The spring is covered by a very tasteful pavilion, which will be noticed just east of the little stream, and in front of the large bottling house beside the grove. The Union Spring is a little northwest of the Excelsior, and but a few steps removed. This valley, in which these two springs are situated, was formerly known as the "Valley of the Ten Springs," but the present owners, after grading and greatly beautifying the grounds, changed its name in honor of the spring to Excelsior Park.

The Excelsior Spring has been appreciated for its valuable qualities by some of the oldest visitors of Saratoga for at least half a century. Many noted cures, among the older residents of the town, were effected by the use of this water before it was introduced to the general public. The water, however, was not much known to the general public until 1859, when Mr. H. H. Lawrence, the former owner, and father of the present proprietors, retubed the Spring in the most thorough manner—the tubing extending to a depth of fifty-six feet, eleven of which are in the solid rock. By this improvement the water flows with all its properties undeteriorated, retaining from source to outlet its original purity and strength. For several years the Excelsior Spring water has steadily increased in public favor, until now its sale has become very large, and it is to be found on draught, or in bottles, in nearly all the principal cities and towns of the United States. We must not fail to notice the perfect

View of EXCELSIOR SPRING, and a portion of EXCELSIOR PARK, SARATOGA SPRINGS, N. Y.

and very ingenious method, invented by the proprietors of this spring, for bottling and barreling the water. In the large and well-lighted cellar of the bottling house is a circular brick vault in whose depths the process of filling is performed. A block-tin tube conveys the water directly from the spring to this vault, at a depth of twelve feet from the surface of the ground. By hydrostatic pressure the water is forced from the main tubing of the spring through the smaller tube to the brick vault into airtight barrels, or reservoirs, lined with pure block-tin. These reservoirs contain two tubes, one of which extends from the top to the bottom of the barrel, the other being shorter. When these reservoirs are connected with the tube leading from the

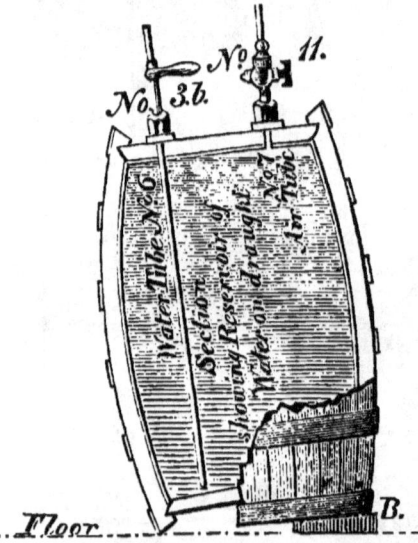

spring, the water is forced by hydrostatic pressure through the long tube into the barrel, and the air is driven out through the shorter tube, while the gas of the water is not allowed to escape. To draw the water from the reservoirs, it is only necessary to attach the draught tube to the long tube of the barrel, and connect the shorter one with an air pump, when the pressure of the air will force out the water, without its being recharged with gas—pure, sparkling, and as delicious as though it were taken directly from the spring. The value of the waters is universally conceded, and they have already attained a world-wide popularity. The familiar trade-mark of the Excelsior water may be seen in nearly all the cities and large villages of America. The water of this spring is a pleasant cathartic, and has also alterative and tonic properties. It is also delicious as a beverage. As a cathartic, two or three glasses before breakfast will be a sufficient dose, while, as an alterative or diuretic, small draughts throughout the day will be found beneficial.

IN BOTTLES.

BOTTLE MARK.

ON DRAUGHT.

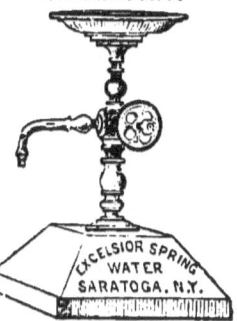

TRADE MARK.

ANALYSIS OF THE "EXCELSIOR" SPRING WATER.

As analyzed by the late R. L. ALLEN, M.D., of Saratoga Springs.

Chloride of Sodium	370.642 grains.	Sulphate of Soda	1.321 grains.
Carbonate of Lime	77.000 "	Silicate of Soda	4.000 "
Carbonate of Magnesia	32.333 "	Iodide of Soda	4.235 "
Carbonate of Soda	15.000 "	Bromide of Potassa	a trace.
Silicate of Potassa	7.000 "	Sulphate of Strontia	a trace.
Carbonate of Iron	3.215 "		

Solid contents in a gallon.....................$514\tfrac{740}{1000}$ grains
Carbonic Acid.......................(cubic inches) 250
Atmosphere................................... 3

Gaseous Contents............................ 253 cubic in.

Union Spring,

Near the centre of Excelsior Park, is about ten rods northwest of Excelsior Spring. It was originally known as the 'Jackson" spring, and is described under that name by Dr. John H. Steele, in his work on the Mineral Waters of Saratoga and Ballston, published by Dr. Steele at Albany in 1819. The water was, however, but imperfectly secured until the present proprietors had the spring retubed in 1868. The water of the Union Spring acts as a mild cathartic when taken before breakfast. Drank at other times during the day it is a very agreeable and healthful beverage. Prof. C. F. Chandler, the distinguished chemist, says: "This water is of excellent strength. It is specially noticeable that the ratio of magnesia to lime is unusually large, which is a decided advantage. The water is also remarkably free from iron, a fact which is a great recommendation." The water is put up in bottles for shipping to any part of the world. It is also sold in Lawrence's Patent Reservoirs (barrels lined with pure block tin), containing about thirty gallons each. These reservoirs are very strong and perfectly gas tight, and retain the water with all its natural Carbonic Acid Gas. From these reservoirs the water can be forced out, under atmospheric pressure, in its natural condition, sparkling with Carbonic Acid Gas as it flows from the spring at Saratoga, in the same manner in which the Excelsior Water on draught is so very widely and favorably known.

ANALYSIS OF THE UNION SPRING WATER,

BY PROF. C. F. CHANDLER.

Laboratory of the School of Mines, COLUMBIA COLLEGE,
New York, March 26, 1873.

The sample of Mineral Water taken from the UNION SPRING, Saratoga, contains in one U. S. Gallon of 231 cubic inches:

Chloride of Sodium.....	458.299 grains.	Bicarbonate of Baryta...	1.703 grains.
Chloride of Potassium...	8.733 "	Bicarbonate of Iron.....	0.269 "
Bromide of Sodium......	1.307 "	Sulphate of Potassa.....	1.818 "
Iodide of Sodium........	0.050 "	Phosphate of Soda......	0.026 "
Fluoride of Calcium.....	trace.	Biborate of Soda........	trace
Bicarbonate of Lithia....	2.605 "	Alumina	0.324 "
Bicarbonate of Soda.....	17.010 "	Silica	2.653 "
Bicarbonate of Magnesia.	109.685 "	Organic Matter	trace.
Bicarbonate of Lime.....	96.703 "		
Bicarbonate of Strontia..	trace.	Total Solid Contents..	701.174 grains

Carbonic Acid Gas in one gal., 384.969 cubic inches. Temp., 48 deg. F.

...yser or "Spouting Spring"

Is a most wonderful fountain of mineral water, discovered in 1870, and situated about one mile and a quarter southwest of the village of Saratoga Springs, in the midst of the beautiful region of landscape scenery now known as "Geyser Lake and Park." To reach it from Saratoga follow Broadway south to Ballston Avenue, which branches off from Broadway in the south part of the village to the right, towards the southwest, and follow this avenue until it crosses the Rens. and Sar. R. R., when the large brick bottling house with the world-wide inscription of " Geyser Spring " will be distinctly seen across the lake to the left. Follow the carriage road across the causeway turning to the left, and you will soon find yourself at the entrance of the spring and bottling house, and in the midst of the most interesting spring region of Saratoga. Visitors are most cordially welcomed to the spring and grounds by the proprietors at all reasonable hours of the day, and perfect freedom is accorded to all visitors to drink the waters, inspect the work of bottling, and to stroll through the beautiful grounds surrounding the springs. As you enter the spring-house, directly in front of you, in the centre of the building, is this marvelous spouting spring, sending forth a powerful stream of water to the very top of the building, which in descending to its surrounding basin sprays into a thousand crystal streams, forming a beautiful fountain ever flowing, and charming to behold.

In the center of the room is the artistical basin, about six feet square, and from the bottom rises an iron pipe. From this leaps, in fantastic dance, the creamy water of the spring. To allow it full play, there is an opening in the ceiling, and here it rises and falls, day and night, continually. At one side, a faucet, with a nose like a soda fountain, enables one to draw a glass. The water boils and bubbles out, mingled with bubbles of gas precisely like cream soda, and all who care may have a free drink. When the bubbles have escaped, the water has a wonderful pearly purity that tempts one to drink bountifully. A glass globe on the well curb has a stream of water flowing through it and escaping at the top. This enables us to see the thick stream of bubbling gas as it rises through the water and makes an extremely pretty display. A large business is here carried on in bottling this valuable and delicious water, and visitors are shown all the processes in detail.

The orifice bored in the rock is five and a half inches in diameter, and 132 feet deep. The rock formation consists of a strata of slate eighty feet thick, beneath which lies the strata of birds-eye limestone in which the mineral vein was struck. The orifice is tubed with a block-tin pipe, encased with iron, to the depth of eighty-five feet, the object being to bring the water through the soft slate formation, as the immense pressure and force of the gas would cut the slate, thereby causing impurities in the water.

Recently the present proprietors became convinced that a large percentage of the Carbonic Acid Gas shown by the phenomenon of spouting, was not present in the bottled water. They recently re-tubed the spring and put in the most approved Bottling Table. The result is that for the first time in the history of the Spring *all the Natural Carbonic Acid Gas is retained to the bottled water*, thereby adding much to its already high medicinal qualities, and making it an EXCELLENT TABLE WATER, the water now being *highly effervescent* and the best mineral water known.

Professor C. F. CHANDLER, Ph. D., of Columbia College School of Mines, visited this spring a few weeks after its discovery, and the following analysis, made from water collected by him at that time, demonstrates the great value of the Geyser as a medicinal spring:

ANALYSIS OF ONE U. S. GALLON.

Chloride of Sodium	562.080 grains.	Bicarbonate of Strontia	0.425 grains
Chloride of Potassium	24.634 "	Bicarbonate of Baryta	2.014 "
Bromide of Sodium	2.212 "	Bicarbonate of Iron	0.979 "
Iodide of Sodium	0.248 "	Sulphate of Potassa	0.318 "
Fluoride of Calcium	a trace.	Phosphate of Soda	trace.
Bicarbonate of Lithia	9.004 "	Biborate of Soda	trace.
Bicarbonate of Soda	71.232 "	Alumina	trace.
Bicarbonate of Magnesia	149.343 "	Silica	0.665 "
Bicarbonate of Lime	168.392 "	Organic matter	trace.

Total solid contents.. 991.546

Carbonic Acid Gas in one U. S. Gal.......................454.082 cubic in
Density.. 1.011
Temperature.. 46° Fahr.

GEYSER SPRING

It may be noticed that the water is charged with medicinal and gaseous properties to a wonderful degree, its total solid contents being 991.546 grains. The amount of gas is excessive, and it is this that enables the water to hold in solution so great a proportion of minerals, and gives to it remarkable preservative properties when bottled, as well as imparts that mysterious power which forces the water from its silent cavern in the earth into the beautiful fountain of the spring. Its properties are permanent in any climate, and for an indefinite time. So long as kept corked, and the bottle laid on the side, it retains its value unimpaired.

As a medicinal agency its effects are marvelous. Testimonials from all quarters are received, bearing witness to its wonderful cures of diseases; especially in *Cutaneous Diseases, or any of the various phases of Scrofula*. It is used with telling effect in *Kidney Disease, Liver Complaint, Dyspepsia, Biliousness, Rheumatism, Acidity of Stomach, etc.* It is a delightful beverage, and when taken as a cathartic leaves none of those unpleasant effects observable in the use of many other of the Saratoga waters.

As an *aperient* or *cathartic* it should be used in the early morning; and, if in bottles, it should stand in the room so as not to be too cool. To give it more ready effect, raise the water to about blood-heat, or 90° Fahr. A pint bottle, or about two glasses, will usually be found sufficiently prompt and effective.

As a *Tonic*, the water should be drank cool and in small quantities. When taken with meals or at lunch, as an ordinary beverage, the system will retain the minerals with strengthening and stimulating effect. After wines or hearty eating, the water is a sure corrective, restoring the stomach to its natural condition, while relieving the system of uncongenial and injurious substances. It cures Biliousness, corrects acidity of stomach, relieves nervous or feverish irritation and headache, and a restless person may be induced to sleep by taking a glass of Geyser on retiring at night. Geyser Water also operates with excellent effect upon the *Kidneys*. The *lithia* found in this water is a specific for gravel or stone, and is effectual in dissolving the chalk or limestone and urate deposits in Rheumatism or Gout. Geyser Water is put up in pint and quart bottles, and in tin-lined barrels of thirty gallons each, and it may be found at any leading druggist's on the continent. In bottles, it is packed in cases of four dozen pints or two dozen quarts.

The spring property is not managed by a stock company, and for the purposes of business the proprietors have adopted only the name "GEYSER SPRING." All orders should be addressed to GEYSER SPRING, SARATOGA SPRINGS, N. Y. The owners of the property are Messrs. George E. Settle and H. F. Cary. The business of the Geyser Spring has increased rapidly since its discovery in 1870, and its waters are now sold in all parts of our country, and in some of the markets of Europe and South America.

By passing through the door, at the east end of the bottling house, we enter upon a piazza which overlooks the stream that dashes by the spring-house. Under the overhanging awning we may enjoy a very charming prospect.

Geyser Park

Embraces a tract of about 100 acres surrounding the Geyser Spring, and is open to visitors who are invited, by numerous rustic chairs and settees, to enjoy the natural beauties of this charming vicinity. Leaving the spring-house by the rear door, we enter upon the ramble and follow the shady path down into the dell. From the rustic bridge is a pretty view of the waterfall near the spring-house, and in the vicinity are several springs of varied mineral properties, more or less undeveloped, but indicating the great richness of this region in mineral waters. Returning to the spring-house, we may pass up the hill towards the west, and obtain a delightful view of the lake and park. From the summit of the slope to the westward the beautiful surroundings of this celebrated locality are brought into view. Standing on the elevation, with our face to the east, a charming prospect is spread before us. The large, beautiful green expanse, studded here and there with trees and cottages, and terminating with the Green Mountain range in the distant east, and the Greenfield Mountains in the west; the silvery water expanding from small proportions into the dimensions of a beautiful lake, fringed with graceful foliage and shaded lawns; the limpid stream plunging over the fall and dashing down into the shaded glen; the strong-arched causeway, and the spouting springs shooting their pearly-white waters into graceful fountains, all unite to form a charming landscape.

Hamilton Spring.

This spring is situated about thirty rods north of the Congress, immediately in the rear of Congress Hall. It was discovered by Mr. Gideon Putnam, one of the early settlers of the place, not long after the discovery of the Congress Spring, and named after the late General Hamilton. The water, when first taken from the spring, is remarkably clear and sparkling. It is saline and acidulous to the taste, and when taken to the quantity of five or six half pints, is usually both cathartic and diuretic.

This water ranks first among the springs as a diuretic, and it has long been celebrated for its good effects in gravelly and calculous affections. In scrofula and indeed all other indolent swellings of the glands, the water of this spring, together with that of the Columbian, will unquestionably take the preference.

It is owing to the iodine which these waters contain that they have become so famous in the cure of strumous affections.

The following ingredients were obtained from one gallon, by an analysis by Dr. John H. Steele in 1831, viz. :

Chloride of Sodium........ 297.3 grs.	Hydrobromate of Potash ... a trace.	
Carbonate of Lime.......... 92.4 "	Solid contents in one gallon.460.326 grs.	
Carbonate of iron........ .. 5.39 "	Carbonic acid gas...........316. "	
Hydriodate of Soda........ 3. "	Atmospheric air.... .... 4. "	
B.carbonate of Soda........ 27.036 "	Gaseous contents in a gallon 320 inches.	
Bicarbonate of Magnesia... 35.2 "		

Address orders for water to C.L. WIGGINS, Saratoga Springs, N.Y.

The Hathorn Spring

Is on Spring Street, directly opposite the north wing of Congress Hall. It was discovered in 1869 by some workmen employed in placing the foundation of the brick block which contains the beautiful ball-room of Congress Hall. It is named in honor of the Hon. H. H. Hathorn, who first developed the spring, and built the famous Congress Hall Hotel. The spring was very securely tubed in 1872, at the large expense of $15,000. The Hathorn is one of the most valuable springs in Saratoga. Great quantities of water are bottled and sold in the leading towns and cities of the United States and Canada. The water contains 888.03 grains of solid contents in a gallon, and combines chloride of sodium, the prevailing chemical element of all the Saratoga Spring waters, with bicarbonate of lithia, and other valuable properties.

Analysis of the Hathorn Spring Water.

Chloride of Sodium.......	509.968 grs.	Sulphate of Potassa.......	none.
Chloride of Potassium....	9.597 "	Phosphate of Soda........	.006 grs.
Bromide of Sodium.......	1.534 "	Biborate of Soda..........	a trace.
Iodide of Sodium.........	.198 "	Alumina...................	.131 "
Fluoride of Calcium......	a trace.	Silica.....................	1.260 "
Bicarbonate of Lithia	11.447 "	Organic matter...........	a trace.
Bicarbonate of Soda......	4.238 "		
Bicarbonate of Magnesia..	176.403 "	Total solid contents....	888.4303
B'carbonate of Lime......	170.646 "	Carbonic Acid Gas in 1 gal., 375.741	
Bicarbonate of Strontia...	a trace.	inches.	
Bicarbonate of Baryta....	1.737 "	Density, 1.009.	
Bicarbonate of Iron......	1.128 "		

The High Rock Spring

Is on Spring Avenue, near the Empire, Star and Seltzer, and is believed to be the first which was discovered in this vicinity. The peculiar mineral formation which gives its name is a great

INTERIOR OF HIGH ROCK SPRING.

curiosity, and early attracted the attention of Indian hunters and the white pioneers of American civilization. The water has built a curb for itself, the foundations of which must have been laid when the continent was in its infancy. The water being impregnated with particles of mineral substances, probably at first saturated the ground about the outlet of the spring. As the water evaporated, a species of rock was formed by the commingling of earth and mineral; and the continual overflow of mineral water, gradually built up the present curious dome shaped rock, which is 3¼ feet high, and 23 feet 4 inches in circumference, and looks like a miniature volcano. There is an Indian tradition that, many years ago, the water ceased to flow over the rock, owing to the displeasure of the Great Spirit. The water, however, remained within reach from the top, and the overflow probably found a way of escape through cracks which eventually have been stopped by deposits from the water. A handsome pagoda has been erected over the spring, and a bottling-house near by contains the usual apparatus for preparing the water for market. It is said that the first white man who used these waters was Sir William Johnson, who was brought in the year 1767 through the wilderness, which then surrounded Saratoga, on a litter, and drank the water a few weeks, when he was able to walk away without assistance. The High Rock Spring, which may therefore be looked upon as the father of all these healing waters, has stood the test of over a century. Its water is a superior tonic, and cathartic as well as alterative. It is useful in Rheumatism, Scrofula, Dyspepsia, Constipation, and is especially beneficial in its operation upon the kidneys and liver; and indeed it purifies and renovates the whole system, clearing and beautifying the complexion and prolonging life.

The High Rock water cures Biliousness, corrects acidity of the stomach, and relieves nervous or feverish irritation and headache

Perhaps there is no class of mineral water drinkers who enjoy a visit to Saratoga so much, or who realize so fully and so speedily the benefits arising from drinking the water, as the class of persons known as "free livers." They suffer from functional disturbance arising from too much food. But when daily drinking the water they are wholly exempt from all inconvenience arising from such surfeit not only, but can use double the quantity of food and drinks previously taken, and experience no inconvenience

The acid products which follow such free living under other circumstances, and which produce sleepless nights, with morbid, nervous, and cerebral symptoms, are wholly prevented by the use of this water, and refreshing sleep, long deferred, is fully enjoyed. All such of the above class as have become more or less diseased from liberal living, may have their stomachs restored to a healthy condition by the use of this water.

As an Aperient or Cathartic the water should be taken in the morning, half an hour before breakfast, its temperature not over cool. For instant action, warm the water slightly.

As a Tonic the water should be taken cool and in small quantities. When drank at meals as a beverage, the system will retain the minerals with strengthening and stimulating effect.

The condition of the system, which marks the early stage of the fearful disease of Scrofula, is usually removed by a timely and faithful use of the High Rock Water. Scorbutic persons, both young and more advanced in life, often witness large scrofulous tumors rapidly pass away under the influence of this mineral water.

The utmost care has been taken in retubing not only to keep out all impure and fresh waters, but also to retain the fixed carbonic acid gas, for which this Spring is so pre-eminently celebrated.

The High Rock Spring is managed by a company of very prominent gentlemen, of which Mr. William G. Fargo, of Wells, Fargo Express Co., N. Y., is the President, and Mr. J. McBride Davidson, of Albany, is Secretary and Treasurer, and Mr. Henry Smith, of Saratoga, is the efficient Superintendent.

The following analysis of the High Rock Spring water was made by Prof. C. F. Chandler, Ph.D., of Columbia College School of Mines, who collected the water at the Spring for analysis.

Analysis of one U. S. gallon:

Chloride of Sodium	390.127 grains		Bicarbonate of Lime	131.739 grains
Chloride of Potassium	8.497	"	Bicarbonate of Magnesia	54.924 "
Bromide of Sodium	0.751	"	Bicarbonate of Soda	34.888 "
Iodide of Sodium	0.986	"	B'carbonate of Iron	1.478 "
Fluoride of Calcium	trace.		Phosphate of Lime	trace.
Sulphate of Potassa	1.608	"	Alumina	1.223 "
Bicarbonate of Baryta	trace.		Silica	2.260 "
Bicarbonate of Strontia	trace.			
Total				628.039 "
Carbonic Acid Gas				409.158 cub. in

The Pavilion Spring

Is situated in the valley, a few rods east of Broadway, between Lake Avenue and Caroline Street, at the head of Spring Avenue.

The Red Spring.

This Spring, so widely and justly celebrated for its curative properties, is located just north of the Empire Spring. It was discovered in 1770, and in 1784 a bath-house was erected at the Spring for the cure of eruptive and skin diseases. The efficacy of the water was thereby demonstrated, and since then, though no particular effort has been made to advertise the water, it has become celebrated throughout the entire country. Hundreds of testimonials from eminent people who have used the water both at the original fountain and at their homes attest its efficacy as a remedial agent. It is a powerful antacid, and is especially adapted to rheumatic and gouty affections. It also neutralizes, by its alkalinity, those acids which produce dyspepsia and its allied diseases. In a general sense its therapeutic effects are alterative, and it is specially adapted to inflamed mucous surfaces. Scrofula, dyspepsia, kidney difficulties, salt rheum, inflamed eyes,

granulated eyelids, are among the diseases which are cured by
this water. Its general effect is to tone up the system, regulate
the secretions, and vitalize the blood, thereby creating an improved
appetite and better assimilation. During the summer season the
Spring is thronged with invalids. More than a hundred gallons
of water are daily taken away by real invalids, besides that which
is drank at the spring. The effect of the water, as an alterative,
is far superior to that of any other spring, and so great that small

quantities produce the desired results, adapting it wonderfully to
the weakest stomachs in cases of extreme chronic disease. This
quality of the water is due to the peculiar combination of its ingredients. Dr. Steele spoke of the wonderful power of this water
in curing salt rheum and skin diseases fifty years ago, in a work he
wrote on the character of "Our Mineral Springs."

The present owners, the Red Spring Co., retubed the Spring a
few years ago and erected a spacious bottling-house provided with
ample facilities for bottling the water, in order to keep pace with
the increasing demand for the water from non-resident patrons.
They have also done much to beautify the surroundings of the
Spring and to improve the drive leading to it. To the mere
pleasure-seeker the Red Spring is "a thing of beauty," while it
is "a joy forever" to the invalid, who finds there the coveted
boon of restored health which he has elsewhere sought in vain.

Saratoga "A" Spring.

The "A" Spring is situated on Spring Avenue, beyond the Empire Spring, and a little north of the Red Spring, on the eastern side of a steep bluff of calciferous sand rock. It is one of the oldest and best springs in Saratoga. A fine, large bottling-house encloses the spring.

The memory of that reverend being, the oldest inhabitant, does not recall the time when the existence of mineral water in this immediate locality was not known. As the merits of spring waters were so little known and understood in the earlier days of their discovery, no attempt was made to introduce this spring to public attention until 1865, when a shaft twelve feet square was sunk to the depth of sixteen feet, and the spring was first tubed. In the spring of the next year the fountain was more perfectly secured by a new tubing, and the water was bottled and sold extensively throughout the country. In 1867 the bottling-house was nearly destroyed by fire; and the spring was again re-tubed to the depth of *thirty-two* feet, going down to the solid rock, where one of the most perfect veins of water was found flowing in all its original purity, which was secured with the greatest care, and brought to the surface through a maple tube.

The SARATOGA "A" SPRING WATER is one of the most effective Mineral Waters found on either continent. It will be observed from the analysis below that it has ten per cent. greater mineral properties than the Congress Spring, four times that of Baden Baden of Austria, five times that of Aix-la-Chapelle in Prussia, twice that of the Vichy of France, nearly three times greater than the Seltzer of Germany, and equally over the Spas of England and Kissengen in Bavaria. The water of the "A" Spring is sold in all the principal cities and towns in the United States, by druggists and others. The great value of the water has been recognized by prominent physicians, and some of the most celebrated men of the country have spoken emphatically in its praise.

The Hon. Horace Greeley said: "I have great confidence in the mineral waters of Saratoga, and can recommend the water of the Saratoga "A" Spring with pleasure."

The Hon. Horatio Seymour wrote, May 1st, 1866: "I have

made use of the Saratoga "A" Spring water with great advantage, and I think the water will prove of great value to the public."

ANALYSIS OF THE SARATOGA "A" SPRING WATER,

BY JULIUS G. POHLE, M. D.,

surviving partner of JAMES R. CHILTON & POHLE.

Chloride of Sodium.....	565.300 grains.	Bicarbonate of Iron.....	1.724 grains
Chloride of Potassium..	357 "	Sulphate of Lime......	448 "
Chloride of Calcium and Magnesia........	trace	Sulphate of Magnesia...	288 "
		Sulphate of Soda.......	2.500 "
Bicarbonate of Soda.....	6.752 "	Sulphate of Potassa.....	370 "
Bicarbonate of Lime....	56.852 "	Silicic Acid..	1.400 "
Bicarbonate of Magnesia...............	20.480 "	Alumina	380 "

Solid contents per gallon...................................656.911 grains
Free Carbonic Acid Gas, per gallon.....................212 cubic inches
Atmospheric air...4 " "

The Star Spring.

To reach this spring from Congress Hall, follow Broadway north five blocks to the railroad. Turn to the right and then to the second left, and in a few steps the long flight of stairs leading down the bluff to the spring will be found. This spring was formerly known as the President and the Iodine. It is over half a century since its waters were first known and used, but their full virtues were not developed until 1862, when the water was traced to its rocky sources, and the spring tubed in the best manner.

Since then the Saratoga Star Spring has greatly increased its popularity as a mineral water, and is now recognized as one of the leading waters in the principal markets. The water is largely charged with carbonic acid gas which renders it peculiarly valuable as a bottling water, since it preserves its freshness much longer than waters containing a smaller amount of the gas.

We give the analysis of this celebrated spring, showing the amount of mineral properties in one gallon of the water as determined by eminent chemists:

Chloride of Sodium	378.962 grs.	Bicarbonate of Magnesia	61.912 grs.
Chloride of Potassium	9.229 "	Bicarbonate of Soda	12.662 "
Bromide of Sodium	55.65 "	Bicarbonate of Iron	7.213 "
Iodide of Sodium of Iodine	20.000 "	Silica	1.283 "
Sulphate of Potass	5.400 "	Phosphate of Lime, a trace	
Bicarbonate of Lime	124.459 "	Solid Contents in a Gallon,	615.685 "

Carbonic Acid Gas, 407.55 cubic inches in a gallon.

The foregoing analysis was made at different times, extended over a period of thirty years, by Prof. C. F. Chandler; also by Dr. Steele and Prof. Emmons. The results show that the great medicinal properties of the Star consist of the large quantity of odine and bromide of sodium, being 5 grs. of iodine and 14 grs. of Bromide to each quart.

While the immediate effects of the Star Spring are cartharctic, its remote effects are alterative, and these, after all, should be considered the most important, as the water thus reaches and changes the morbid condition of the whole system, giving the Star water the high repute which it has maintained from its first discovery. For the following complaints it has been used with marked advantage: Scrofula, Cutaneous Eruptions, Bilious Affections, Rheumatism, Gravel, Calculus, Suppression, Fevers, Dyspepsia, Constipation, Diabetes, Kidney Complaints, Loss of Appetite, Liver Difficulties. The proprietors of the Star were the first to introduce Saratoga Water to the public, on draught, through the United States, Canadas, and Europe, which they did in patent tin-lined barrels which preserve the full purity of the water. They furnish their waters fresh on draught, through the apothecaries of the cities and towns of the United States, enabling patrons to obtain, at home, any quantity at the lowest possible cost, by the glass, gallon or barrel, as well as in pint or quart bottles, knowing that the free use of this water will restore health to invalids away from Saratoga as well as at the springs.

The bottling-house is a handsome brick building, and is supplied with every convenience for business, and visitors are invited to inspect the house and the work of bottling.

The Saratoga Vichy Spouting Spring

Is delightfully located on Ballston Avenue, opposite Geyser Spring, in the midst of a park embracing a beautiful sloping lawn studded with forest trees on one side, and the pretty little Geyser Lake on the other. Its surroundings are very picturesque, and are among the most attractive scenery about Saratoga. It was discovered in the month of March, 1872, by drilling in the solid rock to the depth of 180 feet.

This spring contains more soda and less salt than any other Saratoga water, and takes special rank at once among the valuable mineral waters of this famous Spa, from its wonderful similarity to the Vichy waters of France. It is the only alkaline water found at Saratoga, and a specific in those troublesome affections arising from Acidity of the Stomach, Dyspepsia, Kidney and Bladder Difficulties; several remarkable cases are already recorded of these diseases cured by its use. The following analysis of the Saratoga Vichy, made by Prof. C. F. Chandler, of the Columbia College School of Mines, demonstrates its value as a medicinal agent, and as an alkaline water of equal merit with the celebrated French Vichy.

Contains in one U. S Gallon of 231 cubic inches:

Chloride of Sodium	128.689	Bicarbonate of Strontia	trace.
Chloride of Potassium	14.113	Bicarbonate of Baryta	0.593
Bromide of Sodium	0.990	Bicarbonate of Iron	0.052
Iodide of Sodium	trace.	Sulphate of Potassa	trace.
Fluoride of Calcium	trace.	Phosphate of Soda	trace.
Bicarbonate of Lithia	1.760	Biborate of Soda	trace.
Bicarbonite of Soda	**82.873**	Alumina	0.473
Bicarbonate of Magnesia	41.503	Silica	0.753
Bicarbonate of Lime	95.522	Organic Matter	trace.

Carbonic Acid Gas in one gallon, 389.071 cubic inches. Temperature 50° F.

The Saratoga Vichy is an excellent *table water*, and superior to the French Vichy, as it contains more natural carbonic acid gas, and mixes readily with all wines. It is not a cathartic water, (but mildly laxative if taken in quantity before breakfast,) and can be drank at all times with its good effect as a *Nervous Stimulant*, and in diseases of the *Stomach*, *Kidneys*, and *Bladder*.

Geyser, Congress, Hathorn, and other prominent Saratoga mineral springs are saline waters, but the Saratoga Vichy is an *Alkaline* water; that is, the alkaline properties (lithia, soda, magnesia, lime etc.,) overbalance the saline properties — Chloride of Sodium (salt), and is therefore recommended in an entirely different class of cases. When the blood is impoverished from want of proper assimilation of food, or feeble tone of the stomach generally, when the system is below the normal standard and requires "toning up," the Saratoga Vichy should be used.

One of the most remarkable effects of Saratoga Vichy is the improvement or restoration of impaired digestive functions, increase of appetite and improved tone. Dyspepsia is therefore a special field for use of this water, especially when accompanied

LAWN VIEW OF SARATOGA VICHY SPRING.

with sour stomach, slowness of digestion, loss of appetite, ver tigo, weakness, etc. The Saratoga Vichy is rapidly gaining popular favor, and is much used in our large cities in place of the French Vichy waters, which are frequently stale. Genuine Saratoga Vichy is put up in clear glass bottles, half-pints, pints, and quarts, with "SARATOGA VICHY SPOUTING SPRING, SARATOGA, N. Y.," and large "**V**," in raised letters, blown in the glass, and in block-tin-lined barrels for draught purposes. Circulars containing full directions for its use may be obtained from those selling the water, or the Saratoga Vichy Spring Co., at Saratoga Springs, N. Y. The Company has a wholesale depot at 122 Pearl Street, N. Y., and John Matthews & Co., First Avenue and E. 26th and 27th Streets, New York, are also wholesale agents. It is kept on draught by druggists in the principal cities.

The Diamond Spring

Is just north of the Vichy in its grounds and is a valuable chalybeate or iron spring with ingredients quite unlike those of its near neighbors. It possesses valuable diuretic and tonic properties, and is specially recommended for those suffering from general debility. One glass has the exhilarating effect of champagne and is remarkably efficient in curing many complaints peculiar to the female sex. It contains a large amount of carbonic acid gas and bottles better than any iron water at Saratoga. The Diamond Spring belongs to the Saratoga Vichy Spring Co.

The Washington Spring

Is situated in the grounds of the Clarendon Hotel, on South Broadway. It is a chalybeate or iron spring, having *tonic* and diuretic properties. It is not a saline water, and the peculiar inky taste of iron is perceptible. It should be drank in the afternoon or evening, before or after meals, or just before retiring One glass is sufficient for tonic purposes. Many regard this as the most agreeable beverage in Saratoga. It is frequently called the "Champagne Spring," from its sparkling properties. It is a very popular spring, and in the afternoon is thronged with visitors. It grounds are very picturesque, and in the evening are lighted by gas. The Clarendon band discourses on the neighboring piazza in summer, and fashionably attired people throng beneath the majestic pines, forming one of those peculiar group pictures which render Saratoga so charming.

CHAMPION SPOUTING SPRING.

Champion Spouting Spring.

This phenomenal fountain is about one mile and a half south of the village of Saratoga Springs, near the carriage road leading to Ballston Spa, just east of the Railroad. It is one of the group of celebrated Spouting Springs which have recently been developed and become a wonderful feature of the great watering-place. It was discovered in 1871, after sinking a shaft to the unusual depth of 300 feet. From this deeply-concealed cavern, the precious fountain burst forth to light, sending a column of water six and one-half inches in diameter, 25 or 30 feet into the air, presenting a marvelous and beautiful spectacle. The gaseous force of the water has been checked by a strong iron cap, fastened to the top of the tubing, and only a small jet of water is allowed to escape, except at five o'clock in the afternoon, when this cap is removed, and the water darts forth in large volume to a height of 80 to 100 feet, imitating the wonderful Yellowstone and Iceland Geysers. These Saratoga Geysers are exceedingly interesting, and should be visited. During the winter the water freezes around the tube, and gradually forms a column of solid ice from 30 to 40 feet high, and several feet in diameter. On another page we present an engraving of this wonderful spring, as it appears in winter. This marvelous spring possesses the chemical elements common to the Saratoga spring waters, in larger quantities than any other spring yet developed. We append the analysis by Prof. C. F. CHANDLER, of Columbia College, New York:

SOLID CONTENTS OF ONE U. S. GALLON, 231 CUBIC INCHES.

Chloride of Sodium	702.239	Bicarbonate of Baryta	2.083
Chloride of Potassium	40.446	Bicarbonate of Iron	0.647
Bromide of Sodium	3.579	Sulphate of Potassa	0.252
Iodide of Sodium	0.234	Phosphate of Soda	0.010
Fluoride of Calcium	trace.	Biborate of Soda	trace.
Bicarbonate of Lithia	6.247	Alumina	0.458
Bicarbonate of Soda	17.634	Silica	0.699
Bicarbonate of Magnesia	193.912	Organic matter.	trace.
Bicarbonate of Lime	227.070		
Bicarbonate of Strontia	0.082	Total grains	1195.582

Carbonic Acid Gas, 465.458 cubic inches. Temperature, 46° Fahr.

It contains more mineral properties per gallon than any other spring water in Saratoga. Hence a less quantity will produce the usual effect. It acts very favorably upon the kidneys and liver, and its medicinal value is established by the testimony high medical authority.

The Saratoga Magnetic Spring

Is situated on Spring Avenue, in the valley opposite the High Rock Spring. It is unlike all other springs in Saratoga, having that wonderful magnetic influence which is one of the great marvels of nature. It was discovered recently, but its healing powers and properties have been thoroughly tested, and found to be highly valuable. The waters are not bottled, but are used for bathing purposes. Quite a large number of convenient baths have been built at the spring, and special apartments for ladies have been provided. The baths are found to be highly efficacious in the cure of rheumatism, neuralgia, cutaneous and nervous affections, and have a perceptible tonic influence upon the system. Its valuable qualities are recognized by physicians and residents of Saratoga, and have added another and peculiar feature to this wonderfully rich mineral spring region. All should visit this spring, and while there you may have your knife magnetized by a bath in the spring if you choose. The baths are open from 7 A.M. to 6 P.M. daily, and attendants are at call.

The Seltzer Spring

Is close to High Rock Spring, and in the neighborhood of the Star and Empire. Although in such close proximity thereto, its water is entirely different. This is the only Seltzer spring in this country. The character of the water is almost identical with that of the celebrated Nassau Spring of Germany, which is justly esteemed so delicious by the natives of the "Fatherland."

The Crystal Spring

Is located near the Columbian Hotel, in South Broadway.

The Putnam Spring

Is almost wholly used for bathing, and every facility is provided at the spring. To reach it from Congress Hall, walk along Broadway to the north, and take the second turn to the right.

The Kissingen Spouting Spring

Is a pipe-well, 192 feet deep, on the east side of Geyser Lake.

The United States Spring

Is in the grounds of the Pavilion Spring, and owned by the same company. Its waters are alterative in medicinal effect.

Saratoga White Sulphur Spring.

This valuable spring is situated about one and one-half miles east of the village, and about one quarter of a mile east of the Excelsior Spring. It should not be confounded with a spring of the same name, but which is some ten miles from Saratoga, on the east side of Saratoga Lake. The water of this spring is used for bathing and drinking, but is not bottled. The curative properties of it are fully established, and the proprietors have erected a large and very commodious bathing-house, containing fifty baths, and supplied with every convenience for giving warm or cold sulphur baths at all hours of the day. This spring supplies a very important element to the attractions of Saratoga. The other springs supply valuable mineral waters to be taken internally, while the White Sulphur waters supply that very important element of medicinal effects produced by bathing. Persons afflicted with rheumatism or cutaneous diseases receive positive benefit, and sometimes complete cure, by using these baths. Lady and gentleman attendants are always at hand during bathing hours, and every convenience for luxurious and wholesome bathing are afforded. The baths are open from 7 A.M. to 9 P.M. on week-days, and on Sundays from 7 A.M. to 6 P.M.

Stages run to and from the spring as follows: Leave Washington Hall at 9, 10, 11 A.M., and 3 and 4 P.M. Leave the spring at 9:30, 10:30, 11:30 A.M., 12:30, 4:30, and 5:30 P.M. The stages pass through Broadway, from Washington Hall to Circular Street, through Circular Street to Lake Avenue and the spring. Fare to the spring and return at pleasure, 25 cents.

Invalids and others wishing stages to call at their residences, will please leave word at the office, No. 10 Grand Union Hotel Block, to the man in charge, in ample time to call, as the stages all run on schedule time, and the drivers are not allowed, under any circumstances, to leave their route. Ask for time-table.

A few yards south of the White Sulphur Spring is the mineral

Eureka Spring.

Its water is highly charged with carbonic gas, making it one of the most pleasant to the taste of all the Saratoga waters. It is a superior tonic, diuretic, and mild cathartic.

CHAPTER III.
THE HOTELS.

THE hotels at Saratoga Springs are among the largest, the most costly, elegant, and comfortable in the world. For nearly a century people have journeyed to these springs, to drink their healing waters; and, as one day's visit is hardly worth the while, they have sought a home here during the summer season. It is this that has caused the village to open its doors so freely, and to build up, from a small beginning, a system of hotels and boarding-houses unlike anything else to be found. Added to this came, in time, the demands of the merely pleasure-seeking, fashionable world. People came to the springs for the sake of the gay company gathered here, and from year to year the hotels have grown, expanding their wings and adding room beyond room, till they cover acres of ground, and the halls and piazzas stretch out into miles. They have a bewildering fashion here of repeating the wondrous tale of these things. They talk about the miles of carpeting; the thousands upon thousands of doors and windows; the hundreds of miles of telegraph wires; vast acres of marble floors; and tons of eatables stored in the pantries, till one is lost in admirable confusion. It is all true, and that is the wonder of it. The management that governs it all is more remarkable than the gilding and mirrors. It is a sort of high science, unequaled in the world, combining the "ease of mine inn," and a perfection of detail and freedom from friction that is as pleasant as it is wonderful.

Saratoga's face is her fortune, and it is said that the entire town devotes its days and nights to the comfort of the tourist. The tourist should be indeed happy. If he is not, it is safe to say it is his own fault. In speaking of these hotels, the four great houses are mentioned first. The smaller ones are noticed in the order of their size. The numerous boarding houses will be considered in the next chapter.

Congress Hall

Is built on the site of the old and famous hotel of the same name which was burned in 1866, and occupies the larger part of the square bounded by Broadway, East Congress, Spring and Putnam Streets. Its situation is in the very center of the gay and fashionable hotel world of Saratoga, and is admirably arranged for seeing all the attractive phases of the "great watering-place" life. Its frontage on Broadway, the principal street of the town, is 416 feet, with a high promenade piazza 20 feet wide and 249 feet in length, commanding a view of the most brilliant portion of Saratoga. From the Broadway front two immense wings, 300 feet long, extend to Putnam Street, the northern wing, running along Spring Street and overlooking the celebrated Hathorn and Hamilton Springs on one side, and with the central wing which runs parallel with it, enclosing a very beautiful garden-plot. The southern front commands a full view of the famous Congress and Columbian Springs, and the beautiful Congress Park, owned and adorned by the Congress and Empire Spring Co. Ample piazzas extend around the back of the hotel, overlooking the grass and garden-plots of the interior court, affording cool and shady retreats in the afternoon, when entrancing music is discoursed by one of the best hotel bands in Saratoga.

Congress Hall was purchased in 1878 by Mr. W. H. Clement of Cincinnati, Ohio, President of the Cincinnati and Southern R. R. Co., and Mr. John Cox of New York, gentlemen of large means, who have placed it under permanent management.

Mr. H. S. Clement, lately one of the proprietors of the famous Lindell Hotel of St. Louis, and formerly one of the proprietors of Congress Hall in its palmiest days of 1870 and 1871, has control of the house, and has made it second to none of the hotels of the great watering place in fine appointments. The great success of Congress Hall in 1878, is complete proof of the efficiency and popularity of the management. Owing to the very low purchase price of the hotel, the proprietors feel able to keep up the standard of style of its former glorious years, when Mr. Clement was one of the proprietors, and Congress Hall outstripped all its rivals at Saratoga, and yet keep the prices at the lowest possible, and present popular rates. The hotel opens June 19th.

CONGRESS HALL, Saratoga Springs, N. Y. Clement & Wilkinson, Proprietors.

Opens June 19th, 1880.

H. S. CLEMENT,　　　Rates, $3.50 per day.　　　WILLIAM WILKINSON,

Congress Hall is built in the most substantial manner of brick, with brown-stone trimmings, and presents one of the most graceful architectural appearances in Saratoga. Its walls are 20 inches thick and hollow in the center, thus securing great strength and protection from heat of summer. The roof is a Mansard, with three pavilions, which afford wide and delightful views from the promenades on top. Interior fire-walls are provided to prevent the spread of fire, and Otis elevators afford easy access to all the floors of the house. The rooms are all large, high and well ventilated, and properly provided with annunciators, gas, etc. The halls, dining-rooms, parlors, and offices are of grand proportions, and are furnished with an elegance that bespeaks comfort and neatness in all its departments. The *ventilation* of the dining-room and kitchen has been much improved and a *Steam Heating Apparatus* introduced on the main floor for use whenever changes in the temperature require it. *Hot and cold water* have been carried to every floor, and a large number of baths and closets added for the convenience of guests.

There has also been a complete renovation of the furniture this spring, and the rooms, halls, and parlors have been recarpeted, and 200 rooms refurnished throughout and the walls refinished. The public parlors have been refurnished with new Wilton carpets, and the reception rooms, office, and dining-room renewed. The laundry has been greatly improved and its facilities increased.

The rooms of Congress Hall are all larger, and therefore afford pleasanter and more healthy apartments than any other hotel in Saratoga, and will accommodate over 1,000 guests in the most comfortable style. The beds are the easiest and best spring and hair mattresses to be found in this country, and ample presses, closets, etc., afford all desirable conveniences. The ball-room of the Congress is one of the finest in northern New York, being most exquisitely frescoed and adorned with costly chandeliers and ornaments. It is in the block across Spring Street, but is connected with the north wing of the hotel by a light, graceful iron bridge suspended over the street, properly covered and protected, which when illuminated on hop nights, is very picturesque.

Congress Hall is favored with a superior class of visitors, which annually includes the finest families of our metropolitan cities.

UNITED STATES HOTEL, SARATOGA SPRINGS, N. Y.,
TOMPKINS, GAGE & CO. Proprietors.

United States Hotel.

This magnificent structure was completed in June, 1874, and is situated on the block bounded by Broadway and Division Street, on the site of the old United States Hotel, around which so many pleasant memories cluster, but which was burned a few years ago. It constitutes one continuous line of buildings, six stories high, over 1,500 feet in length, containing 917 rooms for guests, and is the largest hotel in the world. The architectural appearance is exceedingly elegant and beautiful. It is Norman in style, and its Mansard roof is embellished with pediments, gables, dormer windows and crestings, and three large pavilions.

The building covers and encloses seven acres of ground in the form of an irregular pentagon, having a frontage of 232 feet on Broadway, 656 feet on Division Street, with "Cottage Wing" on the south side of the plaza, extending west from the main front for 566 feet. This wing is one of the most desirable features of this admirably-arranged house, as it affords families, and other parties, the same quiet and seclusion which a private cottage would afford, together with the attention and conveniences of a first-class hotel. The rooms of this wing are arranged in suites of one to seven bedrooms, with parlor, bath-room, and water-closet in each suite. Private table is afforded if desired, and the seclusion and freedom of a private villa may be enjoyed here, to be varied, at will, by the gayer life of the hotel and watering place.

The main front and entrance is on Broadway, in which is the elegant drawing-room, superbly furnished with Axminster carpets, carved walnut and marble furniture, frescoed ceilings, elegant lace curtains, and costly chandeliers and mirrors. The room is rich and tasteful in its entire arrangements. Across the hall is the ladies' parlor, furnished with exquisite taste; and beyond, at the corner of the Broadway and Division Street fronts, are the gentlemen's reading-rooms and the business offices of the hotel. To the west of the office in the Division Street wing, is the dining-hall, 52 by 212 feet with $20\frac{1}{2}$ feet ceiling; beyond which are the private drawing-rooms, the children's ordinary, carving-rooms, etc. The grand ball-room, 112 by 53 feet, with ceilings 26 feet high, is on the second floor of the Division Street wing, and is decorated with artistic and appropriate adornments

INTERIOR COURT VIEW OF UNITED STATES HOTEL, Saratoga Springs, N. Y.

The arrangement of the sleeping apartments of this hotel is excellent, and its rooms are furnished with gas, water, and marble basins throughout. It is the only hotel in Saratoga that is thoroughly plumbed and has running water in all its rooms. All the rooms are connected with the office by an electric annunciator The entire building is divided into five sections by thick, fire-proof walls, and the openings through them are protected by heavy iron doors, thus affording great protection in case of fire. There are also fire-hydrants in each section, with hose attached, on each floor. There are ten staircases which afford ample means of escape from fire. Two elevators are used solely for conveying guests to the various floors, and every convenience has been adopted in equipping this elegant hotel for its immense summer business. Upon the Broadway front is a fine piazza, 232 feet long, three stories high, overlooking the center of the village; and one on Division Street, 200 feet in length. Extensive piazzas, 2,300 feet in length, for promenades, encircle the large interior court, which is ornamented with beautiful shade trees, sparkling fountains, graceful lawn-statuary, and meandering walks; and, during the evening, when illuminated with colored lights and lanterns, and enlivened with exquisite music, the scene is brilliant and fascinating in the extreme.

In fact, everything that is needed to make the hotel attractive and convenient is found here, and the United States Hotel stands unexcelled in its furnishing and arrangements by any of the hotels of the great watering-place. As one looks upon this palatial structure, and carefully inspects the detailed arrangements for the perfect convenience and comfort of its guests, he can but be amazed at the enterprise and courage of its owners, who have opened to the world this stupendous establishment. This immense and elegant hotel is managed by gentlemen of great experience. The Hon. James M. Marvin, who is well known to all old frequenters of Saratoga, has the general control of the whole interest, while Messrs. Tompkins, Perry, Gage, and Janvrin, are the lessees and proprietors. Under their able and successful management, the house has steadily gained in favor and become known as the most elegant and aristocratic summer resort in the world. Guests can rely on having everything provided that will conduce to their comfort and happiness.

THE GRAND UNION HOTEL,
SARATOGA SPRINGS.

The arrangement of the sleeping apartments of this hotel is excellent, and its rooms are furnished with gas, water, and marble basins throughout. It is the only hotel in Saratoga that is thoroughly plumbed and has running water in all its rooms. All the rooms are connected with the office by an electric annunciator The entire building is divided into five sections by thick, fireproof walls, and the openings through them are protected by heavy iron doors, thus affording great protection in case of fire. There are also fire-hydrants in each section, with hose attached, on each floor. There are ten staircases which afford ample means of escape from fire. Two elevators are used solely for conveying guests to the various floors, and every convenience has been adopted in equipping this elegant hotel for its immense summer business. Upon the Broadway front is a fine piazza, 232 feet long, three stories high, overlooking the center of the village; and one on Division Street, 200 feet in length. Extensive piazzas, 2,300 feet in length, for promenades, encircle the large interior court, which is ornamented with beautiful shade trees, sparkling fountains, graceful lawn-statuary, and meandering walks; and, during the evening, when illuminated with colored lights and lanterns, and enlivened with exquisite music, the scene is brilliant and fascinating in the extreme.

In fact, everything that is needed to make the hotel attractive and convenient is found here, and the United States Hotel stands unexcelled in its furnishing and arrangements by any of the hotels of the great watering-place. As one looks upon this palatial structure, and carefully inspects the detailed arrangements for the perfect convenience and comfort of its guests, he can but be amazed at the enterprise and courage of its owners, who have opened to the world this stupendous establishment. This immense and elegant hotel is managed by gentlemen of great experience. The Hon. James M. Marvin, who is well known to all old frequenters of Saratoga, has the general control of the whole interest, while Messrs. Tompkins, Perry, Gage, and Janvrin, are the lessees and proprietors. Under their able and successful management, the house has steadily gained in favor and become known as the most elegant and aristocratic summer resort in the world. Guests can rely on having everything provided that will conduce to their comfort and happiness.

THE GRAND UNION HOTEL,
SARATOGA SPRINGS.

The most complete in all its appointments for the comfort and pleasure of its Guests of any Summer Hotel in the World. Rates reduced to $4 per day.

HENRY CLAIR, Lessee.

The Clarendon Hotel.

This excellent house stands on Broadway, a short distance south of Congress Street, on one of the pleasantest sites in the village. Recent improvements have made this part of Broadway one of the most attractive portions of the great watering place. The Clarendon is the only hotel in Saratoga which is painted white, with green blinds, presenting that clean, neat appearance which distinguishes so many New England villages, and produces a truly rural effect among the beautiful shade-trees that surround it. It pleasantly contrasts with the more metropolitan architecture and colors which obtain among the other hotels. It partly incloses within its wings a depression or valley, ornamented with shade-trees, among which stands the tasteful pagoda covering the popular Washington Spring. The Leland Spring, named in honor of the former proprietor of the hotel, is also within these grounds. These spring waters are among the most valuable of the Saratoga waters, the Washington Spring being a *tonic* water, highly prized by Saratoga residents, and popular with the visitors. Congress Grove is immediately opposite the Clarendon, and such of its guests as prefer Congress or Columbian waters to that which springs within their own dooryard can easily reach them. This hotel is largely patronized by a class of visitors who do not desire to mingle with the somewhat promiscuous company which fills the larger hotels. It has a quiet air of refinement about all its arrangements, and one feels quite at home in this cheerful and elegant hotel. The table has always been noted for its excellence. The Clarendon can accommodate about 500 guests, and its arrangement is every way calculated to give satisfaction to those who patronize it as a summer resort. An excellent band discourses delightful music daily, morning and evening, from the piazza overlooking the interior court, which is illuminated in the evening, and presents a very picturesque effect. The Clarendon will be opened as formerly, June 1st. The Proprietorship having been assumed by Mr. J. C. Chamberlain, formerly connected with it for nine consecutive years, associated with Mr. J. B. Powell of New York, is a guarantee that the high standard which has hitherto characterized its management will at least be maintained.

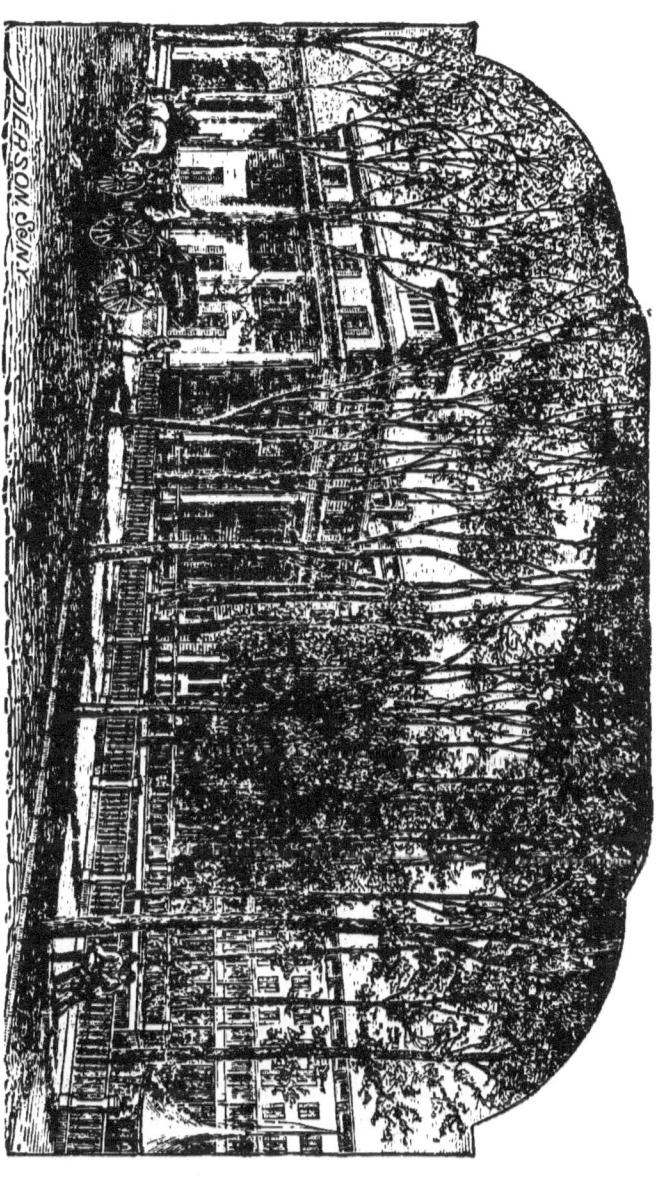

CLARENDON HOTEL, Saratoga Springs, N.Y. Chamberlain & Powell, *Proprietors*.

The old Patrons of the Clarendon Hotel, Saratoga Springs, are respectfully informed that it will be opened as formerly, June 1st. The Proprietorship having been assumed by Mr. J. C. Chamberlain, formerly connected with it for nine consecutive years, associated with Mr. J. B. Powell of New York, is a guarantee that the high standard which has hitherto characterized its management will at least be maintained. Your patronage is respectfully solicited.

JOHN C. CHAMBERLAIN.   JOHN B. POWELL.

Adelphi Hotel.

This elegant hotel, with accommodations for about one hundred and seventy-five guests, was built in the spring of 1877, and is a model modern hotel in every particular. It is centrally located on Broadway, between the two mammoth hotels, United States and Grand Union, within three minutes' walk of the Congress, Hathorn, Columbian, Hamilton, and Washington Springs. The Adelphi has a large piazza, three stories high, fronting on Broadway, and elevated far enough above the street to command a fine view of Saratoga's most brilliant thoroughfare, and at the same time shield guests from street annoyances. There is a very broad sidewalk between it and the carriage-way of Broadway, thus removing it from the noise and dust of the street, and yet being at the head of Phila Street, the view from its piazzas is quite extended and charming.

The rooms are large and are very liberally furnished and some are arranged in suites, for family use, with every modern convenience, marble basins, hot and cold running water, bath-rooms, clothes-presses, closets, etc.

The Adelphi was first opened in the summer of 1877, and at once took rank among the best of the Saratoga hotels, and has maintained a first-class reputation. It is not as large as some of the mammoth hotels, but its modern construction, convenient arrangements, excellent cuisine and central location, have made it a favorite home, both to the visitor for pleasure and the man of business. Its broad piazzas, neat and quiet appearance, and liberal supply of clothes-presses and closets have added special attractions for the ladies, who appreciate its unusually convenient accommodations.

The guests of this fine hotel are of the very best classes of people, and many distinguished visitors have been liberally entertained at the Adelphi, since it was first opened to the public in 1877. The proprietor of the Adelphi is Mr. William H. McCaffrey, who has had much experience as a caterer to the visitors of Saratoga Springs and who knows what tourists require, and how to conduct a first-class hotel. The Adelphi will be kept open all the year, and the prices for board are very moderate, with special terms for commercial travelers.

The Columbian Hotel.

The Columbian opens this season under new and experienced management, and during the month of June the proprietor will offer special terms to excursion-parties. The house will accommodate 250 guests, and is situated on Broadway opposite Congress Park. A more beautiful and central location is not to be found

in Saratoga. Congress, Columbian, Crystal and Washington Springs, are in full view from the piazzas, and the popular drives to Geyser Spring and Ballston, are past this hotel. The house is built of brick, and has a frontage of 121 feet on Broadway, with a wide two story piazza 115 feet long. The back piazza, 115 feet long, overlooks its own beautiful grounds, and as one of these piazzas is always shaded, a pleasant retreat is furnished every hour of the day. All the rooms of the Columbian have pleasant outlooks, and are well furnished. Further information may be obtained upon application to the Proprietor, C. E. PALMER, Saratoga Springs, New York.

DRS. STRONG'S REMEDIAL INSTITUTE, Saratoga Springs, N. Y.

For the cure of Nervous, Lung, Female, and Chronic Diseases, has Turkish, Russian, Roman, Sulphur, Vapor, Hydropathic, and Electro-thermal Baths; Faradic and Galvanic Electricity; the Equalizer or Vacuum Treatment; Oxygen and Medicated Inhalations; also Compressed and Rarified Air, Gymnastics and other varieties of Hydropathy and Medicine. Send for circular. Endorsed by Rev. T. L. CUYLER, D.D.; Ex-Gov. H. H. WELLS, Virginia; Bishop W. L. HARRIS, D.D., LL.D.; General B. D. FEARING, and others.

CHAPTER IV.
INSTITUTIONS AND BOARDING-HOUSES.

THE institutions and boarding-houses of Saratoga afford excellent accommodations, at moderate prices, and are decidedly homelike and healthful. Many of them have beautiful lawns for croquet and out-door sports, and are very attractive in their external surroundings, while the prices for board are very moderate.

The institutions for the special treatment of diseases in Saratoga are few, but one or two are recognized by the medical fraternity as quite superior, and are certainly well supplied with medical appliances, and under competent management. We call attention especially to

Drs. Strong's Remedial Institute.

This excellent institution is situated on Circular Street, the most beautiful avenue in Saratoga, only a short distance from the great hotels, and one block from the Hathorn and Hamilton Springs and Congress Park, in which the famous Congress and scarcely less noted Columbian Springs are located.

It is one of the best-conducted institutions in the world for the treatment of all kinds of nervous, lung, female, and chronic diseases. It is fitting that Saratoga, a place where so many congregate in the summer for recreation, rest, and recuperation of health by the use of the mineral waters, should be supplied with an institution, under able management, where medical advice can be obtained, and the more positive and confirmed cases of disease treated under constant and able medical supervision. Such an one is Drs. Strong's Remedial Institute.

But it is conducted in summer with especial reference to the accommodation of summer boarders, and enjoys a most excellent reputation for its superior advantages as a summer resort. The table is excellent, and the rooms are large and well ventilated, and kept with especial reference to *health*, as well as comfort and luxury. In summer no one would suppose it to be a medical institute from its appearance, and yet there may be enjoyed the most luxurious baths and means of physical exercise, which every summer resort should supply, but which so few, even of the hotels and boarding-houses in Saratoga, afford within their doors. The physicians recognize the superlative importance of the mineral springs in many courses of treatment, and their value may here be tested under skillful and experienced direction. The danger of indiscriminate drinking of the waters cannot be too strongly emphasized. Much of their efficacy and marvellous power over disease is due to their proper administration, and they may become as potent agents for harm as they should be for good, if ignorantly and unscientifically used.

The institution is somewhat removed from the bustle of the large hotels, and affords a delightful retreat for persons of impaired health; while refined and cultivated people will find its society more congenial than that of the more public houses.

Among its patrons are Dr. T. L. Cuyler; Ex-Govs. Wells and Boardman; Bishops Simpson, Robinson, Harris, Haven, Foster, etc.; Judges Reynolds, Drake, Bliss; Editors Monfort, Fowler, Pierce, etc.; College Pres. Haven, Foss, Chadbourne, Tuttle, Payne, Bartlett, etc.; Gens. Fearing, Satterlee, Casey, etc.; Med. Prof. Armour, Ross, Knapp, and others equally well known.

The institution is supplied with new and the most approved appliances now known to medical science, among which are electro-thermal, sulphur, vapor, Turkish and Russian baths, the equalizer or vacuum treatment, oxygen and medicated inhalations; also compressed and rarified air, gymnastics, and other varieties of hydropathy and medicine. Drs. Sylvester S. and Sylvester E. Strong, regular physicians graduated at the Medical Department of the University of New York, supervise the entire institution.

The elegance and convenience of the bath department is unsurpassed in this country or the world. The buildings are heated by steam, so that the temperature throughout the house is moderated to a healthful uniformity, and in winter is brought to the condition of a summer climate.

Circulars, giving a full description of the institution, its remedial agents, and rare appliances, its remarkable success in the treatment of nervous, lung, female, and chronic diseases, with distinguished references, terms, etc., will be sent on application.

Temple Grove Ladies' Seminary.

This fine institution is under the efficient management of Prof. Charles F. Dowd, a graduate of Yale College, and affords the finest advantages for a complete and solid education. During the long vacation of the summer months, from June to September, the building is opened as a summer resort, where, under the efficient management of Dowd & Co., the greatest comforts and luxuries of a summer home are dispensed to the patrons of the house. The delightful grove and grounds, just removed from the bustle and confusion of the great hotels, and its accessibility to all the springs in Saratoga, render the Seminary particularly desirable to lovers of health and comfort.

DRIVES AND RESORTS.

The principal drive, and the only really fashionable one, is that which leads from Saratoga to and along the shores of the lake. There is little which can be termed naturally attractive about this drive, and it is only the brilliant procession of carriages, with their fair occupants and their superb horses, that renders the otherwise uninteresting road one of the sights of Saratoga. *Moon's House*, overlooking Saratoga Lake, is famed for its game and fish dinners, and pre-eminently for its fried potatoes, which are done up in neat paper packages and sold like confectionery, which, in fact, they resemble more than they do the potato of every-day life.

Saratoga Lake is nine miles long and nearly five miles wide. The annual regatta of the American Colleges is held on this lake, as are also several other regattas open to more general competition. The fishing in its waters is excellent, black bass, pickerel, muscalogne, and perch being caught in abundance.

Another drive leads to *Lake Lovely*, a small lake among the hills. It is a pleasant place for picnic excursions. There are other small ponds in the vicinity which form points of interest for those who like to explore the country.

Prospect Hill is 16 miles distant, and from its summit, 2,000 feet high, a wide view may be obtained.

The Saratoga Race Course is on the road to the lake. It is a mile track, kept in excellent order, and largely patronized at the annual races, which take place every summer during the height of the season.

The Saratoga Battle Ground, at Stillwater, is an interesting place to visit. It is about 15 miles from the village, but a fair carriage-road leads to its vicinity, enabling those who desire to visit the scene of the battle and of Burgoyne's surrender to do so without great fatigue.

The Glen Mitchell Hotel and Pleasure Driving Park is situated about one and a half miles from Congress Hall, at the terminus of North Broadway. The hotel was built in 1870, and is constructed with wide piazzas, forming a very delightful and pleasant retreat. The mountain and woods near the house constitute very desirable grounds for picnic parties, and the proprietor is always ready to furnish the necessary equipments for such festive occasions. Game breakfasts and dinners are a specialty, and will be served upon order in the most approved style. A half-mile Driving Park on the grounds is open to the public; and the drive from the village to the Glen Mitchell Hotel and through the Park, returning by the road around Excelsior Lake and by the Excelsior Spring, is one of the pleasantest to be found near Saratoga.

Another beautiful drive is through Excelsior Park, which embraces that portion of Saratoga Springs known as the "Valley of the Ten Springs," with the table-land delightfully situated on either side of this valley. The higher portions of this table-land have been divided into Villa Plots, many of which command fine views of the mountains of Vermont and the hills around Lake George.

The Park lies about a mile north-east of the R. R. Depot, and is reached by broad avenues running directly to it from the center of the village.

ADIRONDACK COMPANY'S RAILROAD.

This railroad, connecting with the Rensselaer and Saratoga R. R. at Saratoga Springs, runs in a northerly direction towards the great hunting and fishing grounds of Northern New York. From Thurman, stages run to WARRENSBURG and LAKE GEORGE, in connection with the trains from Saratoga. The distance from Thurman to Fort William Henry Hotel at Lake George is exactly the same (9 miles) as from Glen Falls, and the route is over a fine plankroad through a wild and mountainous country.

The Railroad is projected, through the heart of the **Great Wilderness**, to Ogdensburg on the St. Lawrence River, and is intended to open up these vast wilds of 150 miles in diameter to civilization, and afford convenient access for travellers to this picturesque and interesting country. It will also, when completed, form one of the great lines of communication between the States and Canada, and will become one of the great outlets of the vast cereal productions and mineral resources of Canada and the Great Northwest. The whole Adirondack region is intersected and diversified by a network of lakes and streams which render it picturesque and beautiful in an almost unequalled degree. These systems of water communication afford very convenient means of transit for hunters and pleasure-seekers, the lakes being connected by streams, most of which are navigable for small light boats, though some are broken by falls and rapids, around which the light boats are easily carried by the guides who accompany travellers through this wild region. Abundance of deer and other game may be obtained by hunters, while the streams and lakes abound in various species of the skilful delicious trout.

Iron ore is found in large quantities among the mountains, and some of the most accessible beds are profitably worked. Valuable qualities of marble are also found in some portions of the mountains. The Railroad is already completed several miles beyond North Creek, which is 57 miles from Saratoga Springs. A splendid line of stages runs from Riverside Station to Schroon Lake, daily, on arrival of trains.

THE ADIRONDACK RAILROAD.

The Railroad connects at various points with stage lines running to all of the innermost hotels in this whole Sacondaga and Schroon Lake tract. Starting from the Rensselaer and Saratoga Railroad depot at Saratoga Springs, the traveller passes over a plain and sterile farming country until he reaches

KING'S,
Greenfield, Saratoga Co., N. Y.,
10 *miles from Saratoga Springs.*

A station for the accommodation of the people of North Greenfield, Greenfield Center, and Porter's Corners.

SOUTH CORINTH,
Corinth, Saratoga Co., N. Y.,
13 *miles from Saratoga Springs.*

The small village lies a little to the west of the Railroad, and contains a small tannery, saw-mill, bolt factory, two churches. The inhabitants are chiefly engaged in agricultural pursuits.

JESSUP'S LANDING,
Corinth, Saratoga Co., N. Y.,
17 *miles from Saratoga Springs.*

This is a village of about 600 inhabitants, and is situated on the west bank of the Hudson, about three-quarters of a mile east of the Railroad station. It contains the extensive manufactory, **Hudson River Pulp Company**, for making pulp from wood for the manufacture of paper.

At this point the traveller reaches the edge of the wild and mountainous Adirondack Region, and also approaches the west bank of the Hudson, river along which the Railroad continues until it reaches its present terminus. The scenery from this point north is grand and delightful.

At Jessup's Landing is a magnificent waterfall in the Hudson, which here plunges over perpendicular rocks 70 feet in height. The falls, with the rapids extending half a mile above, afford a scene of remarkable grandeur and sublimity.

HADLEY,
Hadley, Saratoga Co., N. Y.,
22 *miles from Saratoga Springs*

Just before reaching this station, the Railroad crosses the Sacondaga river, a branch of the Hudson, on a bridge 450 feet long, and 96 feet above the bed of the river.

The valley of the Sacondaga contains several thriving villages, and the river affords an almost limitless amount of water-power, much of which is being converted to manufacturing uses. Six miles above Hadley, the Sacondaga is navigable

LUZERNE,

Luzerne, Warren Co., N. Y., is on the east bank of the Hudson, ¼ mile from Hadley Station on the Adirondack Railroad.

This delightful little village is charmingly situated amidst some of the finest scenery to be found in Northern New York. The mountains on either side rise about 600 feet, and the boisterous Hudson plunges through a deep and rocky gorge, forming the most beautiful rapids and delightful prospects.

At Luzerne is the well-known Rockwell's hotel, kept by Messrs. George T. Rockwell and Son. It is one of those houses which are a delight to all lovers of good living, and "where the happiness of the landlord is in exact ratio to the appetite of his guests."

The house is nicely furnished throughout, and the table is always spread with an abundance of trout, game, and other luxuries, prepared in the most inviting style. The Messrs Rockwell make a specialty of preparing *game dinners*, and parties from Saratoga will find every accomodation for their comfort and enjoyment, by sending notice to the proprietors a little in advance of their coming. A free carriage conveys the guests to and from the hotel, and will be in waiting for all the trains at the Railroad depot. A more enjoyable hotel or resort cannot be found in Northern New York. Terms according to rooms and time of occupancy.

Lake of Luzerne, seven hundred feet above the sea level, and surrounded by hills, is a picture of beauty in itself.

Parties who early seek the exhilarating and oxygenated air of the mountains, will find at the well-known and popular Wayside Hotel all the conveniences and luxuries of a first-class hotel. Its facilities for the accommodation of tourists are among the best. It is just before the lake and is built in the style of Swiss architecture. It possesses a fleet of 24 row-boats, a unique livery of single and double buckboards and a Centennial building, which is now a pretty opera house, for private theatricals and other entertainments of the guests. The Plateau of "The Wayside" is seven hundred feet elevation above tide water. The dry and invigorating atmosphere is a tonic. The soil, sandy, and an absorbent. The water, soft and pure, from granite rocks. No miasma, or malaria. And the hygienic conditions are believed to be perfect. The breezes blow over living timber—over pine-spruce, and other gummy and resinous trees—which statistics show are conducive to long life. The place is recommended by the best physicians as good for rheumatism; good for throat and lung difficulties; good for dyspeptics; good for general debility; good for all who desire relaxation, rest and quiet. No better recommendation for the house can be given than the very liberal patronage it has received in the past, and the exceptional number of families distinguished for culture and refinement who annually make the place their summer home.

WAYSIDE HOTEL.

The Wayside Cottages, nine in number, erected like the hotel, and containing from five to twelve rooms each, rent at from $200 to $900 for the season, and have been christened by Col. Butler with appropriate names.

STONY CREEK,

Stony Creek, Warren Co., N. Y., 30 *miles from Saratoga Springs.*

Just before reaching the station, the Railroad crosses Stony Creek on a bridge of 125 feet span. The village is about two miles above the station, and contains a comfortable hotel, an extensive tannery, one church, and about 300 inhabitants.

THE ADIRONDACK RAILROAD.

THURMAN.

Thurman, Warren Co., N. Y.
36 miles from Saratoga Springs.

This is the stopping point for passengers wishing to reach Warrensburg or Lake George. The station is at the junction of Schroon river and the Hudson. Warrensburg is a prosperous village of about 1,000 inhabitants, and contains several stores, manufactories, saw-mills, a large tannery, four or five churches, and the Warrensburg Academy.

The Warrensburg Hotel and the Adirondack House are very comfortable hotels. Stages run daily from Thurman to Warrensburg and Lake George on arrival of trains from Saratoga. This affords a delightful trip for parties who desire to enjoy the variety and wildness of the mountain scenery, to or from Lake George and Saratoga.

"THE GLEN."

Johnsburg, Warren Co., N. Y.
44 miles from Saratoga Springs.

At this station the Hudson river is spanned by a large wooden bridge.

RIVERSIDE.

Johnsburg, Warren Co., N. Y.
50 miles from Saratoga Springs.

Riverside is situated close by the bank of the river, and has been brought into importance by being made the station where passengers leave the cars for Chester, Pottersville, Schroon Lake, Johnsburg, and other points north. A magnificent line of stages runs from this station to these several points. The distance to Schroon Lake is only about 6 miles, and hence, this route is decidedly the most desirable and pleasant. The steamers on the lake make close connections with the stages, and tourists will find the route one of the most delightful and entrancing to be found in this country. Schroon Lake is rapidly growing in popularity as a resort, and though not as large as Lake George, the beauty of its surrounding mountains, and the picturesqueness of its scenery is by no means inferior to its popular rival.

NORTH CREEK.

Johnsburg, Warren Co., N. Y.
57 miles from Saratoga Springs.

This is the present northern terminus of the Adirondack Railroad, and is a base or starting point for the excursionist or sportsman visiting the Adirondack country. The entrance from this point is the easiest and quickest to Raquette Lake, the heart of the Wilderness. Raquette, Blue Mountain, Moose, Mohican, Three Cedar, Sumner, and Shedd Lakes and Moose River, in the heart of the Wilderness, and in the midst of the finest Trout Fishing and Hunting grounds of the whole Adirondack region, are all readily reached from this point

BATES HOUSE,

Rutland, Vt.

This new, elegant and capacious hotel, so deservedly popular with the traveling public, is now, more than ever, complete in every appointment, having just added 30 new rooms, richly furnished, and conveniently arranged, and other comforts and embellishments throughout the entire structure. The house stands to day without a rival in the State, and surpassed by few in the large cities. The location of the "Bates House" (being diagonally opposite the depot), is most desirable, and stands on the most valuable ground, by far, in the State. The *Cuisine* is of the high st order, and is universally commended by guests visiting the house. Large sample rooms, with strong light, lead from the office. The billiard room, containing four new and elegant tables, is a popular f ature connected with the house, and is undoubtedly the largest and most airy room connected with any hotel in Northern New England. The most attentive service will always be given to guests, and rates are very reasonable. The house is warmed throughout by steam. The finest turnouts are promptly supplied by a new livery stable connected with the house.

J. M. HAVEN,

Proprietor.

RENSSELAER & SARATOGA R. R.—*Continued.*

GANSEVOORT.

Northumberland, Saratoga Co., N. Y.
193 *Miles from New York.*

Is a small post-village, named after Colonel Peter Gansevoort, of the Revolutionary army, who lived here after the war was over. The village stands upon the banks of *Snook Kil*, which the railroad crosses just north of the station. The country in this vicinity is a rolling table-land, and the view is bounded on the one side by the southern spurs of the Adirondacks, and on the other by the hills east of the Hudson.

MOREAU.

Moreau, Saratoga Co., N. Y.
193 *Miles from New York.*

The townships of this name lies along the western bank of the Hudson. It is intersected by numerous ravines and small streams which give the country a somewhat rugged aspect. The range of mountains seen at times to the westward is the Palmerstown range, a continuation of the Adirondacks. The soil is a light, sandy loam. The town was named after General Moreau, of France. The trains stop at this station only on signal. It was formerly the station for passengers leaving the cars for Lake George, but the stage line to the Lake is now discontinued, and tourists visiting Lake George will leave the R. & S. R. R. at Fort Edward.

FORT EDWARD.

Fort Edward, Washington Co., N. Y.
199 *Miles from New York.*
HOTEL—*St. James.*

This town is of considerable importance and activity. It stands on the left bank of the Hudson near where that river changes its course from east to south. An island of considerable size divides the river opposite the town. The railway crosses this island, and the two channels afford a good view of the town along the river. The large buildings near the midst of the town are those of the *Washington County Seminary*, a large school for both sexes. Fort Edward was an important military point in the Indian, French, and Revolutionary wars. A fort called Fort Nicholson was built here in 1709 but was soon after abandoned. In 1755, in pursuance of the plan of military operations against Canada, a fort was erected here, called at first Fort Lyman, but the name was afterward changed to Fort Edward in honor of Edward, Duke of York, the brother of George III. of England. Being on the great carrying place to Lake Champlain, it became a very important depot for arms and rendezvous for armies in the expeditions against Canada. It also served as a hospital for the sick and wounded. During the Revolution it was again occupied by both British and Americans. It stood on the bank of the river, north of the creek, within the present limits of the village.

The murder of Jane McRea took place near a spring a little east of the village, July 27, 1777. The tragedy served to intensify popular feeling against the British and has passed into our national history. The remains of Miss McRea are interred in the Union Cemetary.

Passengers wishing to reach the Fort William Henry Hotel, at the head of Lake George, or to take the Lake George route northward, leave the Rensselaer and Saratoga Railway at Fort Edward, and take the cars on the branch for Glens Falls, whence the lake is reached by stage, through wild and interesting scenery.

(For description of the route via Lake George, see page—.)

DUNHAM'S BASIN.

Kingsbury, Washington Co., N. Y.
202 Miles from New York.

A small village on the Champlain Canal.

SMITH S BASIN.

Washington Co., N. Y.
207 Miles from New York.
HOTEL—*Smith's Hotel.*

A small station with few houses.

The station bears the name of a large landowners of this vicinity and proprietor of the large hotel near the station.

FORT ANN.

Fort Ann, Washington Co., N Y.
211 Miles from New York.

This village bears the name of an old colonial fort which stood on the west side of Wood Creek, about half a mile from the railway station. The Champlain Canal now crosses the spot where it stood. The fort was one of a chain of works erected in 1709, at the joint expense of England and the colonies, to facilitate expeditions against Canada during the French war, and was the scene of several encounters between the hostile forces. An engagement occurred here in 1777 between Burgoyne's advance and a detachment of Americans. The latter held their ground until their ammunition was exhausted, and then retreated, felling trees, burning bridges, and otherwise obstructing the roads. Burgoyne was several weeks in overcoming the obstacles so that his heavily equipped troops could continue their march

As we pass along the railroad towards Whitehall, we may notice the high, steep, and rocky mountains on the north and west of us, which are called Fort Ann Mountains.

COMSTOCK'S LANDING.

Fort Ann, Washington Co., N. Y.
215 Miles from New York.

For some miles the railway follows the course of a rocky ledge of limestone, between which and the track is the Champlain Canal. At Comstock's Landing the ridge is quite high and precipitous. A road, however, ascends through a break in the cliff, and part of the village may be seen. The large and handsome house, which is so beautifully situated on the wooded summit of the cliff, is the residence of Mr. I. V. Baker, Superintendent of the R. & S. Railway.

WHITEHALL.

Whitehall, Washington Co., N. Y.
223 Miles from New York.

Hotel—*Hall's Hotel.*

The village of Whitehall stands at the head of Lake Champlain, and a short branch of the R. & S. Railway runs through the pleasantly shaded street, from the station to the steamboat landing. High hills rise on both sides the village, but the country is level and open to the southward. Whitehall is the largest lumber market on the lake, and owes its prosperity principally to that branch of industry. The R. R. train divides at this station, a part of the cars carrying the passengers to the steamboat wharf, and a portion going on to Rutland. (For description of Lake Champlain and route by steamer, viz lake steamers, see p 110.)

FAIRHAVEN.

Fairhaven, Rutland Co., Vt.
229 Miles from New York.

The village stands on an elevated plateau, overlooking the open country along the base of the hills along Lake Champlain. Close by the station, and in sight from the car windows, are beautiful falls in the Castleton River. Slate is quarried and worked in large quantities at this place. Here also is the westward limit of the great marble beds of Vermont.

HYDEVILLE.

Castleton, Rutland Co., Vt.
231 Miles from New York.

The village is largely engaged in marble and slate works. It is pleasantly situated among lofty hills. Immediately north of the village is a large lake called Lake Bomoseen. It affords good fishing, and is a pleasant place of resort for the inhabitants of the vicinity.

CASTLETON.

Castleton, Rutland Co., Vt.
234 Miles from New York.

Is on a small river of the same name. Killington Peak, among the Green Mountains, may be seen at intervals to the eastward. The peculiar bold eminence in the same direction is known as Spruce Knob, and its immediate neighbor is Herrick Mountain.

WEST RUTLAND.
Rutland, Rutland Co., Vt.
241 *Miles from New York.*

Extensive marble works are in operation at this place. The quarries, to which a branch railroad track leads, may be seen on the hillside to the north. The whole ridge surrounding the alluvial flat on which the village stands is composed of marble of greater or less degrees of fineness.

RUTLAND.
Rutland, Rutland Co., Vt.
244 *Miles from New York. From Montreal,* **150½.**
HOTELS—*Bates and Bardwell.*

The name of Rutland is probably best known in connection with the marble which is quarried from various places within its limits, and carried thence to all parts of the country. The town and village are the centres of the marble region, and large quantities of fine white marble are annually shipped thence by railroad. Rutland is the county town, and is important as the central market for a large region of country. Its population is about 10,000. It has one daily and three weekly newspapers, two iron foundries, large marble-sawing works, and some other factories. On the principal street are a number of fine stores of all kinds, well stocked with supplies for local trade. The railroad depot is a fine brick building in the central part of the town, and is used by the three railroads which meet here, namely, the *Rutland R.R.*, the *Rensselaer and Saratoga R.R.*, and the *Bennington and Rutland R.R.* Pleasant drives and walks abound in the vicinity, among which may be mentioned the roads leading to *Clarendon Springs*, *Middletown Healing Springs*, and the various marble quarries. The Green Mountains surround the valley in which Rutland stands, and add greatly to the beauty of its scenery. The three highest peaks are known by the names of *Shrewsbury*, *Killington*, and *Pico*. *Otter Creek* flows through the northern part of the village, and furnishes excellent water-power at various points.

(For description of the Rutland R.R. and continuation of **railroad** route, see page 99.)

BARDWELL HOUSE,
Rutland, Vermont.
J. W. CRAMTON, Proprietor.
A good Livery connected with the House.

ADDISON HOUSE,
MIDDLEBURY, VERMONT.

DARWIN RIDER, - - - - Proprietor.

Having again assumed the management of the Addison House, altered and improved the building by enlarging the windows with awnings attached, building new large piazzas, and refurnishing the rooms, I beg leave to call your attention to the attractions it offers to those seeking pleasure, retreat from business, and a quiet home. The house stands on rising ground, surrounded by the parks of this beautiful village, but a few miles from the base of the Green Mountains, and in full view of the Adirondack range of Northern New York.

The village of Middlebury, Vt., has scarcely a superior in beauty in New England, and in its immediate vicinity are numerous pleasant walks and drives to various localities that have become famous for their attractions— Lake George, Lake Dunmore, Lake Champlain, Grand View Mountain, Ticonderoga, Belden's Falls, Mountain Drive, &c. The mountain streams, but a few miles east of the house, abound in trout to a degree unequaled by any other portion of New England.

Connected with the House is a Livery Stable, where fine equipages, with careful drivers if desired, can be procured. The house has a Billiard Hall, where ladies and children can amuse themselves with almost the same privacy as at their own homes.

The Rutland & Burlington Division of the Central Vermont R. R. passes through the village, trains leaving in each direction three times daily.

DARWIN RIDER, Proprietor.

CLARENDON HOUSE,

CLARENDON SPRINGS, VT.

B. MURRAY & SONS, - - - - - Proprietors.

Open from May to November.
Hotel and Three Cottages accommodating 200 Guests.
Farm of 170 acres connected with the Hotel.

TERMS:

Board, per week, - - - - - - -	$8.00 to $10.00
Children under Twelve, going to first Table, -	5.00 and 6.00
Servants, - - - - - - - - - -	5.00
Day Board, - - - - - - - - -	2.00

☞ Carriages at West Rutland to meet all regular Railroad Trains. *Telegraph* communication, Livery and Boarding Stables connected with the House. Warm and Cold Baths. Cool nights, and no mosquitoes. Music, Billards, Bowling, etc. Pleasant drives and *beautiful* scenery in every direction. References, if desired, in all principal cities.

Send for Pamphlet with description.

CLARENDON SPRINGS,

DISCOVERED IN THE HISTORIC YEAR 1776, ARE

Unequaled for Curing all Impurities of the Blood, Liver Complaint, Dyspepsia, Dropsy, and for Restoring Appetite and Physical Strength.

This water has no sediment, is delicious to drink, health-giving, and is a fine water for bathing. As a choice table water helping digestion and sharpening the appetite, these waters will be found invaluable.

ANALYSIS:

One gallon, or 235 inches of water contains:

Carbonic Acid Gas	46.16 cubic inch.
Nitrogen Gas	.96 " "
Carbonate of Lime........................	3.02 grains.
Muriate of Lime, Sulphate of Soda, and Sulphate of Magnesia.	2.74 "

One hundred cubic inches of the gas which was evolved from the water consist of—

Carbonic Acid Gas........................	0.05 cubic inch.
Oxygen Acid Gas.........................	1.50 " "
Nitrogen Acid Gas.	98.45 " "

DR. AUGUSTUS A. HAYES, State Assayer for Massachusetts, says: "It is a remarkable water, containing nitrogen dissolved."

CLARENDON SPRINGS, VERMONT,

Clarendon, Rutland Co., Vt. 3 Miles from West Rutland.

These springs are on the west side of the Tinmouth river, among the beautiful hills of Vermont, three miles from West Rutland Station, on the Delaware and Hudson Canal Co's Railroad. They are about 170 miles from Boston, 90 from Albany, 60 from Saratoga Springs, and 25 from Whitehall. The scenery about the springs is of peculiar beauty, even for Vermont, while the splendid roads afford excellent opportunity for drives and views of this delightful region. Many prominent peaks and spurs of the Green Mountains are within a few miles, and may be seen from the lower hills that surround the springs. Killington, Pico, Little Pico, and Shrewsbury Peaks of the Green Mountains, Spruce Knob and Bird's-Eye Peaks, add grandeur and picturesqueness to this region. Amid this charming scenery, nature has sent forth one of her life-giving fountains, rarely excelled in rich medicinal properties or healing efficacy. The following, taken from the Geological Survey of Vermont, Vol. II, describes the discovery of these valuable waters. "These springs were doubtless among the first ever visited for their medicinal virtues, and are more resorted to than any others in the State. Tradition informs us that their medicinal character was first discovered in 1776, by Asa Smith, who resided in the town. He is reported to have 'dreamed' of a spring in the western part of the town, and, full of faith, started in search of the water that would restore him to health. Arriving at this spot, he recognized it as the one he had seen in his dream, and accordingly drank of the waters, and bound clay saturated with it upon his swollen and inflamed limbs. The scrofulous humor which for years had been a source of continual annoyance, at once yielded to the potent influence of the water, and the man was soon restored to perfect health." Many residents of Rutland and vicinity testify to a number of cures of obstinate diseases by drinking this water. The best effects are obtained by taking it fresh from the spring, where all its mineral properties, combine with the fresh mountain air, to restore health and strength. The large hotel and some cottages near the Springs, supply all the conveniences of our best summer resorts. Warm and cold baths, billiards, bowling, a livery and boarding stable, and telegraph communication to all parts of the country are connected with the hotel.

HORSESHOE AND BIRMINGHAM FALLS,
AU SABLE CHASM, N. Y.

Middletown Healing Springs.

Middletown, Rutland County, Vt.

8 *Miles from Poultney.*

The Middletown Healing Springs are situated on the north bank of the Poultney River, a tributary of Lake Champlain, in Middletown, Rutland county, Vermont. The village lies on both sides of the river. The springs are about fifteen miles south-west from Rutland; but Poultney is the nearest railroad station, and the proper point of RR. departure. Stages connecting with trains run between Poultney and the springs. The road between Middletown and Poultney, winding around the foot of mountains and along the margin of the river, is a charming drive. The springs are less than an hour's drive from Poultney, and their beautiful surroundings and rare medicinal virtues are destined to make them a favorite resort for the invalid and pleasure-seeker.

Spruce Knob Mountain, four miles north of the town, is abundant in extensive and charming views.

Bird's-Eye, three miles west of Spruce Knob, seven miles from the springs, and *Lover's Rock*, one quarter of a mile from the springs, are said to "present scenery which would excite admiration even in Switzerland."

These springs were known previous to 1811, and their waters used to a limited extent as a remedial agent. In that year, according to old residents of the county, a flood changed the bed of the Poultney river at Middletown, filling up the old channel with gravel, and depositing an immense layer of it against the north bank, out of which the springs issued. From this time nothing was seen of them until June, 1868, when another flood of unusual volume occurred, which washed away the deposit of gravel, and again laid them bare.

When the springs were re-discovered, a number of individuals, afflicted in various ways, commenced drinking the waters. They drank indiscriminately from all the springs, and in many cases a complete cure and restoration to health resulted. The fame of the springs grew rapidly, and from the neighboring towns the people began to come with every variety of pail, jug, and barrel for the water. Cures of many cases of long-seated chronic diseases have been reported. They act as a tonic and stimulant, giving tone and strength to the system, stimulating the digestive organs, and promoting the full and healthful action of the organs of the body. They have not the weakening and painful harshness and unnatural quickness of effect which characterize the action of many mineral waters, natural and artificial.

The springs are seven in number, but the waters of only three have as yet been analyzed, and their medicinal properties ascertained. Although situated within a few yards of each other, their properties are distinct.

The water from Spring Number One has been analyzed by Prof. Peter Collier, of the Agricultural College of Vermont, and is found to contain the following mineral constituents:—

Carbonic Acid, Sulphuric Acid, Chlorine, Nitric Acid, Lime, Magnesia, Iron, Manganese, Alumina, Potash, Soda.

These elements are found in the following combinations: Sulphate of Lime, Carbonate of Lime, Carbonate of Magnesia, Carbonate of Iron, Carbonate of Manganese, Alumina, Chloride of Potassium, Chloride of Sodium, Carbonate of Soda.

Of these, iron and manganese are found to exist in unusual abundance. Immense quantities of these waters are shipped daily, and movements are on foot to erect additional hotels and bathing-houses.

THE CENTRAL VERMONT RAILROAD.
RUTLAND DIVISION.

BELLOWS FALLS TO BURLINGTON, PLATTSBURG, AU SABLE RIVER, AND PROVINCE (CANADA) LINE.

The *Rutland Railroad* and the *Vermont Valley, Montreal & Plattsburg, Whitehall & Plattsburg*, and the *Addison* Railroads* are now controlled and operated by the Vermont Central R. R., having its headquarters at St. Albans.

The lines of these several roads extend from Brattleboro via Bellows Falls to Burlington, and from Plattsburg to Au Sable River, and Province (Canada) Line.

The Rutland R. R. proper, extending from Bellows Falls to Burlington, was finished in 1849, and has very materially assisted in developing the manufacturing resources of the State, as well as increasing its mineral and agricultural wealth.

The railroad passes through the only two cities in Vermont, namely, *Vergennes* and *Burlington*, having its northern terminus in the latter place. At Rutland it connects with *The Rensselaer and Saratoga*, and *The Harlem Extension* railroads, all which roads meet in a spacious depot near the center of the town.

The line passes through the richest marble district in the State, of which district, perhaps, Rutland may be called the center. Large quantities of marble are transported to market over the railroads which center here, and this valuable mineral is an important source of income to the railroads, and of wealth to the State. Soapstone and slate are also exported in large quantities, and in suitable forms for the various purposes to which each is adapted. Lumber, also, is constantly brought by rail from Burlington, which is one of the greatest lumber shipping towns in the country.

The scenery throughout the line is ever varying in its beauty. The Green Mountains, with their ravines and cataracts, are a constant source of interest and pleasure while passing through them and when the track leaves the mountain range, and tra-

* For description of Addison R. R. see page 103*b*.

verses the level land near Lake Champlain, the mountains still remain in sight, as a grand background to the more quiet landscape along the railroad. For twenty miles south of Burlington the line is on or near the shore of Lake Champlain, of which, with the Adirondack Mountains beyond, fine views are afforded.

CENTRE RUTLAND.

Rutland, Rutland Co., Vt. Fr. Montreal, 148¼. 245¼ *M. fr. N. Y.*

A suburb of Rutland on the banks of *Otter Creek*, which we here cross for the first time. There are here some large marble-works.

SUTHERLAND FALLS.

Rutland, Rutland Co., Vt. 249 *M. fr. N. Y. Fr. Montreal,* 145.

Otter Creek here plunges through a rocky chasm on the right of the track. When the water of the creek is high, a glimpse of th' falls may be caught in passing, but a fair sight at their great beauty can only be obtained by stopping for the purpose. A large marble company has its works here. The buildings stands at the right among the rocks. A few hundred yards beyond the station a superb view opens on the right. A broad and beautiful valley surrounded by lofty mountains is spread before us. The railroad follows the hillside along the edge of this valley for some distance, gradually sinking to the level of the meadows, until it crosses them just before reaching the next station.

PITTSFORD.

Pittsford, Rutland Co., Vt. 252 *M. fr. N. Y. Fr. Montreal,* 142.

On the north of the valley just mentioned are the station and village of Pittsford. The village is on a hill not far from the station. Near this place were two American block-houses during the Revolutionary War, known as forts *Moot* and *Vengeance*. Iron ore is found in the town in considerable quantities. There is a large marble quarry at this place, and another before reaching Brandon.

BRANDON.

Brandon, Rutland Co., Vt. 260 *M. fr. N. Y. Fr. Montreal,* 134.

HOTEL.—*Brandon House.*

Brandon is built on both sides of a small stream, and is a thriving village. It is especially celebrated for the manufacture of *mineral paints*, which are made of various colors, mostly browns and yellows, and are very durable. There is a scale factory and a large marble quarry in the town. Population, 4,000.

LEICESTER JUNCTION.

Whiting, Addison Co., Vt. 265 M. fr. N. Y. Fr. Montreal, 129.

This station is at the junction of the Addison Branch R. R., which runs to Ticonderoga and Port Henry, N. Y., and the Rutland R. R. For description of the branch, see page 103b. At the station we have a fine view of the Green Mountains, a few miles to the eastward.

SALISBURY.

——, *Addison Co., Vt. 279 M. fr. N. Y. Fr. Montreal,* 124.

Salisbury is in the midst of extensive level fields, many of which are only partially cleared, but give promise of great richness when properly cultivated. Stages leave this station on arrival of trains during the summer season for

LAKE DUNMORE.

Salisbury, Vt., 5 miles from Salisbury Station.

Lake Dunmore, named in honor of the Earl of Dunmore, is a beautiful sheet of water situated about eight miles north of Brandon, and eight miles south-east of Middlebury, among the Green Mountains of Vermont. The Lake is about five miles long, one mile wide, covering a space of about 1,400 acres, at an altitude of 358 feet above the level of the sea. Its waters are clear as crystal, and its shores skirted with a variety of scenery rarely seen and seldom equalled, even in the beautiful mountain regions of New England and northern New York. On the western shores, the country rises in undulating meadow and wooded hills, while on the eastern side two or three spurs of the Green Mountains rise to a height of 1,500 to 2,000 feet, thus uniting, in charming variety, the bold, majestic mountain scenery with the lovelier features of lake and meadow. From these elevations on either side, which are accessible by pedestrians or on horseback, the most charming views of the surrounding country are obtained, embracing Lake Champlain and the Adirondack Mountains on the west, and several of the most prominent peaks of the Green Mountain range on the east and south; the view extending 70 or 80 miles from north to south, is not surpassed in grandeur and beauty by any prospect this side the summits of

Mansfield and Washington. As a summer resort it is unexcelled. The pure mountain air, the beautiful lake, abounding in trout and other fish, and affording excellent opportunity for rowing and bathing, the many delightful walks and drives to falls, caves, and prospective points, the bold mountain scenery, together with the excellent large hotel, furnished and conducted in a style corresponding with the superior natural advantages of its location, all combine to render Lake Dunmore one of the pleasantest and most delightful resorts in America. Among the more prominent points of interest, and which are well worth visiting, are Mountains Gnomon and Moosalamoo on the east, the latter rising to a height of 1,959 feet, Mount Bryant on the north, 500 feet above the lake, on the top of which is Prospect Rock, easily reached and commanding magnificent views of Lake Champlain and Adirondack Region, Sunset Hill on the west—one of the most delightful spots in Vermont—Warner's Cave—noted in the history of the Green Mountain Boys—Pleasure Island in the center of the lake, Wolf Hill, and other places delightful and interesting in their association with the history of the native Indians and early settlers of this portion of Vermont. The Lake Dunmore House is the only hotel near the lake, and it is most delightfully situated, commanding a full view of the steep and rugged mountain side, and the beautiful crystal lake at its feet. Several cottages occupied by prominent families of New York, New Haven, Boston, Philadelphia, and other cities: billiards, bowling, hunting, fishing, and a good livery, add to the other attractions of the place. To reach the lake, leave the cars at Salisbury station and take the coach five miles across the country.

MIDDLEBURY.

Middlebury, Addison Co., Vt. 276 *M. fr. N. Y. Fr. Montreal,* 118.
HOTEL.—*Addison House.*

Otter Creek flows through the village, which is large and prosperous. A fall in the creek affords fine water-power in the midst of the village. There are near this place two large marble quarries, from one of which the marble for the new Custom-house and Post-office at Portland, Me., is taken.

MIDDLEBURY COLLEGE is situated here. This college was organized in 1800 by private subscriptions, and has at present about one hundred students. It has an able faculty, and a good standing among the educational institutions of the country. The standard of scholarship is high, and the management of the college is in "orthodox" hands. Just after leaving the station, the falls may be seen on the left. On the right are *Camel's Hump* and *Mt. Mansfield*. A few miles north of Middlebury we cross New Haven River, which joins Otter Creek just below the bridge. Picturesque rapids and bends in the river may here be seen on the left.

BROOKSVILLE.
New Haven, Addison Co., Vt.   280 *M. fr. N. Y.   Fr. Montreal*, 114.

A small farming village in a rolling country, well adapted for stock-raising.

NEW HAVEN.
New Haven, Addison Co., Vt.   284 *M. fr. N. Y.   Fr. Montreal*, 110.

The face of the country is gently undulating. On one of the hills to the right of the railroad is the village of New Haven. The Green Mountain range is a few miles beyond.

VERGENNES.
Vergennes, Addison Co., Vt.   289 *M. fr. N. Y.   Fr. Montreal*, 105.

HOTEL.—*Stevens House.*

Vergennes is the oldest city in Vermont, which fact does not necessarily imply a great age, as the only other city in the State, *i.e.*, Burlington, was incorporated in 1866. Vergennes has, however, a good old age, having been incorporated as a city in 1788. The city limits are a little more than a mile square, enclosing a tract of land located just at the head of sloop and schooner navigation on Otter Creek, and including excellent water-power. The city may be seen on a hill half a mile west of the railroad station; beyond it are high hills along the lake, and still farther the blue outline of the Adirondack Mountains may be seen. Otter Creek is navigable to Vergennes for vessels of 300 tons burden. In fact, vessels of that size can lie almost alongside the bank anywhere below the city. Commodore Macdonough's fleet was fitted out here during the war of 1812, and a United States Arsenal is still established here, containing supplies of ordnance and munitions of war. Vergennes has manufactories of farming implements and an iron foundry. A weekly market is held here, to which the neighboring inhabitants resort in large numbers. The *Fort Casson House* is a summer resort on Lake Champlain, a few miles from Vergennes, whence it may be easily reached by stage or boat.

FERRISBURG.
Ferrisburg, Addison Co., Vt. 295½ *M. fr. N. Y. Fr. Montreal*, 102¼.

We here cross a bridge under which are falls; the name of the stream is Lewis Creek. The village is on the right, a short distance from the station. After leaving Ferrisburg, a fine view of Lake Champlain and the Adirondacks opens on the left, while on the right may be seen *Camel's Hump* and *Mt. Mansfield*. On the latter mountain a hotel is kept open during the summer.

NORTH FERRISBURG.
Ferrisburg, Addison Co., Vt. 295 *M. fr N. Y. Fr. Montreal*, 98.

A small village with hardly any houses in sight from the railroad station. The main village is two or three miles east of the railroad.

CHARLOTTE.
Charlotte, Chittenden Co., Vt. 390 *M. fr. N. Y. Fr. Montreal*, 94.

The village stands on a hill, east of the station, and broad meadows stretch to the lake shore on the west. Some remarkable fossil bones were found here while the railroad was being built. They were classified by the *savans* as belonging to an animal of the whale species.

SHELBURNE.
Shelburne, Chittenden Co., Vt. 305 *M. fr. N. Y. Fr. Montreal*, 89.

This is a small village, with pleasant houses overlooking the lake. A curious ledge of stratified rock, of different colors, is near the track on the right of the road.

BURLINGTON.
318¼ *M. fr. N. Y. Fr. Montreal*, 82½.

From Burlington the route continues by Lake Champlain Steamers to Plattsburg, connecting with the Whitehall and Plattsburg Road for Au Sable River Station, where stages will be in waiting for passengers for the Adirondack region; from Plattsburg to Rouse's Point, and thence by railroad to Montreal.

(For description of Burlington, see page 116.)

SOUTHERN DIVISION OF THE
WHITEHALL & PLATTSBURG AND ADDISON RAILROAD.

The Addison Railroad was completed in the year 1871, and extends from Leicester Junction, on the Rutland R. R. through Whiting, Shoreham, Orwell, Larabee's Point in Vermont, where it crosses Lake Champlain, and connects with the southern division of the Whitehall & Plattsburg R. R. at Ticonderoga in the State of New York, thence passing through Crown Point to Port Henry. The entire road is operated by the Vermont Central Railroad Company. Trains run between Leicester Junction and Port Henry to connect with the trains on the Rutland R. R.

LEICESTER JUNCTION.
Whiting, Addison County, Vt.

This station is at the junction of the Addison Railroad with the Rutland Railroad. There are only a few houses at the junction, the village of Whiting being about 3 miles to the west. Passengers going to Ticonderoga, Crown Point or Port Henry change cars at this place.

WHITING.
Whiting, Addison County, Vt.

This village is in the midst of a rich agricultural district, and contains a small population. Fine views of the Adirondack and Green Mountain Ranges and Lake Champlain may be obtained near this place.

SHOREHAM.
Shoreham, Addison County, Vt.

An agricultural town, with no especial attractions except the beautiful and delightful views of mountain and lake scenery which it commands.

ORWELL.
Orwell, Addison County, Vt.,

is a small town devoted to agricultural pursuits.

LARRABEE'S POINT.
Shoreham, Addison County, Vt.
HOTEL, UNITED STATES.

This station is on the shore of Lake Champlain about 2 miles. It is unimportant in history, but since the railroad was built it has risen somewhat in interest. At this point the Railroad crosses Lake Champlain to Ticonderoga on the New York side of the Lake. There is a good hotel here, and good fishing grounds are near at hand.

TICONDEROGA.
Ticonderoga, Essex County, N. Y.

For description of Ticonderoga, Crown Point, Port Henry, see pages 114, 115.

A Delightful Summer Resort among the Green Mountains.

THE BROOKS HOUSE,
BRATTLEBORO, VT.
(The Half-Way House between New York and the White Mountains.)

TO SUMMER TOURISTS.

VERMONT, as is shown by its statistics, is the healthiest State in the Union. The purity of its air and water, and the grandeur of its scenery, have always made it a favorite resort of the tourist.

BRATTLEBORO, on the banks of the Connecticut, is pronounced by experienced travelers to stand unrivaled in natural and enjoyable attractions. Long a favorite Summer Resort, the thousands of visitors, from all parts of the country, who have thronged here during the summer and autumn months for health and pleasure, will bear witness to its beautiful and varied landscapes, its charming drives and walks, and its delightful health-giving climate and pure water. Surrounded by hills and mountains, its scenery is grand and picturesque; and new drives may be enjoyed for weeks, over roads winding along the banks of swift-running brooks, through groves and over hill-tops, within a radius of a dozen miles, each with its distinctive features of interest and beauty.

THE BROOKS HOUSE, which was opened on the first of June, 1872, is situated at the corner of Main and High Streets, and is within three minutes' walk of the depot, and but five hours by rail from Boston, and seven from New York. It is provided with all the modern improvements, and no expense has been spared in furnishing, to make it a pattern home for city families.

The building, which has cost $150,000, is of a modern style of architecture, three stories high, surmounted by a French roof and towers. The length on Main Street is 175 feet, and on High Street, 120 feet, while the depth is 70 feet. The building thus forms nearly a right-angle, whose total lenght is almost three hundred feet. A spacious veranda, 90 feet in length, fronts the centre on Main Street, beneath which is the main entrance of 20 feet front, and 70 feet depth. The Parlors, Dining Rooms, and Sleeping Apartments, are all spacious, handsomely furnished, and arranged for the complete accommodation of guests. All the rooms are in telegraphic communication with the office, are heated by steam radiators, and are mostly arranged in suits, parlor and bedroom adjoining. The stabling is ample. A fine livery stable is connected with the house. Most liberal terms made with permanent boarders for one month or for the season.

LAKE GEORGE ROUTE,

VIA GLENS FALLS.

THE traveler going north, and wishing to visit Lake George, or to take the route by that lake, will leave the main line of the R. & S. R. R. at Fort Edward, and take the cars of the Glens Falls Branch R. R. to Glens Falls, about six miles distant, and thence take stages to Caldwell and the Fort William Henry Hotel, at the head of the lake, distant nine miles from Glens Falls. In continuing the journey from Caldwell, the route is by steamer down Lake George to Baldwin (Ticonderoga), where a railroad ride of five miles around the rapids connects with the steamers on Lake Champlain at Fort Ticonderoga.

Of course this route is only available during the season of summer travel, but it is much frequented by lovers of nature, as the scenery of Lake George has an almost world-wide reputation for beauty and attractiveness.

If, however, one has plenty of time, or only wishes to visit Lake George, and not go farther north, it will perhaps be as well for him to go on by rail to Fort Ticonderoga, take the branch R. R. to Baldwin on Lake George, and thence pass up Lake George to Fort William Henry. By this means he secures the best introduction to the scenery of the lake of "The Silvery Waters," amid the glory and deepening shadows of a sunset on the lake. Two trips are made daily by the steamers during the season after the middle of June.

A tarry over night at the Great Hotel, and a stage ride to Glens Falls, or a return down the lake to "Fort Ti," will bring one back again to the commercial thoroughfare with anything but regret for the short delay at the beautiful lake.

SANDY HILL.

Kingsbury, Washington County, N. Y.

This village contains about 3,000 inhabitants. A dam 1,200 feet long across the Hudson affords great water-power, which is extensively used by various sorts of manufactories and mills. The town was the scene of numerous adventures during the French and Revolutionary wars. At one time 17 soldiers captured by the Indians were at this place seated on a log, and all but one deliberately tomahawked. In August, 1758, Major Rogers and Major (afterwards Gen.) Putnam encountered and repelled a party of French and Indians within the town. Putnam was made a prisoner in the engagement.

Traces of a road cut by Burgoyne's army are said to be still visible in the township.

GLENS FALLS.

Queensbury, Warren County, N. Y.

HOTEL—ROCKWELL' HOUSE.

Glens Falls is an important incorporated village of about 9,000 inhabitants. It is the present terminus of the Glens Falls branch of the Rensselaer and Saratoga R. R., and a branch of the Champlain Canal, and aside from its business importance, is a place of much interest to the tourist and traveler. The village is divided by the Hudson River which at this point makes a descent of about fifty feet, producing a scene of surpassing grandeur. The river is spanned by a bridge just below the falls, and from it a delightful view may be obtained. These falls in the river afford valuable water power, which is largely improved by extensive saw mills, which may be seen in operation on either side of the river. The lumber trade of the place is immense, and millions upon millions of feet of lumber are annually sawed at these extensive mills. Above the falls is a dam across the river, built by the state, and a navigable feeder from above the dam supplies the summit level of the Champlain Canal with water. In the Hudson River at this point are several large booms, where logs floated from the upper woods are sorted and distributed. It is no uncommon thing to move a million or more of logs at one time at this place. Below the falls is a small island, from which a cave extends from one channel to the other. This island has been made famous by Cooper in his "Last of the Mohicans." The tourist will find Glens Falls well worth visiting, and the picturesque scenery, the excellent hunting and fishing grounds in the adjacent mountains, the walks and beautiful drives render the place very attractive as a summer resort. Besides the above attractions there is a most excellent hotel, the "Rockwell House," which was erected and opened in the spring of 1872. It is built of brick, four stories in height, surmounted by a mansard roof, and is situated in the centre of the village. It is furnished throughout in elegant style, with brussels carpeting, marble top and black walnut furniture, and the rooms are supplied with hot and cold water, gas, plenty of closet room, &c. Some of the apartments are arranged in suites suitable for family use. In the rear of the house is a large and beautiful lawn, with croquet grounds, walks, and garden. We commend it from experience to our readers as one of the best hotels to be found in northern New York. It is kept by Rockwell Bros., who formerly kept the Lake House at Lake George, and whose experience in hotel keeping is widely known, and is a guaranty that its patrons will be well entertained. Passengers going through Glens Falls will find the comfort and enjoyment of their trip very much enhanced by stopping over at the Rockwell House, either for dinner or the night, and visiting the falls and vicinity. Carriages are in waiting for passengers at the R. R. Depot, and at Lake George, for conveying guests to the house.

CALDWELL.

Caldwell, Warren County, N. Y.

This place is the country seat of Warren County, but derives its principal importance from its position at the head of Lake George, and the delightful scenery which surrounds it. As these are spoken of in the description of Lake George, we omit them here. Caldwell is connected by stage with Warrensburg, Chester, Schroon Lake, Long Lake and other points in the lower Adirondack region, and with Thurman, on the Adirondack R. R.

ARLINGTON HOTEL,

At WASHINGTON, D.C.

T. ROESSLE & SON, Proprietors.

THE *Arlington Hotel* is well worthy of the first-class patronage which it receives. It is situated on the corner of 15th and H streets, in one of the most interesting portions of the city. The southern wing fronts the beautiful Lafayette Park, in which is the celebrated bronze equestrian statue of Jackson, and opposite which are the "White House," U. S. Treasury Building, and the U. S. War and Navy Departments. The residence of the Secretary of State is a few rods to the north of the hotel—and all the public buildings are within easy distance. The hotel is five stories high, with brown stone front, and is furnished in elegant style, and supplied with a fine passenger elevator—closets on all the floors, signal bells, etc. The dining hall is one of the handsomest and most pleasantly situated in Washington. A large number of the rooms are arranged in suites, with all the conveniences for family use. The proprietors of the Arlington, also conduct the magnificent *Fort William Henry Hotel at Lake George*, the finest summer resort in America. To the patrons of the *Fort William Henry* we need only say that what *it* is in the *summer resort* world the *Arlington* is among the hotels of the Capital.

Prices, $3.00 and $4.00 per day.

LAKE GEORGE.

"Horicon" (the Silvery Waters) is an Indian name often ap plied to this unrivaled gem of American lakes. The Indians themselves called it Can-i-a-déri-oit—the tail of the lake. The French discovered it in 1609, and named it Saint Sacrément.

The loyal Britons afterwards re-christened it Lake George, in honor of George I., their sovereign, and the English name still prevails, though, to most Americans, Horicon, the euphonious and significant Indian title, is more satisfactory, and the wish is often expressed that it might prevail.

The renown of its wild and picturesque beauty has spread throughout the world, and thousands yearly come to view its charms, and go away to praise them.

The lake is almost surrounded by steep and rugged mountains and its pellucid waters are studded with numerous islands. The passage up or down the lake presents an ever-varying panorama of beautiful and distinct views. Sometimes the mountains rise abruptly from the banks, at others quiet valleys scooped among the hills reveal the grand proportions of more distinct heights, and vistas of Arcadian beauty.

The numerous islands—said to equal in number the days in the year—add beauty to magnificence in the scenery of the lake.

Some are of considerable size, inhabited (in summer at least) and partially cultivated. Some are rugged cliffs crowned with shrubs or meagre vegetation; others, low bare rocks, or mere points just rising above the water, only useful because, in their place and multitude, they are beautiful.

The whole region of the lake is full of historic interest, and islands, waters, glens, and mountains have witnessed many a scene of martial glory, strife, and slaughter.

Fort William Henry, at the head of the lake, is the principal point of attraction and resort on its shores, not only on account of its unequaled scenery and beauty of situation, but because of the excellent hotel, which can accommodate twelve hundred guests, and supply their wants on a most liberal scale. THE FORT WILLIAM HENRY HOTEL has long been known and patronized by lovers of Lake George. Under its original proprietors it gained an enviable reputation among the hotels of this region. It is now in the possession of the Messrs. Roselle, who have effected such changes and improvements in the hotel and its surroundings, that its guests of former years would hardly recognize its once-familiar features.

The building has been enlarged and improved on a generous scale. A mansard roof has been raised above the old building, affording a new series of rooms commanding the most entrancing views of the lake, while from the top of the roof still more extensive prospects can be obtained. Besides this, great alterations have been made in the interior arrangements and furniture. Not content to confine their improvements to the hotel, the proprietors have built a number of neat and convenient cottages in the immediate vicinity, which are intended to accommodate those who wish for more private as well as more rooming apartments than can be obtained in the hotel. The ornamental grounds, which have always added so much to the attractions of this resort, have been improved and re-arranged, so that this most desirable feature of the establishment adds to its beauty more than ever.

The Fort George Hotel is a fine house, east of the old Fort George ruins. It has extensive grounds on the lake shore, and cottage accommodations for more than 50 guests. The house is handsomely furnished, and is one of the best on this famous lake.

In 1775 Sir Wm. Johnson, with an army of 5,000 men, operating against the French, encamped at the head of Lake George, near where the hotel now stands. The French, under Baron Dieskau, who had occupied Ticonderoga, passed up South Bay —the southern limit of Lake Champlain—and across the rocky

Fort William Henry Hotel.

PRICE, $3.00 PER DAY.

T. ROESSLE & SON, Proprietors.   LAKE GEORGE, CALDWELL, N. Y.

peninsula to the rear of the English, and, having ambuscaded and overcome Col. Williams and King Hendrick, who with 1,000 troops and 200 Indians had been sent out to meet them, fell upon the English camp, but after a sanguinary fight the French were totally defeated. Johnson and Dieskau were both wounded in the fight. The English loss was 262 killed, wounded, and missing, while the French loss was variously estimated at from 500 to 800. After this the English built Fort William Henry on the site of their camp.

In 1757, 9,000 French under Montcalm invested the fort, which, after a siege of nine days, surrendered, Col. Munro, the commander, having stipulated that the garrison should march out with the honors of war, and one of the four cannons of the fort, and their baggage and baggage wagons, and an escort of 500 men to Fort Edward. But the terms of surrender were disregarded, and the disarmed and defenceless troops were surrounded and attacked by the Indians of Montcalm's army, and a most horrible slaughter ensued. A few survivors fleeing for their lives escaped to Fort Edward. "The revolting scenes of this day have stained the memory of Montcalm with the blackest infamy." The French did not attempt to hold the fort.

In 1758 Gen. Abercrombie, with 7,000 regulars and 10,000 provincials, embarked on 900 bateaux and 135 boats, and passed down the lake, with all the glittering pageantry of war, to assail Fort Ticonderoga. They failed of their purpose, and four days after returned, shattered and broken, with a loss of 2,000 killed and wounded, to Fort William Henry.

In 1759 Gen. Amherst, with 12,000 men, advanced to Lake George, and, while waiting to complete his arrangements, commenced to build Fort George, about one-half mile east from Fort William Henry. When Gen. Amherst advanced against Fort Ticonderoga, the French withdrew to Crown Point, and afterwards to Isle aux Noix. Quebec fell soon after, and the conquest of Canada being completed the following year—1760—the vast military works of Fort William Henry, Forts George, Ticonderoga and Crown Point were of no further use.

The steamer Horicon, Capt. C. P. Russell, which plies during the summer season on the lake, starts from the wharf at Caldwell, near the Fort William Henry Hotel, at an early hour in the morning, and, making the trip to the outlet of the lake, returns in the afternoon.

A new steamer called the "Ganouskie," Capt. A. Hulett, built in 1869, runs on the lake as a pleasure and excursion boat. She is elegantly furnished, and is managed very skillfully and with especial reference to the comfort and entertainment of the passengers. Both these boats are owned by the Champlain Transportation Co.

The lake is 36 miles long and from 1 to 3 miles in width. Its whole extent furnishes a ceaseless succession of pictures which have for years engaged the pencils of our best landscape artists, and which will for many a year to come continue to charm the eye with their peculiar beauty.

On the shores of the lake are several places of resort, where excursionists may find very comfortable accommodation.

BOLTON, at the north-western end of the North-west Bay, has a very commodious hotel, and is quite a resort for families and excursion parties. It is situated on the west side of the lake, commanding a very delightful view of Lake George scenery. On the east side, opposite Bolton, is a favorite resort for fishing parties, where is a good hotel—Trout Pavilion—and near which are the best fishing-grounds on the lake.

Fourteen-mile Island, just above the Narrows, has a very good hotel, and is a convenient stopping point for fishing and excursion parties.

At other points on the shores are fishermen's homes, but the most of them lack accommodation for tourists or pleasure-seekers who desire comfort and luxury.

THE LAKE CHAMPLAIN ROUTE.

GOING north, diverges from the old line of the Rensselaer and Saratoga Railroad at WHITEHALL, to the new Railroad, completed in 1876, on the west side of Lake Champlain. The Champlain Division of the Delaware and Hudson Canal Co.'s R. R. runs from Whitehall to Rouse's Point, a distance of 122 miles, and now forms the chief route *via* the D. and H. Canal Co.'s Line from New York and Albany to Montreal. Drawing-room cars are run though from New York to Montreal without change, and in less time than by any other route.

The R. R. runs from Whitehall through Fort Ticonderoga, Crown Point, Port Henry, Westport, where stages connect for Elizabethtown, Essex, Port Kent, Plattsburgh, West Chazy, to Rouse's Point, and thence by Grand Trunk Line to St. John's, Victoria Bridge, and Montreal. These places are described more at length hereafter. At Fort Ticonderoga, in summer the tourist has the choice of the Railroad Route, or the more delightful trip on Lake Champlain, on the elegant steamers of the Champlain Transportation Co., which run from Ticonderoga to Plattsburgh, touching at Burlington and other landings on the Lake. At Fort Ticonderoga, the tourist wishing to make the Lake George trip will take the branch R. R. to Baldwin, 4 miles distant, thence by Lake George steamer up the Lake to Fort William Henry Hotel, and thence stages to Glenn's Falls, and railroad south to Saratoga and New York

The trip on Lake Champlain is very delightful. The elegant and commodious steamers; the pure, bracing, and healthful atmosphere; the ever-varying and ever-beautiful landscape, embracing on the east the verdant Green Mountains, the rich farms and quiet villages of Vermont, on the west the rugged lofty summits of the Adirondacks, and, between them—now narrow and stream-like, again expansive, but ever placid—the long and beautiful lake,—these all combine to make the Lake Champlain route very charming to the tourist.

LAKE CHAMPLAIN.

No name can be found more aptly describing this beautiful lake than that which was given it by the Indians who once dwelt along its shores. To them it was "The Gate of the Country," and was as important in their rude warfare as it afterward proved to be when England and France expended life and treasure in fighting for its possession.

To us it is known by the name of its discoverer, Samuel Champlain, who, in order to gain the friendship of the Hurons and Algonquins, joined them, with two of his companions, in a warlike expedition against the Iroquois.

Champlain named the lake *St. Sacrément*, and straightway proceeded to inaugurate the long series of conflicts which have taken place along the shores.

The first account that we have of Lake Champlain is the history of the warlike expedition on which Champlain went, with his Indian guides, against the Iroquois; and from that time until the close of the last war with England the lake was often the scene of conflicts,—involving Indians, or French, or English, or Americans, or all four together. The most important battle was that of Plattsburg, which took place on September 11, 1814. The American and British fleets were engaged in a fierce fight on the lake, while their respective armies were at the same time in action on shore, close at hand. This double combat ended in the total defeat of the British, and was one of the most hotly-contested battles of the war. A more particular account of this engagement may be found under the sketch of Plattsburg (page 119).

Plattsburg is but one of the many places on the lake which are of great historic interest. During the "Old French War," while France still held possession of the Canadas, the English maintained garrisons along the shores, and flotillas on the water. These two great European Powers brought their ancient feuds across the Atlantic with them, and were constantly seeking one another's destruction. The horrors of this desultory warfare were increased by the barbarities perpetrated by the Indian allies of both parties. Crown Point and Ticonderoga, near the outlet of Lake George, are both famous—the latter as the site of the old fort, which was captured, with its British garrison, by Ethan Allen and his brave Green Mountain Boys.

Valcour Island, a few miles south of Plattsburg, is near the scene of Arnold's disastrous engagement with the British, in 1776. That officer then stood high in public estimation, and on this occasion fully sustained his reputation for skill and bravery, in covering the retreat of his flotilla. The battles of Bennington and Hubbardston, and the line of Burgoyne's march, were all on or near the shores of Lake Champlain, and add a never-dying interest to the magnificent scenery which surrounds it.

Lake Champlain is 150 miles long, and varies in width from a few hundred yards to thirteen miles. Its waters are clear, deep, and cold, and it is well stocked with fish of various kinds, affording excellent sport for the angler. In the spring and fall thousands of wild ducks make this their feeding-ground, and the wild lands west of the lake abound with all kinds of game.

Large quantities of lumber are shipped through this lake, Burlington being the chief mart on the shores.

The steamer A. Williams runs from Burlington *via* Port Kent and Plattsburg to St. Alban's, leaving Burlington at 8 A. M., and St. Alban's to return at 1:15 P. M., arriving at Burlington at 4:30.

The elegant, large steamer Vermont plies between Plattsburg and Fort Ticonderoga, stopping at Burlington. Leaves Plattsburg at 6:50 A. M., and Burlington 8:40 A. M., reaching Fort "Ti." at 12:15 P. M. Returning leaves "Ti." at 1:15 P. M., and arrives at Plattsburg at 7 P. M.

SENTINEL AND TABLE ROCK, AU SABLE CHASM, N. Y.

The route from Whitehall is past *Chub's Dock, Dresden,* and *Putnam,* three unimportant stations between Whitehall and Fort Ticonderoga. The R.R. runs on the west side of the lake.

FORT TICONDEROGA.

Ticonderoga, Essex Co., N. Y. 24 *M. fr. Whitehall,* 247 *M. fr. N. Y.*
HOTELS.—*Burleigh's and Pavilion.*

At this point the traveler going north takes the splendid steamers of the Champlain Transportation Co., or, if he wishes to visit Lake George, will take the branch R. R. to Baldwin Station, five miles distant, and thence the beautiful little steamers on that lake.

"Fort Ti." is a favorite resort for summer tourists, and is full of historic interest. The old fort, on the high bluff near the steamboat wharf, is in a dilapidated condition, but enough remains of its ruined bastions to make it a most interesting subject for the study of those who revere the memory of our early days as a nation.

Ticonderoga is a corruption of the Indian name Tisinondrosa, meaning "the tail of the lake," and referring to the narrow portion of the lake south of this point. The French were the first to fortify Ticonderoga. They built a fort there in 1755, and named it Carillon. The same year it was strongly garrisoned, and was held by them until 1759. In 1758, General Abercrombie sailed down Lake George from Fort William Henry, and attacked Carillon with a force of 17,000 British regulars and provincials. He was repulsed with a loss of 2,000 killed and wounded; Lord Howe, his second in command, being among the killed. The battle-ground is passed on the rail route between the two lakes, and the disposition of the forces in the battle can be ascertained by inquiring of residents. In 1759, General Amherst advanced against the fort with a force of 12,000 men, regulars and militia, and the French were obliged to abandon it. It was greatly strengthened by the English, and was held by them until 1775, when, on May 10th, Ethan Allen and his Green Mountain Boys surprised and captured it. (The centennial of this event was celebrated with appropriate exercises and much enthusiasm.) On Burgoyne's advance down the Hudson, in 1777, it again fell into British hands, and was occupied by them until Burgoyne's surrender to Gates in October of that year.

Ticonderoga is at the mouth of the outlet of Lake George, and trains run regularly to that lake. There is an excellent hotel at

LAKE CHAMPLAIN ROUTE.

"Fort Ti," as the place is called by the inhabitants.

Ticonderoga is the point of departure from Lake Champlain for passengers wishing to visit Lake George. A R.R. conveys passengers from the landing, around the rapids, five miles to the Lake, where they meet the beautiful steamer HORICON, which will convey them the whole length of lake, through the most beautiful scenery in the world, to Caldwell and the Fort William Henry Hotel.

LARABEES' POINT.
Shoreham, Addison Co., Vt.
26 *M. fr.* Whitehall, 249 *M. fr. N. Y.*
HOTEL—*United States.*

This landing is in Shoreham, Vt., and is about two miles from the village. It is unimportant in history, and of no especial present interest.

CROWN POINT.
Crown Point, Essex Co., N. Y.
35 *M fr.* Whitehall, 258 *M. fr. N. Y.*
HOTELS.—*Gunnison's and Crown Point.*

The village of Crown Point is about 1 mile west of the landing. A small village called Hammond's orners is about a mile west of the landing. Near the landing is a new hotel, built in 1869, where good accommodation may be obtained. This is one of the starting-points for hunters and tourists entering the Adirondack region. The grading of the Whitehall and Plattsburg Railroad, in course of completion, can be seen along the shores of the lake at this point. An iron mine is about to be worked in the rocky mountains south of the landing. Opposite is Bridport, Vt., where the steamers formerly stopped at Frost's Landing, but no landing is now made.

As we proceed north on our journey, and before we reach Port Henry, we pass Crown Point, a high promontory, on which is a light-house and the ruins of Fort Frederick, built by the French in 1731, but which was captured by the English in 1759. It fell into the hands of the Americans under Ethan Allen, at the same time and under the same circumstances as did Fort Ticonderoga. West of this point lies Bullwagga Bay, and south of the bay is the high rocky mountain of the same name. The lake widens at this point to a width of about two miles.

PORT HENRY.
Moriah, Essex Co., N. Y.
42 *M. fr.* Whitehall, 265 *M. fr. N. Y.*

This is a very pleasant and picturesque village—the scenery of the mountains in its vicinity being exceedingly beautiful. The Port Henry Iron-works, distinctly seen from the steamboats, are quite extensive. Iron mines are abundant, and largely worked just west of the village. After leaving Port Henry the views of the Adirondack Mountains to the westward and of the Green Mountain range to the eastward are very grand. On the west the most prominent elevation is Bald Peak.

WESTPORT.

Westport, Essex Co., N. Y.
52 *M. fr. Whitehall*, 275 *M. fr. N. Y.*
HOTELS. — *Well's and Richard's.*

A very pleasantly located village on the west shore of the lake. The iron business is carried on extensively in the towns west of this, and much iron and ore are shipped from this port. Jay Cooke & Co. have extensive works in Elizabethtown, a few miles west of this village.

As we leave Westport, going north, the spires of the city of Vergennes, Vt., are visible to the eastward. The lake narrows again as we proceed, and opposite its narrowest part are the ruins of Fort Casson, named in honor of an officer of McDonough's fleet. It is situated at the mouth of Otter Creek, where was formerly a steamboat landing for the city of Vergennes. The creek is navigable for 20 miles as far as Vergennes, where McDonough fitted out his fleet.

On the west is Split-Rock Mountain, and at its north end is a light house. Near this mountain and light the lake is very deep and has never been correctly fathomed. Bottles tightly corked have been sunk to a great depth, and on being raised to the surface were found full of water, though the corks were not removed.

ESSEX.

Essex, Essex Co., N. Y.
64 *Miles from Whitehall*, 287 *Miles from New York.*
HOTEL—*Royce's.*

The landing may be seen soon after the boat rounds the point of Split-Rock Mountain. The village is romantically situated at the foot of the hills which render the whole western shore so picturesque. Essex is one of the points on the lake whence hunters take their departure for the Adirondacks.

The islands which lie in the middle lake, a few miles north of Essex, are the *Four Brothers.*

BURLINGTON.

Burlington, Chittenden Co., Vt.
85 *Miles from Whitehall*, 308 *Miles from New York.*
HOTEL—*Van Ness House.*

Soon after passing the Four Brothers, Burlington may be seen on the Vermont shore, the tin-covered dome of its university building shin-

VAN NESS HOUSE, Burlington, Vt.
D. O. BARBER & CO., Proprietors.

The Van Ness House is a fine hotel, central in location, with a beautiful outlook upon Lake Champlain and the Adirondack Mountains. It is the largest hotel in Burlington, and will rank as one of the best hotels in New England.

AUSABLE CHASM.

ing like a beacon above the roofs of the city. It was incorporated as a city in 1866, and is delightfully situated on a hill which rises from the lake shore, and commands a wide view of water and landscape. The city has a population of about 16,000. It has two daily and two weekly papers, three banks—having an aggregate capital of $1,000,000—cotton, flour, and rolling mills, machine-shops, and a furniture factory. Its heaviest business is in lumber, large quantities of which are brought from Canada and from along the lake shores, and are shipped by rail to various markets.

In the centre of the city is a large public square, containing a fountain and shade trees. Near by are the custom-house, city and county buildings, banks, and other business offices. The *University of Vermont* stands on the crest of the hill overlooking the city.

From the dome of the chief building an extensive and very beautiful view may be obtained, including the ranges of the Adirondack and Green Mountains, while Lake Champlain, with its bays and islands, stretches north and south, as far as the eye can reach. The large island in front of Burlington is *Juniper Island*. To the south of this may be seen *Rock Dunder*, which is said to have excited the suspicions of the British commodore, while cruising here during the war with England, to such an extent that he opened fire upon it. *Colonel Ethan Allen*, the gallant Vermonter, who, with his Green Mountain Boys, rendered such good service during the Revolution, was often in Burlington while living, and now lies in the Green Mount Cemetery, near the city, where a granite monument has been erected by the State to perpetuate his memory. Burlington is the residence of several distinguished men and prominent politicians. *John G. Saxe*, the well-known author of poetry and prose, Judge Smalley, and U. S. Senator Edmunds, have resided in Burlington for many years. Mr. Le Grand Cannon, President of the Champlain Transportation Company, has a summer residence on a commanding eminence overlooking the lake and city. The view of the Adirondacks, lake, and city from this elegant resort is one of surpassing beauty and grandeur. In the country surrounding the city are many romantic drives and walks; those leading along the *Winooski River* are, perhaps, the most attractive.

The charming and picturesque residence of the late Bishop Hopkins, and his Seminary, at Rocky Point, two or three miles down the shore of the lake, will well repay a visit.

The best hotel is the Van Ness House, kept by D. C. Barber & Co. It is situated in the center of the city overlooking the Park, and commands a delightful view of Lake Champlain and the Adirondack Mountains. The table is excellent, and the rooms are newly furnished and very comfortable.

Mallett's Bay, 8 miles distant, is a beautiful sheet of water, celebrated for its bass and pike fishing. The drive to the bay is delightful.

From Burlington tourists start for the White Mountains and Mount Mansfield by rail. The general offices of the Champlain Transportation Company are located in Burlington, fronting the public park.

The steamboat wharf is close beside the railroad station. From here the traveller crosses the water late in the afternoon, when the surroundings of mountain and lake are most beautiful.

PORT KENT.

Chesterfield, Essex Co., N. Y.
90 *M. fr. Whitehall,* 313 *M. fr. N. Y.*

Port Kent is a small village, situated on the shore of Lake Champlain, near the mouth of the *Au Sable River*. It is important chiefly as the port from which the products of the iron-works at *Keeseville* and *Au Sable Forks* are shipped to various markets, and as the terminus of the stage-route to the Adirondacks, by way of Au Sable.

Thousands annually visit these mountains, to enjoy the sports peculiar in this wild region, or to derive health from its pure and invigorating atmosphere. The *Au Sable River*, between Port Kent and Keeseville, passes through a remarkable chasm, forming what are known as the "Walled Banks of the Au Sable River." The river plunges over a precipice, Birmingham Falls, seventy feet in height, and rushes for a distance of two miles through a chasm which is in some places one hundred and thirty feet deep. The river is at one point forced through a channel only a few feet in width, and the water can hardly be seen from the top of the rocks. The geological formation which the river thus passes is the *Potsdam Sandstone;* and the whole chasm forms an object of great interest to the tourist.

At *Keeseville* are two good hotels, namely, the *Adirondack House* and the Lake View House, Au Sable Chasm. Thence stages run to Paul Smith's, Bartlett's, Martin's, and the other houses on the Saranacs.

From *Au Sable Forks* a road leads into the mountains through the famous *Wilmington Notch.* Throughout this part of the mountains good hotels are established at favorable localities.

Upon the hill just above the lake

is a fine old stone house where live the descendants of *Colonel Elkanah Watson*, the founder of the first agricultural society of New York. In 1777, the year of Burgoyne's surrender, Colonel Watson, then aged 17, made a tour through the country, and wrote a very interesting and accurate account of his experiences. This account forms one of our most valuable histories of those Revolutionary times.

PLATTSBURG.

Plattsburg, Clinton Co., N. Y.
328 *M. fr. N. Y. Fr. Montreal*, 63
HOTELS—*Fouquet's, Cumberland, and Witherell's.*

The village of Plattsburg is situated at the mouth of Saranac River, on a plateau some fifty feet above the level of the lake. It has about 8,000 inhabitants, and is in every respect a flourishing place. The Saranac River furnishes water-power for several mills, one at least of which—a saw-mill—is well worthy of a visit. It is worked day and night, and the interest is perhaps enhanced by a visit after nightfall, when everything is more or less mystified by the surrounding darkness. Plattsburg is the county town, and contains the usual buildings for judicial purposes. The U. S. Government has barracks and keeps a garrison here. Plattsburg is the southern terminus of the *Montreal and Plattsburg Railroad*, which extends to the Canada line, where it joins a branch of the *Grand Trunk Railroad of Canada*. Steamers touch daily at the wharves, conveying passengers across the lake, or to various places on its shores.

FOUQUET'S HOTEL is a house which every traveler who has ever patronized it remembers with pleasure. It is a new building, finished in the best manner, and kept admirably. The piazzas and promenade command extensive views of the lake and surroundings, and every effort is made to supply everything required or wished for by travelers and summer guests. This hotel fronts the lake and overlooks Cumberland Bay.

Beyond the bay is *Macdonough's Point*, just inside of which, in September, 1814, was anchored the American fleet, awaiting the attack of the British, while on shore lay the two hostile armies, watching one another, and ready at any moment for either attack or defence Commodore Macdonough commanded the American fleet, and Commodore Downie the British. The land forces were commanded by General Macomb on the American side, and General Provost on the British. The British fleet had 1,000 men, and 95 guns. The American, 880 men, and 86 guns. On shore, the Americans had one brigade of regulars and several thousand militia, and the British had about 14,000 men.

The battle was opened on the water by a shot from the American vessel *Eagle*, and very soon the engagement became general. The roar of artillery was heard far off in Vermont, and a long distance down the lake. The fight lasted with the greatest fury for two hours and a half. Commodore Macdonough with his own hands sighted one of his guns, from time to time throughout the action, and after one battery of his flag-ship, the U. S. frigate Saratoga, had been disabled by the superior artillery of the *Confiance*, her adversary, she was swung round so as to bring her other battery to bear. This decided the fight, for the British ship was soon compelled to surrender, and the victory was soon after rendered complete by the surrender of the remaining ships. The British gunboats alone, being worked with sweeps, effected an escape.

On shore the assaults of the British were repelled, and when it was seen that the day was lost on the lake, General Provost retreated from the field, leaving the Americans victorious by land and water. In one of the houses of Plattsburg is still to be seen a twelve-pound shot, which entered the house during the engagement, and lodged in the wall over the staircase, where it has remained ever since.

From Plattsburg, the Whitehall and Plattsburg R. R. conveys passengers to Point of Rocks (Au Sable station), 20 miles distant, where travelers may take stages to the hunting and fishing grounds of the Adirondack region. This forms the most convenient and comfortable route to the North Woods, and is the most popular starting-point on the lake.

THE FLUME, AU SABLE CHASM, N. Y.

ADIRONDACK MOUNTAINS

In traversing Lake Champlain, and while following its eastern shores on the railway, the traveler is constantly in sight of the mysterious wild region of Northern New York. The line of blue summits against the western sky is in the heart of this region, and any one who is acquainted with the mountains can readily point out *Tahawus*, *Whiteface*, and others of the great mountain brotherhood which watches over the country from Ontario to the Green Mountains. This wilderness is nearly a hundred miles in diameter, and is nominally divided into several tracts, such as *The Saranac*, the *Chateaugay*, &c. The *Adirondacks* are, properly, the mountainous region occupying the eastern part of the wilderness, but the name is often used in referring to the whole uninhabited district. Notwithstanding the numerous hunters and fishermen who annually go into the woods, game and fish are still abundant. Deer are protected by law during the breeding season, and as their natural foes, the panther, the bear, and the wolf, are outlawed by common consent, they are rather increasing in number. They are, however, becoming very shy, and much caution is necessary in hunting them.

The whole Adirondack region is intersected and diversified by a network of lakes and streams, which render it picturesque and beautiful in an almost unequaled degree. These systems of water communication afford very convenient means of transit for hunters and pleasure-seekers, the lakes being connected by streams, in some cases navigable for bateaux, and in others broken by falls and rapids, around which boats and luggage must be carried

Iron is found in large quantities among the mountains and

ENTRANCE TO THE FLUME, AU SABLE CHASM, N. Y.

some of the most accessible beds of ore are profitably worked
Marble is also found, of a valuable quality. It is probable that
a large portion of this tract will always be wild and almost uninhabited, save by the hunter or pleasure-seeker, for it is so inaccessible that the traffic which invites a large population could
hardly ever reach its central portions, even if the land were sufficiently fertile and easily cultivated to invite settlers.

The wilderness may be easily reached by several different
routes, partly by carriage-roads and partly by boats, which latter
will convey the tourist to almost any part of the woods which he
wishes to visit. A favorite route to the woods is from Port
Kent, whence stages convey the tourist to Keeseville, Au Sable
Forks, and the Saranac Lakes, whence by boats and "carries"
he can penetrate to the heart of the wilderness.

The recent completion of the White Hall and Plattsburg Railroad, from Plattsburg to the Au Sable River, at Au Sable Station,
opposite Point of Rocks, on the Au Sable River, 10 miles above
Keeseville, makes Plattsburg the natural rendezvous on the east
for visitors to either the Saranac or Chateaugay region. By this
route the traveler will save about 14 miles of stage travel.

Stages leave Point of Rocks for Whiteface Mountain and for Lower
Saranac and Lower St. Regis Lakes daily, on arrival of trains from
Plattsburg, and returning connect with trains for Plattsburg.

Through tickets by this route for the Adirondacks can be procured
at the principal railroad ticket offices, on the Lake Champlain steamers,
and at Fouquet's Hotel, Plattsburg.

Telegraph lines extend to the Adirondack region, and most of the
principal hotels have telegraph offices connected with them.

Camp equipage and stores and provisions, for parties going into the
wilderness, can be procured at these hotels, rendering it unnecessary for
visitors to burden themselves with such things before arriving at the
lakes.

It would be impracticable, in a work of this kind, to give any minute
directions for exploring the wilderness. Indeed, a large portion of this
vast wild is as yet substantially unexplored. Perhaps the greater number of visitors strike directly for Lower Saranac Lake, and from thence
make different trips to the lakes and mountains. For a general course,

CATHEDRAL ROCK, AU SABLE CHASM, N. Y.

to be as inclusive as possible, we might indicate the route *via* Whiteface Mountain, up the West Branch of the Au Sable River from Point of Rocks, stopping at Whiteface to ascend the mountain, from the top of which most splendid views are afforded, including fine views of Moun Marcy, Mount Seward, Nipple Top, and the whole range of Adirondacks. Sixty-four different bodies of water—lakes, ponds, and rivers—are said to be visible by the naked eye from this summit, and, with the aid of a glass, Lake Ontario and the White Mountains can be seen.

There is a hotel near the foot of the mountain, and a small one is being erected on the summit. By this route the traveler will pass a natural flume and the falls on the Au Sable River, and go through the "*Wilmington Pass*," a deep and very narrow gorge with mountains several hundred feet high towering almost perpendicularly on both sides.

From Whiteface the route continues to North Elba, the home and burial-place of John Brown, whose "soul is marching on," and whose exploits are known to all Americans. The stages pass in sight of his grave. From North Elba the stages will turn from the Branch of the Au Sable and pass over to Lower Saranac Lake, distant by this route 22 miles from Whiteface and 12 miles from North Elba. If the traveler wishes he can pause at North Elba and explore the region of the Upper Adirondacks, among which are Mount McIntyre, Walltace, Mount Martin, Mount Marcy, Mount Seward, and a host of other peaks of great elevation. A number of these peaks are over 5,000 feet in height— Mount Marcy is said to be 5,467 feet. The Adirondack or Indian Pass, 7 miles above North Elba, is a most majestic natural wonder, and well repays the toil of its difficult approach. Passing over to Lower Saranac Lake the traveler will find several hotels and excellent accommodation for a rest preparatory to the tour of the lakes.

From this point the route is by water, up through the Saranac chain of lakes. Between the Saranac and the St. Regis Lake there are but two *portages*, and at these horses are kept, in the season of pleasure travel, for transporting parties across.

The passage of the lakes may be prolonged to enjoy the fishing and hunting, and by detours among the innumerable lakes, ponds, and streams, according to the leisure or inclination of the tourist, and on arriving at the Lower St. Regis a stage-ride of 36 miles from the hotel there brings you back to the railroad at Point of Rocks.

Those who prefer to do so may leave out the detour to Whiteface and North Elba, and go by stage from Point of Rocks direct to Saranac, o

ADIRONDACK MOUNTAINS.

may reverse the trip by staging up to Lake St. Regis and returning *via* Saranac Lake.

From the Upper Saranac Lake a portage of 3 miles reaches the Raquette River, down which the traveler may find his way through the wilderness to Potsdam, in St. Lawrence County.

Westward of the St. Regis lakes are the innumerable lakes and ponds emptying into the St. Regis River, and the river itself, all abounding with fish and fowl, and forests alive with deer and other game; and to the northward for 20 miles stretches another chain of lakes equally attractive to sportsmen, turning from which one may emerge at Malone, at the north, or bearing eastward from Loon Lake may descend the West Saranac and Saranac Rivers, viewing the Great Falls above Saranac Village, and reach Plattsburg by the old stage route.

Still further north lies the Chateaugay region, which is accessible from Plattsburg *via* Dannemora and Chazy Lake, or from points on the Northern or Ogdensburg and Lake Champlain Railroad.

FOUQUET HOUSE, Plattsburgh, N. Y.

Starting point for the Adirondacks—under new management. Free excursion to St. Albans Bay and return offered to tourists stopping at this House two days or longer, season 1880. D. McBRIDE, Proprietor.

CAPITOL, Montpelier, Vermont.

MONTPELIER,

Washington Co., Vt., 209¼ *m. fr. Boston. Pop.* 3,500. *Stages to Calais, Hardwich, Greensborough, Glover, Barton, Cabot, Danville, Barre, Orange, and Chelsea.* HOTEL—*Pavilion.*

Montpelier, the capital of Vermont, is beautifully situated at the junction of the Winooski River with its north branch. It is surrounded by a hilly but highly cultivated region, and is the active centre of a rich farming and grazing country. The town was first settled in 1787, and has been the capital of the State since 1805.

The Capitol building is of granite, and is built upon the site of the first building, which was burned in 1857. The present edifice is cruciform in its general plan, 176 feet long, and surmounted by a dome 124 feet high. In the portico, surrounded by Doric columns, stands a marble statue of Ethan Allen, of whose fame Vermont is so justly proud. In the State House may be seen the regimental flags which were borne by Vermont regiments during the civil war. Most of them show signs of having been often under fire, and many bear long lists of the battles through which they were carried. The geological and historical rooms are especially interesting in specimens of the mineral wealth which is so remarkable a feature of Vermont. There is also a large and well-selected public library. Several newspapers are published in the town, and it contains two banks and three insurance offices.

The Winooski River and its tributaries furnish abundant waterpower, which is employed in driving the machinery of lumber mills, carriage factories, large flouring mills, and other smaller manufacturing establishments. It is here spanned by a fine stone bridge of great strength and durability.

Montpelier has been visited by some disastrous fires, which have swept over the business part of the town; but though bringing great distress temporarily upon its residents, they have had the ulterior effect of beautifying the town. Upon these ruins have sprung up substantial brick business blocks and beautiful church buildings, such as few country towns can boast. Montpelier is also provided with one of the best hotels in New England. The

Pavilion Hotel overlooks Capitol Park, upon which are the State Buildings, and commands the most beautiful portion of the town. It was opened to guests in January, 1876, equipped with all the appurtenances, including bath-rooms, closets, wardrobes, etc., which are essential to a first-class hotel. It is elegantly fur-

PAVILION HOTEL, T. O. BAILEY, Proprietor.

nished, and each room is heated by steam—thus regulating the temperature to the comfort of each guest—lighted by gas, and connected by automatic speaking tubes with the principal office. Extensive piazzas around the house afford delightful promenades and lounging places for summer guests, and every attention needed to enhance the pleasure and comfort of guests, is given by the popular proprietor, Mr. T. O. Bailey, and his efficient Mr. Sibley. No place in Vermont combines more attractions as a summer resort than the beautiful village of Montpelier. From the hills around beautiful views of the village and Winooski val'ey may be obtained. The fine roads, through rich and varied scenery, afford charming drives. Mr. Bailey has this year completed a carriage road to the top of Capitol Hill, 1¼ miles from the hotel opening a delightful drive to a commanding summit. He has also built a carriage-road to the top of Mt. Hunger, 11 miles from the Pavilion. Mt. Hunger is one of the highest peaks in New England, and affords a view of marvellous extent and beauty, limited only by the Adirondacks on the west and the White Mts. on the east.

There are other drives to Benjamin Falls, 1¼ miles; Middlesex Narrows, 5 miles; Williamstown Springs, 12 miles; Plainfield Springs, 12 miles; and Mt. Mansfield, 20 miles from Pavilion Hotel.

Carriages and careful drivers may be obtained at the Pavilion, and ample accommodations for boarding private teams.

Montpelier is on the direct line between the White Mountains and Saratoga, Lake George, Lake Champlain, and Montreal.

The Montpelier and Wells River Railroad, running 38 miles between this town and Wells River, opens up a rich agricultural and lumber region, and speedy connections east, south, and north. The towns of Plainfield, Marshfield, the largest and most important of the route, Groton, and Ryegate are all intersected by this route. The scenery is varied by mountain, lake, stream, woodland, hamlet, and the rich bottom-land along the valley of the

MIDDLESEX NARROWS, Winooski River, Vt.

Wells River. Tourists will find Montpelier a convenient and delightful place to spend a short time in their summering. Leaving Lake George and Saratoga in the morning, and Montreal in the afternoon, they may take tea here, remain over night, and, leaving Montpelier after breakfast, they can dine at any of the White Mountain houses the same day. This forms one of the most delightful and comfortable ways of making the journey to the mountains.

GRAND TRUNK RAILWAY OF CANADA.
MONTREAL AND CHAMPLAIN DIVISION.
Rouse's Point to Montreal—49 Miles.

THE Montreal and Champlain Railroad now forms a part of the direct line from New York to Montreal *via* Delaware and Hudson Canal Co.'s R. R. and Lake Champlain. It is almost entirely in Canada, crossing the line between the United States and the Dominion of Canada about one mile north of the depot at Rouse's Point. The railroad runs on the West side of the Richelieu River in a northerly direction to St. John's whence it diverges towards the northwest to St. Lambert, on the St. Lawrence River, where it joins the main line of the Grand Trunk and crosses the St. Lawrence on the wonderful Victoria Bridge.

ROUSE'S POINT.
Champlain, Clinton Co., N.Y., 352 miles from New York. From Montreal, 49.

The scenery of the north part of the lake is very fine, embracing a view of numerous islands and points of lands of much beauty. Rouse's Point is a village of about 2,000 population, and contains several churches. The village was named in honor of Jacques Rouse, a Canadian, who settled here in 1783. The Ogdensburg and Lake Champlain Railroad operated by the Central Vermont R. R. runs to Ogdensburg, and the Vermont Central Railroad to St. Alban's and the East. The latter railroad crosses the lake on a bridge one mile in length. A floating draw of three hundred feet, opened and shut by steam, admits the passage of vessels. About one mile north of the village, upon the banks of the lake, Fort Montgomery is situated. This fort commands the entrance to the lake. It was begun soon after the war of 1812, but in 1818 it was found to be within the limits of Canada, and the work was abandoned. It became known as "Fort Blunder," but by the Webster Treaty of 1842 it was ceded again to the United States. Work upon it was resumed, and the fort completed at the cost of about $600,000. Between Rouse's Point and St. John's the railroad passes through three small but uninteresting villages in the Canadian Territory.

LACOLLE.
St. John's Parish, Quebec Province, Dominion of Canada, **355** *miles from New York. From Montreal,* 43.

STOTTSVILLE.
St. John's Parish, Quebec Province, Dominion of Canada, 36º *miles from New York. From Montreal,* 39.

GRAND LIGNE.
St. John's Parish, Quebec Province, Dominion of Canada, 368 *miles from New York. From Montreal,* 33.

ST. JOHN'S.
St. John's Parish, Quebec Province, Dominion of Canada, 374 *miles from New York. From Montreal,* 27.

This village contains about 1,000 inhabitants and some manufactories. On the west side of the Richelieu or Sorrel River, is a small military barracks, and on the parade ground near the railroad depot may be seen a large cannon captured by a Canadian regiment from the Russians at Sebastopol. St. John's is the terminus of the Central Vermont Railroad, which crosses the river at this place. This stream is the outlet of Lake Champlain, and falls into the St. Lawrence forty miles below Montreal. It is navigable for its whole length, with the exception of certain rapids which are passed by means of canals and locks.

LACADIE AND BROSSEAUS.
La Prairie Parish, Quebec Province, Dominion of Canada, 381 *m. fr. New York. Fr. Montreal,* 20.

These are small and unimportant villages, the inhabitants of which are chiefly farmers, who send the products of their labor to the Montreal markets. The former place is on Montreal River.

ST. LAMBERT.
St. John's Parish, Quebec Province, Dominion of Canada, 385 *m. fr. New York. Fr. Montreal* 6.

This station is opposite Montreal, and at the eastern end of *Victoria Bridge.* Entering the bridge, little can be seen except iron plates and braces, until after a space of six to ten minutes the train emerges from the western end of the bridge and following a descending grade soon reaches the level of the streets, and in a few minutes enters the Montreal Depot. The Victoria Bridge is nearly two miles long, It is built on the tubular plan, and rests on two abutments and 34 piers. It cost $6,300,000.

MONTREAL.

Quebec Province, Dominion of Canada, 391 *miles from New York.*

HOTELS.—*Windsor, Ottawa House, St. Lawrence Hall, Albion, and Canada Hotel.*

The chief city of British America stands on Montreal Island, at the head of natural navigation on the St. Lawrence River. It was founded in 1640, on the site of an Indian village called Hochelaga, which was visited by French Jesuit missionaries in 1542, nearly a hundred years before a permanent settlement was made. The French held the island until 1760, when it was captured by the British, and has been held by them ever since. The Canadian government was formerly established here, but was removed to Quebec in 1849, in consequence of a political mob which burnt the parliament houses and library. At that time Canada was under the royal government, but it is now more independent and governs herself, with certain restrictions, under the title of *The Dominion of Canada.* Montreal Island is thirty-two miles long and about ten miles broad. Near the city it rises into a considerable elevation known as Mount Royal. The soil of the Island is good, and especially favorable to the growth of pears and apples.

The city is principally built on the level ground between Mt. Royal and the river, along which it extends nearly three miles. The population of the city is about 120,000 and is rapidly increasing. On the high ground near Mt. Royal are many elegant private residences, and a fashionable drive extends around the mountain, bordered by gardens and ornamental inclosures, and affording fine views in all directions. The principal buildings in Montreal are of gray limestone, which is of a delicate neutral tint, very pleasing to the eye. The great number of buildings of this material gives a more solid look to the streets than we are accustomed to in the States. Architecturally, many of the buildings are very fine, especially the new church of the Jesuits. The cathedral of Notre Dame is of great size, and well worth visiting. The view from one of the towers, in which hangs "Gros Bourdon," the great bell, is very extensive and interesting. Admission may be gained to the cathedral and tower at almost all hours. At certain times, interesting services are performed in the cathedral, at which the nuns of the seminary of St. Sulpice assist. The music at these services is very fine. Many other fine buildings, public and private, may be seen, especially in Great St. James and Notre Dame streets, the two finest business streets in the city. The stranger will take great pleasure in visiting such places of interest as the English Cathedral, Jesuit College, McGill College, Viger Square, the Post Office, New Court House, Bank of Montreal, Bank of British North America, Molsom's Bank, Merchants' Bank, Bonsecours Market, Hotel Dieu Hospital, Mount Royal Cemetery, Place D'Armes, Champ de Mars, Bon Parteur Nunnery, and many others. The stone quays of Montreal are an object of interest to every one, and ought to excite a spirit of emulation in New York. The Victoria bridge over the St. Lawrence is a splendid piece of engineering skill, and should be visited. It is the longest bridge in the world, being nearly one and a half miles in length, and is built entirely of iron, over 8,000 tons of which were used in its construction. The Grand Trunk Railway crosses the St. Lawrence river upon it, and passengers going to or from the States pass over it. A pass to go upon the bridge may be obtained at the office of the Grand Trunk Railway. The trip to Lachine Rapids is one of the most interesting excursions from the city. By driving to Lachine, about nine miles, and taking the steamboat which descends the Rapids, the tourist will soon find himself in the midst of exciting adventure, as the bold craft reels and dashes down the stream and shoots unharmed upon the placid waters below. The trip is full of pleasant excitement, and has a spice of danger about it especially pleasing to the Anglo-Saxon temperament.

The business houses of Montreal are worthy of the reputation which enterprise, integrity, long experience, and substantial financial basis have given them. Many of them are found on St. James and Notre Dame streets, and others in different parts of the city. Prominent among these is the Jewelry House of Savage, Lyman & Co., Nos. 226 and 228 St. James street.

HOTELS OF MONTREAL.

The new Windsor Hotel is the most elegant hotel in Canada, and is not excelled by any in America in the completeness and extent of its modern improvements. It has a fine location on elevated ground near the mountain, overlooking the city and the St. Lawrence River, and fronts one of the finest streets in Montreal. All its surroundings are attractive and elegant. The hotel has many rooms en suite with bathroom attached, and the bridal parlors are luxuriantly and elegantly furnished. Special care is taken to have its cuisine unexcelled, and the best caterers to be found are employed at the Windsor. The dining hall is the most beautiful in America, and with its luxurious cuisine offers the most inviting repast of any hotel on this continent.

The new Ottawa Hotel on Great St. James and Notre Dame Streets, is in the business portion of the city and is kept on the European plan. Mr. J. F. Warner manages the hotel in excellent and liberal style. It has an entrance from both St. James and Notre Dame Streets. It has lately been entirely re-arranged and greatly improved, and been refurnished throughout with Queen Anne and Eastlake furniture, a passenger elevator, electric bells, bathrooms, etc. The cuisine is excellent, the service polite and the charges very moderate.

St. Lawrence Hall, situated on St. James Street, in the most central part of the city, is kept in very good style, at moderate prices. It has been patronized by the Government on all public occasions, and was the former residence of the United States Consul. It is kept more in the style of English hotels than any in Montreal, and is managed by Mr. H. Hogan, the Proprietor, who provides excellent accommodations at moderate prices.

The Albion House is a good hotel, on the corner of McGill and St. Paul Streets, and has been for twenty years a favorite resort of the general traveling public of the United States when visiting Montreal. It will accommodate nearly 500 guests, and is well supplied with modern conveniences, and commands a fine view of St. Lawrence River and the Victoria Bridge. Its charges are very moderate, but its accommodations are equal to those of its higher-priced competitors.

The Canada Hotel is on St. Gabriel Street, between Notre Dame and St. Paul Streets. It has been thoroughly renovated and refitted recently, provided with the modern conveniences, and is kept in good style by Mr. A. Beliveau at very reasonable prices.

RIVER ST. LAWRENCE, FROM MONTREAL TO QUEBEC.

Our choice of courses to Quebec lies between the railway ride of eight hours and the sail down the river by night. We can economize time, strength, and money by the sail. We will, therefore, take passage in one of the splendid steamers of the Richelieu and Ontario Navigation Company's Mail Line. Either the "Montreal" or the "Quebec" makes the passage from Montreal to Quebec every night except Sunday. These steamers are the most elegant in Canada, and approach closely in accommodations the magnificent floating palaces of the People's Line on the Hudson River, and Fall River Lines from New York. With staterooms secured, we are free to move about the boat, dine, watch the scenery, or gaze at the stars, until our weariness invites repose, and we seek Nature's sweet restorer. Before daylight is gone we shall enjoy many miles of delightful river scenery. As we pass out from the wharf, the shores of the military island of St. Helen's —named from the wife of Champlain, the first Governor of Canada, and the founder of Quebec—appears. Just below the island is the village of Longueuil, a favorite summer resort of the citizens of Montreal. At the mouth of Richelieu, the outlet of Lake Champlain into the St. Lawrence, is

SOREL,

a town with about 5,000 population. It was for many years the summer residence of the English Governors of Canada, and here Victoria's father once resided. Immediately below Sorel the river widens into a lake called Lake St. Peter, about thirty-five miles long by ten miles wide. This is shallow, except in a narrow channel; and in a storm its waves become very turbulent, and engulf the unfortunate rafts exposed to its fury. Half-way to Quebec is the port of

THREE RIVERS,

at the confluence of the St. Maurice and the St. Lawrence Rivers, ninety miles from Montreal This town is one of the oldest settled towns in Canada. It is well laid out, contains many good buildings, and a population of 9,000. The celebrated St. Maurice Forges, near the town, have been in operation more than a century.

BATISCAN,

a village of little importance, is the last stopping place before reaching Quebec. Seven miles above Quebec we pass the mouth of the Chandière River on the right. The celebrated Chaudière Falls are a short distance up this river, and are annually visited by a large number of tourists. The Falls are 125 feet high, the river being 400 feet wide, studded with forest-covered islands, which make a picturesque and beautiful scene. The banks of the St. Lawrence present little variety as we proceed. The villages are French, the buildings being small, the better class painted white or whitewashed, and having red roofs. As we approach Quebec, we first behold the tin-covered spires of the Catholic churches. In the river, we see the shipping and the frequent rafts lying at rest in the coves, awaiting shipment to different parts of the world. Passing the frowning rock-walls of the citadel, we touch the pier and are speedily ashore and breakfasting.

QUEBEC.

Hotel.—*St. Louis.*

The Gibraltar of America, and the only walled city on the Continent, is situated at the confluence of the St. Charles and St. Lawrence Rivers, 400 miles from the Gulf of St. Lawrence, and 180 miles from Montreal. It is the second city in the Dominion, and was until recently the capital of United Canada.

Quebec has about 70,000 inhabitants, chiefly engaged in handling and exporting lumber, of which some $6,000,000 worth a year is sent away. It has also a fine export trade in grain, and, being the terminus of transatlantic shipping, it is a depot of immigration. The city is nearly in the form of a triangle, bounded by the two rivers and the "Plains of Abraham," and is divided into the Upper and Lower Towns—the former being walled, strongly fortified, and standing partly on a bluff 350 feet high; the latter being built on the narrow strip of land between the cliffs and the river. The suburbs of St. John's and St. Roche's extend along the St. Charles to the "Plains of Abraham." The houses are mostly built of cut stone, and severely plain. The streets are narrow, and often steep, and are said to follow, in many instances, the foot-paths of the Indian village once on the same site.

THE ST. LOUIS HOTEL

is the prominent and best hotel in the city. It is situated on St

Louis Street, in the upper town, near Durham Terrace, Governor's Garden, and many of the principal points of interest in the city. It is a long established and favorite house, complete in all its arrangements, efficient and liberal in its management, affording to its guests all wished-for accommodations. The location is central, near the delightful and fashionable promenades and terraces of this grand old city. The management is the best, and substantial plenty and commendable neatness in every department are characteristics of the house. The accommodations are for five hundred guests, and, with the recent enlargements and improvements, the most exacting cannot fail of satisfaction. Carriages at reasonable rates for the tour of the city and surroundings may be had at the hotel, and valuable information regarding the attractions within and around the city.

The Citadel, on Cape Diamond, is one of the most interesting objects to visitors. The area within the fortifications is more than forty acres, and the line of fortification around it and the Upper Town is about three miles long. Formerly there were five massive gates to the town, two of which remain.

The churches, convents, colleges, and public buildings of Quebec will interest strangers. Among the Roman Catholic churches they will wish to see the Cathedral and the adjoining Seminaries, fronting on the Upper Town Market Place. This is very large, seating 4,000 persons; unpretentious outwardly, it is inwardly handsomely fitted up. The Cathedral and Seminary Chapel have many fine paintings of the old masters well worth inspection. These churches and institutions of mercy and learning in Quebec have become rare picture galleries. Permission to visit them and catalogues will be given, on application, at proper hours. St. Patrick's, St. Roch's, St. John's, The Church of Notre Dame des Victoires, with its pictures by Vandyke, are all worth visiting. The Hotel Dieu, both hospital and church, built mostly in the seventeenth century, has fine paintings. It has thirty or forty nuns, and the hospital is free to the sick and infirm of any sect, with attendance of the best doctors in the city. The Gray Nunnery near St. John's Church, and the Black Nunnery near St. Roch's, will interest the stranger. At the Ursuline Convent, a very old building, there are forty nuns, devoted to teaching girls, and also to working in embroidery, painting, etc. The parlor and chapel are open to visitors. In the latter are some good paintings. The General Hospital is an extensive pile of buildings founded in the seventeenth century, and conducted by forty or fifty nuns of St. Augustine. The Laval University is second to none on this continent in its museum of Huron antiquities, its collection of Canadian birds, its library, its fine scientific instruments, and its extensive and comprehensive curriculum. It is adjoining the seminary whose chapel, mentioned above, has the celebrated paintings of Champlain and others.

Among the Protestant churches the English Cathedral is the largest, accommodating about 4,000 people. It is a handsome structure, neatly fitted up. The monument of Jacob Mountain, D. D., first Anglican Bishop, is in the church. King George is said to have expressed a doubt, in the presence of Dr. Mountain, as to whom to appoint bishop of the new See of Quebec. The Doctor replied, "If your majesty had faith, there would be no difficulty." "How so?" said the king. Mountain answered. "If you had faith, you would say to this Mountain, 'be thou removed into that See,' and it would be done." The witticism won him the appointment. There are many other churches and public buildings worthy of mention.

Durham Terrace, in the Upper Town, is a platform commanding a splendid view of the river and the Lower Town, as well as Point Levi and the bold peaks of the Laurentian Range. The Terrace is the favorite promenade of the citizens. The monument erected to the memory of Wolfe and Montcalm in the Public Garden is chaste and beautiful in design, 65 feet high, and should be seen by strangers. The Place d'Armes and the Esplanade are open pieces of ground, beautiful and well worth a visit. We have room only to mention the Court-House and City Hall on St. Louis Street, the Gaol, St. Ann Street, Upper Town, the Marine Hospital on the river St. Charles, capable of accommodating 400 patients, the Lunatic Asylum at Beauport, two and a half miles from the city, and the Music Hall.

Every step in this city seems to be over a tradition, or a history. Every wall and tower seems ancient. Indeed the seventeenth century is here largely transformed into the nineteenth. The quaint style of vehicles and very many of the customs of the people have come down from the long-ago. Yet here is a city of thrifty, busy, contented people. Living is cheap here. Protected from enemies by its scowling defiant fortresses and rocks, rich in one of the best harbors on the continent, with her piers loaded with the commerce of all nations, Quebec enjoys a position among the cities of the continent, unique and interesting.

Many places of interest and many fine drives are in the neighborhood. Among these we mention Cap Rouge, nine miles from Quebec, reached by the Grand Allée. On the drive we pass a monument near the toll-gate; the inscription says, "Here died Wolfe victorious." The Plains of Abraham are on the south, and the scene of the battle on either hand. Many objects of interest are along this route, and the whole distance is lined with fine old villas of the Canadian aristocracy. Returning from Cap Rouge

FALLS OF MONTMORENCI.

by another route, the tourist is treated to varied but equally interesting sights. Indian Lorette, nine miles from Quebec by the Little River Road, is an ancient village of the Hurons, in whom Indian blood predominates, and who hunt, fish, make bead-work moccasins, etc., and live a rude but religious life. The Lorette Falls are near the village, and a few miles inland are the Beauport and St. Charles Lakes, the latter famed for its red trout and remarkable echoes.

One of the principal drives is to the Falls of Montmorenci, eight miles from the city. We cross the St. Charles River—notice in succession the extensive ship building, the curious market wagons and ponies of the French women, who mostly make the gardens and market their products; the old cottage where Montcalm had his headquarters, and near the scene of the first struggle for the possession of the city; the neat Canadian cottages on either side with their huge chimneys, out-of-door ovens, and steep roofs—until we reach the Montmorenci River and the field of the battle of Montmorenci. We register at the little hotel, pay the admittance fee, and by a short path reach the Falls, 250 feet high, and 50 feet wide. A solid mass of water rolls over the black bluff of rocks, is shattered into feathery foam, falls like a gossamer veil of beauty into the stream below, and disappears in the St. Lawrence. Small streams on each side, parted strands of light, follow the rocky seams in a delightful tangle down the chasm. A suspension bridge erected over the Falls fell some years ago while a laborer and his family were crossing in a rude cart. The towers stand as monuments of the mournful tragedy. The Falls are in winter the scene of the rare fun of coasting, known in local phrase as "tobogginiug." The spray from the river forms lofty cones, down which gentlemen and ladies slide on their "toboggins," or long, thin, narrow pieces of wood. The Isle of Orleans, reached by ferry, is a point of interest, and should be visited.

Below Quebec are many popular resorts. The Saguenay River, 132 miles below, is a famous river, much frequented by both Americans and Canadians. During the pleasure season, steamers of the St. Lawrence Steamboat Navigation Co. leave Quebec every day except Sunday and Monday, on the arrival of steamers from Montreal. These steamers are elegant and comfortable, thoroughly furnished and carefully handled. On the trip, nine miles from Quebec, we pass the Island of Orleans, sometimes called Isle of Bacchus, from its abundant wild grapes. It is twenty miles long, and at its greatest width six miles wide, very fertile, and dotted with villages. Sixty or seventy miles below we pass the mouth of St. Anne River and a village of the same name. About two miles from the village are the Falls of St. Anne, and the scene above the cataract is very grand. The natural scenery of the vicinity is delightful, and the place is frequently visited. Five miles below we pass Grosse Isle, the "Quarantine," a spot full of the wreck of human hopes. Here in one grave the bodies of about 6,000 Irish emigrants lie interred. Ninety miles from Quebec the first landing-place is Malbaie or Murray Bay, a favorite watering-place for the better class of French Canadians. The Lorne House, with its connected cottages, is a comfortable hotel. Steaming across the river, which is twenty miles wide with eighteen-feet tides, with seals, porpoises, and whales playing in its water, we strike Riviere du Loup on the south shore, and the eastern terminus of the Grand Trunk, as it is the western terminus of the Intercolonial Railroad from St. John, Halifax, etc. About six miles pleasant drive from here is

CACOUNA,

the Newport of Canada, where thousands of visitors enjoy sea bathing in the summer.* The temperature of the air is always delightful here. St. Lawrence Hall accommodates 500 guests in large, airy rooms, fitted with every comfort and convenience. Every provision is made for indoor and outdoor amusement. The house commands from its windows and balconies magnificent seaward views; vessels being distinctly visible at a distance at sea. Guests here combine driving, fishing, boating and seabathing. The hotel omnibuses meet the trains at Cacouna Station, and the steamers at Riviere du Loup wharf.

Opposite Riviere du Loup, about two-hours' sail, is Tadousac, at the mouth of Saguenay. Here is a fine hotel and sea-bathing. Many handsome villas have been erected here, including one built by His Excellency Earl Dufferin. The place was, from an early period, the capital of the French settlements, and of the chief fur-trading posts. The ruins of a Jesuit establishment are found here; and on this spot the first stone and mortar building erected in America stood, the home of Father Marquette, the explorer of the

Mississippi Valley. A cluster of pine trees over 200 years old, in the centre of these ruins, marks the spot.

CAPE ETERNITY, Saguenay River.

The Saguenay, the largest tributary of the St. Lawrence, is unquestionably one of the most remarkable rivers on this continent. Its source is in St. John's Lake, which is forty miles long and lies 150 miles from the St. Lawrence, and nearly due north of Quebec. The scenery is wild and romantic in the highest degree, especially in its upper half, which runs through unbroken wilderness, over rapids and falls, so as to be navigable only for the Indian canoe. The lower half has wonderful scenery. The granite shores, the imposing bluffs—some of them towering high in air, and seeming ready at any moment to precipitate their huge mass upon you—the smooth-sided rocky promontories, 600 to 900 feet high, the echoes—all make a picture of awful grandeur that no description can reproduce. Ha! Ha! Bay is the limit of steam navigation, sixty miles from the St. Lawrence. This Bay is a beautiful expanse of water, receding from the river several miles. At the head of it is the village of Grand Bay, the usual resort for those who wish to remain a few days.

ST. LOUIS HOTEL,
St. Louis Street, Quebec, P. Q.

The ST. LOUIS HOTEL, which is unrivalled for size, style, and locality, in Quebec, is open only during the Season of pleasure travel.

It is eligibly situated near to and surrounded by the most delightful and fashionable promenades,

THE GOVERNOR'S GARDEN,

THE CITADEL,

THE ESPLANADE,

THE PLACE D'ARMES.

DURHAM and DUFFERIN TERRACES.

which furnish the splendid views and magnificent scenery for which Quebec is so justly celebrated, and which is unsurpassed in any part of the world.

The Proprietors in returning thanks for the very liberal patronage they have hitherto enjoyed, inform the public that this hotel has been thoroughly renovated and embellished, and can now accommodate about 500 visitors; and assures them that nothing will be wanting on their part that will conduce to the comfort and enjoyment of their guests.

THE RUSSELL HOTEL COMPANY,

WILLIS RUSSELL, *President.* *Proprietors.*

ST. LAWRENCE HALL,

MONTREAL.

HENRY HOGAN, - - Proprietor.

For the past thirty years this hotel, familiarly known as the "St. Lawrence," has been a "household word" to all travellers on the continent of North America, and has been patronized by all the Royal and noble personages who have visited the City of Montreal.

This Hotel has been recently re-taken by MR. HENRY HOGAN, the former proprietor, who has handsomely and appropriately decorated and renovated the interior, and completely refitted the whole of the apartments with new furniture.

The Hotel is admirably situated, being in the very heart of the city, and contiguous to the General Post Office, the principal Banks, Public Buildings, Law Courts, Commercial Exchanges, Railway and Telegraph Offices.

The Hotel will be managed by MR SAMUEL MONTGOMERY, under the immediate personal supervision of MR. HOGAN, than whom no one is better qualified to conduct an hostelry of such magnitude as the St. Lawrence Hall, and than whom no one has gained a better reputation as an obliging, generous, and considerate host.

PLACES OF INTEREST IN AND AROUND MONTREAL.

The Churches of Notre Dame and the Gesu; the English Cathedral; the Grand Seminary; the Mount Royal and St. Helen Parks; the Victoria Bridge, and Harbor; the Art Gallery; the Academy of Music; the Hotel Dieu; the City Hall, or Hotel de Ville; the various Convents, including the far-famed Villa Maria and Sacred Heart, Sault au Recollet; the McGill College, with its Library and Museum; the Mount Royal Cemetery, &c.

ALBION HOTEL,

McGill and St. Paul Sts., Montreal, Canada.

The Proprietors of this Hotel take this opportunity of thanking the public, for the patronage so liberally given for a period considerably over twenty years, and beg to announce that they have just completed redecorating and refurnishing, and have spared no expense to make the "Albion" the most comfortable, as it has for so long been the best patronized hotel in Montreal.

Being situated on McGill Street, the great business thoroughfare of the city, the "Albion" is in the midst of the greatest business houses of Canada, and at the same time commands an unequalled view of the St. Lawrence River, Victoria Bridge, Victoria Square and Mount Royal.

Prices, $1.50 to $2.00 per day, according to location of room.

STEARNS & MURRAY, Proprietors.

NATIONAL EXPRESS CO.

Forwarder to Stations on the Harlem R. R.,

TROY, SARATOGA, SHARON SPRINGS,

RICHFIELD AND LEBANON SPRINGS,

COOPERSTOWN, LAKE GEORGE,

ADIRONDACK MOUNTAINS,

MT. MANSFIELD AND GREEN MOUNTAINS,

MONTREAL, QUEBEC,

AND ALL POINTS IN

NORTHERN NEW YORK,

VERMONT AND CANADA.

Every variety of Merchandise, Specie, Bank Notes and Jewelry forwarded and delivered with promptness and despatch. Especial attention paid to forwarding and delivering *Wash Hampers and Family Baggage* for those *visiting Summer Resorts.*

Offices in New York, Troy, Albany, Cooperstown, Saratoga, Plattsburg, Rutland, Burlington, St. Albans, Montreal, etc.

THE TROY TIMES

RANKS WITH THE
Best Advertising Mediums
IN AMERICA FOR
QUICK RESULTS.

More than 30,000 persons read it daily.

All advertisments advantageou-ly displayed, and matter changed often. Interesting reading matter on every page.

Price from twelve and one-half to forty cents per line, according to location.

☞ Special Rates for Adverti-ing Summer Resorts and Educational Institutions.

Information cheerfully furnished, and rates and sample papers promptly sent upon application.

J. M. FRANCIS & TUCKER, Publishers, Troy, N. Y.

THE
SPENCER HOUSE,
NIAGARA FALLS, N. Y.

This well-known hotel, with additional attractions, continues ready to welcome its patrons. The Spencer, from its desirable situation, offers greater inducements to the tourist than any other hotel at Niagara. It is the only first-class hotel

OPEN SUMMER AND WINTER,

And combines all the elegance of the modern hotel with the quietness and comfort of a home. Its table has always been distinguished for its excellence, and its apartments are the best ventilated and most commodious at Niagara. Of all the first-class hotels, the Spencer only has reduced its prices for 1879 to $3.00 and $2.50 per day, according to location of rooms.

ALVAH CLUCK, Proprietor.

COSMOPOLITAN HOTEL,
EUROPEAN PLAN,
Cor. Chambers St. and West Broadway, N. Y.

One of the best hotels in New York for the traveling public. Centrally located and most economical in prices.

This Hotel has been recently re-fitted and is complete in all its appointments.

It is centrally located, the principal City Railways pass the door, is five minutes' walk of the New Jersey Central, Pennsylvania, Delaware, Lackawanna and Western, Erie Rail-Roads, all Hudson River Steamboats; within fifteen minutes' ride of Grand Central Depot and Central Park by Elevated Railroad. An Otis Brothers' Elevator carries guests to every floor, rendering all rooms easy of access. The house contains a Barber's Shop with range of Baths, a Railroad Ticket Office where Tickets may be obtained at the same prices as at the depots, a Billiard Room, and a News Office for the sale of Daily and Weekly Papers, Periodicals, Etc.

Rooms $1.00 per Day and upwards.

Rooms for Two, $1 50 per Day and upwards, according to Location of Rooms.

N. & S. J. HUGGINS, Proprietors.

First-Class RESTAURANT, at Popular Prices.

ST. DENIS HOTEL,

Cor. Broadway and Eleventh Street,

NEW YORK,

IN CONNECTION WITH THE WELL KNOWN

TAYLOR'S SALOON.

THE MOST CENTRALLY LOCATED HOTEL IN THE CITY.

Being in the vicinity of all the leading Retail Stores and Principal Places of Amusement—of easy access from all the Depots and Ferries by Horse-Cars, Stage, or the Elevated Rail-Roads. Stages from Grand Central Depot pass the door.

PRICES IN ACCORDANCE WITH THE TIMES.

WILLIAM TAYLOR, Proprietor.

FLEISCHMAN'S VIENNA MODEL BAKERY (of the Centennial Exposition),
Now at BROADWAY and 10TH STREET. NEW YORK (Opposite Stewart's).

THE MOUNTAIN HOME,
WERNERSVILLE, PA.

The "MOUNTAIN HOME," one of the most noted and best located health institutes in this country, is situated on the Eastern slope of Cushion Mountain, at an elevation of one thousand feet above tide water at Philadelphia; one and a half miles from the station at Wernersville, on the Lebanon Valley R. R., and nine miles from the city of Reading, Pa.

The "Home" is easy of access from all parts of country

PIAZZAS.

These extend the whole length and breadth of the building, thus affording extensive walks or promenades under cover in all kinds of weather and at all seasons of the year.

The panoramic view from the piazzas is most beautiful, stretching out North and East fifty to one hundred miles.

CLIMATE.

The climate here is the finest in the world.—*Bayard Taylor*.

It is all that can be desired by either invalid or guest, being free from all foul and miasmatic contaminations, which are so conducive to disease.

The air the year round is dry and bracing. In the hot season of summer the temperature is generally 12° to 15° lower than at Philadelphia, and considerably lower than that of our neighboring city of Reading.

This place is unusually well located and adapted for the successful treatment of throat and lung affections, as well as Rheumatism, Dyspepsia, Nervous Diseases, and all forms of diseases of debility, &c. Consumption a specialty, and is treated successfully here.

SCENERY.

The grandeur of the scenery is indescribable. It must be seen to be appreciated. Besides the above there are many points attracting attention from strangers—besides numerous walks and drives to points of interest at a distance.

WATER.

The water which abundantly supplies the "Home," is soft, pure, unusually cool. It is derived from a number of springs which are all of unvarying and the same temperature throughout the different seasons of the year.

BATHING FACILITIES.

Our facilities for bathing are ample. Besides two large bath rooms on each of two floors of the building, used for ordinary and general bathing, we have two separate rooms where the douche, shower and spray can be conveniently given. We have also an electric bath conveniently arranged for such as may require or desire it, either for health or pleasure. In addition to the above variety of baths, we have also lately introduced that Queen of baths, "The Turkish," which we have reason to believe, there is none better or equal as a depurative in disease, and none more grateful to the well as a luxury when properly administered.

THE TABLE.

It will be a specialty in our institution to have the table well supplied with such things as are in season, most healthy and most relished by patients and guests. An abundance of small fruits and vegetables are raised on the grounds belonging to the "Home" for its special use. Rich fresh milk, cream and butter, produced from our own well regulated dairy will be constantly supplied for table use. Only select meats will find their way to the table.

TELEGRAPH IN THE HOUSE.

For further information, reference, &c., send for circular to

DRS. WENRICH & DEPPEN,
Mountain Home, Wernersville P. O., Berks Co., Pa.

THE MOUNTAIN HOME, WERNERSVILLE, PA.
DRS. WENRICH & DEPPEN, Proprietors.
OPEN ALL THE YEAR.

FEW EQUALS.

NO SUPERIORS.

LOGAN HOUSE,

ALTOONA, PA.

On main line of Pennsylvania R. R., 1,200 feet above sea level; nine hours' ride from New York and Washington; seven from Philadelphia and Baltimore, without change. Open all the year. Capacity 400. First-class in all its appointments. Tourists can obtain a good night's rest and a daylight view of the matchless scenery of the Alleghenies. Health and pleasure-seekers find pure air, good fishing, and hunting, and rides and drives of great beauty and interest. No mosquitoes. Hay Fever unknown. A parlor orchestra of rare excellence has been secured.

For circulars and terms, address

W. D. TYLER, Sup't.

Mountain House,

Cresson Springs, Cambria Co., Pa.

This famous mountain resort will open June 14th, 1880. On the summit of the Alleghenies, 2,200 feet above sea level, pure air, unsurpassed scenery, and valuable Medicinal Spring Waters combine to render it the finest mountain resort in Pennsylvania. Elegant Cottage Residences in a park of rare beauty may be rented by those desiring the quiet and seclusion of home. First-class music. Out-door amusements. Hunting, Fishing, Riding and Driving, Lawn Tennis, Croquet, Archery, etc.

For circulars, terms, etc., address

W. D. TYLER, Sup't.

LOGAN HOUSE, Altoona, Pa., W. D. TYLER, Supt.

CRAWFORD HOUSE.

BOSTON, MASS.

STUMCKE & GOODWIN, Proprietors.

This hotel is at the corner of Court and Brattle Streets, or Scollays Square, and is one of the most conveniently situated hotels in the city, being centrally located for all depots, horse-cars, theatres and all points of interest. It is built of brick and stone, five stories high, is well furnished, and has all modern conveniences. The rooms are supplied with running water, the house has a steam elevator, is heated by steam, and is amply protected against fire. It is kept on the European plan, and will accommodate two hundred persons. Single Rooms, from $1 to $2. Double Rooms, from $2 to $4. Two very large and pleasant Ladies' and Gent's Dining-Rooms attached to the house.

PRICES VERY REASONABLE.

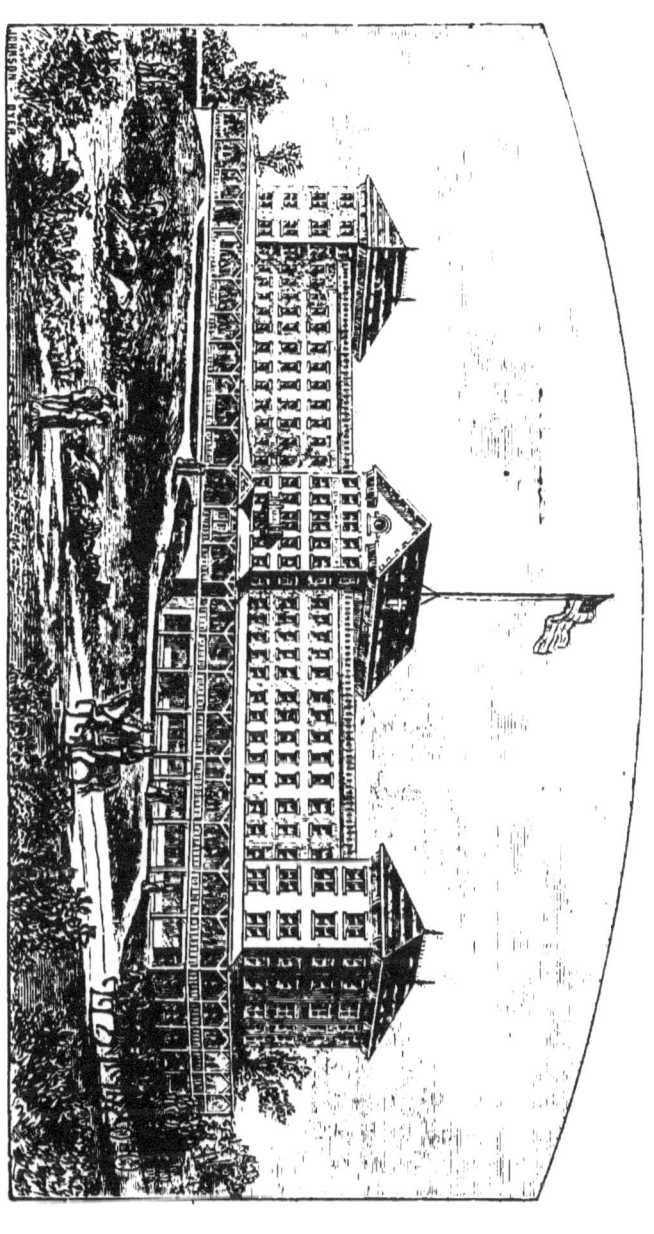

OLD ORCHARD HOUSE. OLD ORCHARD BEACH, Me. E. C. STAPLES, Proprietor.

WESTFIELD, Mass.

R. V. COOLEY, Proprietor.

This excellent hotel is situated in the delightful village of Westfield, Mass., which is six miles west of Springfield, on the Boston and Albany R. R., at its junction with the Canal R. R. running from Northampton to New Haven and New York. The hotel is well furnished, has good spring beds in its sleeping-rooms, and offers a most excellent table to its patrons. Besides the many attractions of the village of Westfield as a summer resort, there are several points of interest within short driving distance from the Wilmarth, among which are Southwick Ponds, which afford excellent fishing grounds and bathing, and are rapidly becoming attractive as resorts for picnic and excursion parties.

The famous Blanchford Hills are but six or eight miles distant; and many other drives among the hills of Western Massachusetts, render the vicinity of the Westfield and the Wilmarth House peculiarly attractive. The terms for board at the Wilmarth are very moderate for the accommodations afforded.

TRADE MARK.

H. VOULLIEME,
Manufacturer of Rich and Choice Confections,
ICE CREAM, SODA WATER AND FRUIT ICES.
CONGRESS PARK CARAMELS A SPECIALTY.
GENERAL DEPOT FOR VOULLIEME'S CONGRESS PARK CARAMELS.

Also, importer of Precious Stones and Jewelry, Onyx, Cameo, Amethyst, Blood Stone, Smoked Topaz, Calcedony, Amber, Lapis Lazuli, Agate, Cornelian, Malachite, etc. Splendid Specimens in the rough state.

No. 361 Broadway, Saratoga Springs, N. Y.
UNDER ADELPHI HOTEL.
☞ Goods shipped to any part of the United States and Canada. ☜

SHELDON HOUSE,
Ocean Grove, N. J.

Largest and most Central House in the Grove, and the only one having a PASSENGER ELEVATOR, and other important First Class Modern Improvements.

Warm Salt Water Baths. Entire Freedom from Mosquitos.

Perfect Drainage by a large new Sewer, on the most elaborate and Modern Plan.

WELCOME E. SHELDON, Proprietor.

WEST END HOTEL.

ASBURY PARK, N. J. Will open June 10th, 1880.

Handsomely located near the Surf and Wesley Lake, with full view of each.

HAS LARGE AIRY ROOMS HANDSOMELY FURNISHED.

Extra Wide Halls entire length of Building; Wide Open Stairway to each floor, giving fresh and Cool Sea Breezes to all parts of the House. Bed-Rooms all thoroughly ventilated. Wide Verandas, etc.

For particulars, address, **MRS. JOHN S. COOK, Proprietress,**
ASBURY PARK, N. J.

SHELBURNE HOUSE,

ATLANTIC CITY N. J.

On Michigan Avenue, 100 yards from the SEA, and near the WARM BATHS, with unobstructed OCEAN FRONT and SEA BREEZES; a Comfortable and Pleasant Summer House. Will be open until October.

EDWIN ROBERTS,
Proprietor.

CONGRESS WATER.

This famous Water is a well-known specific for Constipation, Indigestion and all disorders of the Stomach, Liver, Kidneys, Bladder, etc. Other *coarse-crude* Mineral Waters, *foreign* and *domestic*, not only aggravate such disorders when they exist, but being *irritants positively induce* them by their effect on the mucous membrane.

Congress Water contains none of those deleterious ingredients found in so many of the foreign imported waters, which intelligent foreigners carefully avoid, as do the intelligent residents of Saratoga, the coarse, irritating waters found in some of its numerous springs.

All Mineral Waters that are dangerous *irritants* may be known by their *acrid-acid* like *after-taste*.

For sale, in bottles only, by all leading Druggists, Grocers and Hotels.

CONGRESS & EMPIRE SPRING CO.,
Saratoga Springs, N. Y.

OCEAN BLUFF HOTEL,

Cape Arundel, Kennebunkport Maine.

This most delightful resort on the Atlantic Coast, situated on high ground overlooking the finest ocean scenery, will open early in June, under the same popular management as last year.

The healthiest section, in N. E. Excellent facilities for yachting, boating, bathing and fishing. Easily reached by express trains. Will accommodate 200 guests. Address

Stimpson, Devnell & Davis, Prop's.
Kennebunkport, Maine.

CARLETON HOUSE,

Jacksonville, Florida.
Open from November to May.
THE SARATOGA OF THE SOUTH.
All the Northern Comforts with a Warm and Equable Climate.

New Brick Hotel. Fire Hose on each Floor.

Passenger Elevator, and all Modern Improvements.

STIMPSON, DEVNELL & DAVIS,
Proprietors.

GO TO THE

WHITE MOUNTAINS,

VIA

Central Vermont R. R. Lines.

THE ONLY

All Rail Line from New York to the Summit

OF

MOUNT WASHINGTON.

Trains leave Grand Central Depot daily (except Sunday) at **8 o'clock A.M.**, with new and luxurious Drawing Room Cars (built expressly for this line), running through to Fabyans without change, arriving at Littleton, Profile House, Bethlehem, Twin Mt. House, Fabyans, Crawford House, and Jefferson, in season for supper.

The Only Route through the lovely and Picturesque **CONNECTICUT VALLEY.**

The Old-Established and Popular All-Rail Route between NEW YORK and MONTREAL, via New York Central and Hudson River R. R., Troy and Boston, Bennington and Rutland, *Central Vermont* and Grand Trunk Railroads.

Wagner Day and Sleeping Cars on all Express Trains running through between New York and Montreal without change.

Two Through Express Trains daily (except Sundays) between Boston and Montreal, with Pullman Cars through without change. No other Line does it.

TO THE TOURIST, TRAVELER AND PLEASURE SEEKER.

This Company issues annually a book entitled the "Summer Excursionist," handsomely illustrated, giving a list of routes and rates for "*Excursion Tickets*," also a full description of all routes and summer resorts, which is now ready for distribution, and can be obtained "*FREE*" on application in person or by letter, at all Ticket offices in Boston, New York, Philadelphia, Baltimore, Washington, Albany, Utica, Syracuse, E ni ra, Rochester, Buffalo, Niagara Falls, Montreal, Ottawa, Quebec, and White Mountains.

Tourists' and Excursion Tickets at greatly reduced rates, for sale at all the principal Stations and Ticket Offices of the PENNSYLVANIA RAILROAD; also, at all the leading Hotels and Ticket Offices in New York, Philadelphia, Baltimore and Washington, and in all the principal cities of the South, West, Middle, and New England States. Also, at the Company's Offices, *417 Broadway, corner Canal Street, New York;* 260 Washington Street, Boston; and 136 St. James Street, Montreal, where seats and berths in Drawingroom and Sleeping Cars can be secured.

ST. ALBANS, VT., *May 22th*, 1880.

J. W. HOBART, Gen'l Supt.

   W. F. SMITH, Gen'l Pass'r Agent.

      D. McKERNZIE, Ass't Gen'l Pass'r Agent.

GENERAL OFFICES, ST. ALBANS, VT.

WAUKEAG HOUSE,
SULLIVAN, MAINE.

This house, comparatively new, is situated at the head of Frenchman's Bay, within a few rods of the water, on a site commanding one of the grandest views in N. E. Mt. Desert, only a few miles distant, with all its wonderful panorama of grandeur and beauty, greets the gaze.

Sea-shore and country are here combined.

The drives are many and varied.

Superior trout and sea fishing. The very best facilities for boating, yachting and bathing.

A first-class livery, connected with the house.

This section is in the centre of the richest mining region of the State.

The Waukeag, with ample accommodations for one hundred guests is now open, and rooms may be secured by early application.

Terms, $9 to $12 per week.

Steamer Mt. Desert will land guests within a few rods of the house. Telegraph office near.

STILLMAN F. WHITE, Proprietor.

SPRINGFIELD
FIRE AND MARINE INSURANCE CO.

Incorporated 1849.   Charter Perpetual.
No Marine Risks Taken.

Capital, ...	$750,000.00
Cash Assets, Jan. 1st, 1880. .	$1,858,477.34

LIABILITIES.

Capital Stock all paid up,	$750,000.00	
Outstanding Losses,	75,245 95	
Re-Insurance Fund,	573,972.05	
All other Claims,	14,925.00	$1,414,143.00
Surplus over all Liabilities,		$444,334.34
Surplus as regards Policy Holders,		1,194,334.34

DWIGHT R. SMITH, President.
SANFORD J. HALL, Sec'y.   ANDREW J. WRIGHT, Treas.

GEO. M. COIT, Agent,	New York.
WISTER & PETERSON, Agents.	Philadelphia.
REED & BROTHER, Agents,	Boston.

Agencies in all the principal Cities and Towns of the United States.

A. J. HARDING, Gen'l Agt. (Western Department), Chicago, Ill.

PEOPLE'S EVENING LINE

BETWEEN

NEW YORK AND ALBANY

During the Season of Navigation, the Magnificent Steamers

DREW, or ST. JOHN,
Capt. S. J. ROE.   Capt. T. D. CHRISTOPHER,

WILL LEAVE NEW YORK
Daily, Sundays excepted, at 6 P.M., from Pier 41, North River.

ARRIVING IN ALBANY
In time to connect with morning trains **NORTH, EAST, and WEST.**

LEAVE ALBANY
Every week-day at 8:15 P.M., from Steamboat Landing, connecting at New York with **ALL EARLY TRAINS** for the **SOUTH** and **EAST**. Meals on the European Plan. Rooms heated by Steam during the cool months.

FOR TICKETS IN NEW YORK
Apply at the Company's Ticket Office on the wharf (Pier 41, North River); at Dodd's Express Co., 944 Broadway — 786 Sixth Avenue — 4 Court Street, Brooklyn, Jersey City and Hoboken, and at all principal Hotels and Ticket Offices in New York, and on board the Steamers.

W. W. EVERETT,   **J. C. HEWITT,**   **M. B. WATERS,**
President.   *Gen. T. Agt.*   *Gen. Pass. Agt.*

ARE YOU INSURED?

ORGANIZED 1853.

RUTGERS FIRE INSURANCE CO.,

CASH CAPITAL, - - - $200 000.
SURPLUS, - - - - - $240,000.

Office, 180 Chatham Square,

Branch Offices, 58 Wall Street, and 1295 Broadway

NEW YORK.

Losses immediately adjusted and promptly paid.

JOS. F. HANFORD, Sec'y. EDWARD B. FELLOWS, Pres't.
HENRY C. KREISER, Ass't Sec'y, CHARLES D. BAILEY, Vice Pres't.
LEWIS S. WATKINS, Surveyor.

A LIFE INSURANCE COMPANY

SOLID AS GRANITE.

The Hartford *Post*, commenting on the Annual Statement of the ÆTNA LIFE INSURANCE COMPANY, says: "The management of the company has been eminently successful from the outset, but never more so than during the past year. This is clearly demonstrated by the interest account, which shows an income of more than 7¼ per cent. on the gross assets of the company at the beginning of 1879 The remark of Insurance Commissioner Stedman several weeks ago, after finishing the examination of the company as required by law, that 'the Ætna's assets are as solid as granite,' is sustained in every respect by the thirtieth annual statement. The Policyholders in the Ætna Life have the best reasons for feeling that they are insured in one of the strongest and most reliable companies in the world."

HUDSON RIVER BY DAYLIGHT.

NEW YORK AND ALBANY
DAY LINE STEAMERS,

"ALBANY" and **"C. VIBBARD,"**
(*built* 1880)   (*re-modelled* 1880)

Leave New York, Vestry St., Pier 39, N. R. (adjoining Jersey City Ferry), 8.35 A.M., and foot 24th St., N. R., 9 A.M., landing at Nyack and Tarrytown, West Point, Newburgh, Poughkeepsie, Rhinebeck, Catskill and Hudson. Returning, leave Albany, 8.30 A.M., from foot of Hamilton St., connecting in New York with trains for Philadelphia, South and East.

CONNECTIONS.

BROOKLYN—Annex leaves Fulton Street at 8:00 A.M. Leaves Vestry Street Pier on arrival of down boat.

WEST POINT—With Stages for **Cozzens'** and **West Point Hotels.**

POUGHKEEPSIE—With Stages for **Lake Mohonk**, and with Poughkeepsie, Hartford & Boston R. R.

RHINEBECK—With Ferry for **Rondout**, and Ulster & Delaware R. R., all *Catskill Mountain resorts*, and Wallkill Valley R. R. for **Lake Mohonk.**

CATSKILL—With Stages for **Prospect Park Hotel, Mountain House** and all Stage Lines.

HUDSON—With Boston and Albany R. R., for Chatham, Pittsfield, North Adams, etc.

ALBANY—With New York Central R. R., for **Niagara Falls, Buffalo, Watertown, Thousand Islands,** and Western points. With Rensselaer & Saratoga R. R., for **Saratoga, Montreal,** and points North. With Albany and Susquehanna R. R., for **Elmira, Watkin's Glen,** etc.

DINING SALOON ON THE MAIN DECK.
Meals served on the European plan.

TICKETS or COUPONS good on Hudson River R. R. received on board for passage. ☞TRIP TICKETS from New York to West Point, or Newburgh, returning same day, $1.00. To Pougheeepsie and return $1.50.

C. R. VAN BENTHUYSEN, General Ticket Agent.

Vestry St. Pier, New York City.

FRENCH'S HOTEL.
EUROPEAN PLAN,
Opposite City Hall, Court House, and New Post Office,
NEW YORK.

PRICES REDUCED.
ROOMS—75 CENTS, AND UPWARDS

THIS HOTEL has all modern improvements, including Elevators, Gas, Running Water, and Burglar Proof Locks on every door. It is convenient to all Theatres, and within three minutes walk of both the Elevated Railroad Stations. Horse Cars for all parts of the city pass the door.

The Saratoga Geyser
NATURAL MINERAL WATER,
Saratoga Springs, N. Y.

As a Cathartic, Alterative and Diuretic this water SURPASSES ALL OTHERS, and is highly recommended in the treatment of DYSPEPSIA, CONSTIPATION, FEVER AND AGUE, and all disorders of the BLOOD, LIVER and KIDNEYS.

It is HIGHLY EFFERVESCENT, a great aid to Digestion, and an Excellent Table Water.

As a CATHARTIC it is Mild yet Thorough. The usual Cathartic dose is one pint, taken rather warm, before breakfast.

For an ALTERATIVE or DIURETIC, drink in smaller quantities during the day or at night.

For DYSPEPSIA take with or after meals.

EVERY CORK WIRED AND BRANDED.

WEBSTER'S UNABRIDGED
NEW EDITION.

Now added a **Supplement** of over **4600** NEW WORDS and Meanings, These include such as have come into use during the past fifteen years—many of which have never found a place in any English dictionary before,

AND A NEW
BIOGRAPHICAL DICTIONARY,
of over 9700 NAMES.

of Noteworthy Persons, ancient and modern, including many now living, giving the Name Pronunciation, Nationality, Profession and date of each.

☞ In meeting names in reading, how frequently the thought is in mind, "Who was he? Where was he? What was he? and When was he?" This **New Biographical Dictionary** in Webster just answers these questions in brief.

Published by **G. & C. MERRIAM**, Springfield, Mass.

ALSO

WEBSTER'S NATIONAL PICTORIAL DICTIONARY.
1040 Pages Octavo.   600 Engravings.

HOP BITTERS.

(A Medicine, not a Drink,)

CONTAINS

HOPS, BUCHU, MANDRAKE, DANDELION.

AND THE PUREST AND BEST MEDICAL QUALITIES OF ALL OTHER BITTERS.

THEY CURE

All Diseases of the Stomach; Bowels, Blood, Liver, Kidneys, and Urinary Organs, Nervousness, Sleeplessness and especially Female Complaints.

$1000 IN GOLD.

Will be paid for a case they will not cure or help, or for anything impure or injurious found in them.

Ask your druggist for Hop Bitters and try them before you sleep. **Take no Other.**

D. I. C. is an absolute and irresistible cure for Drunkenness, use of opium, tobacco and narcotics.

Send for circular.

All above sold by druggists.
Hop Bitters Mfg. Co., Rochester, N. Y.

HEMORRHOIDS OR PILES.

My Treatment is Original, Painless and Uniformly Successful.

The Hemorrhoids, or Piles are permanently eradicated in two to three weeks, without the knife, ligature, caustic, or any of the old painful and dangerous methods used by the general profession. It is a permanent and perfect cure. It is free from all danger of hemorrhage.

A GREAT CONSIDERATION

Is the short length of time required in affecting a cure and not preventing patients from attending to their usual business.

REFERENCES.

Francis Rew, editor Rochester *Evening Express*, Rochester, N. Y.
C. D. Tracy, Secretary and Treasurer Rochester *Evening Express*, Rochester, N. Y.
H. S. Greenleaf, of Sargent & Greenleaf, Lock Makers, Rochester, N. Y.
Rev. Newton Mann, Pastor Unitarian Church, Rochester, N. Y.
Geo. Cramer, Proprietor Flour City Bag Works, Rochester, N. Y.
Judge Sill, Municipal Court, Rochester, N. Y.
Henry Powis, Esq., Rochester, N. Y.

Ex-Judge Buell, Rochester, N. Y.
J. G. Wagner, Contractor and Builder, Rochester, N. Y.
J. B. Crocker, Cashier First National Bank, Waterloo, N. Y.
T. E. Kuhn, Cashier First National Bank, Dansville, N. Y.
E. A. Mills, Cashier, Genessee Bank, Mt. Morris, N. Y.
J. R. Murray, Mt. Morris, N. Y.
Gen'l Geo. W. Palmer, 112 Broadway.
James Sargent, of Sargent & Greenleaf, Lock Makers, Rochester, N. Y.

CONSULTATION FREE!   **NO CURE NO PAY!**

HOWARD STRONG, M.D.,

Room 30, Elwood Memorial Building, Rochester, N. Y.

SARATOGA OFFICE, Open from July 1st to September 1st.

EXCELSIOR SPRING,

SARATOGA SPRINGS, N. Y.

The Water of the Excelsior Spring is thought to be unequalled by that of any other Spring at this world-renowned Watering Place.

Its virtues are such as have secured it the high encomiums of Physicians and others who have used it, possessing, as it does in an eminent degree, Cathartic, Diuretic, Alterative, and Tonic qualities.

This Water produces its beneficial effects without the injurious results which so commonly follow the use of artificial curatives; and, as a general regulator and preservative of the tone of the system, the Water of the "Excelsior" Spring is invaluable, removing and *preventing*, by its aperient and alterative effects, the *incipient forms* of disease.

THE "UNION" SPRING

Is situated about one mile east of the Town Hall, at Saratoga Springs, near the centre of Excelsior Park, and about ten rods north-west of the Excelsior Spring.

The water of each of the above two Springs is put up in Pint and Quart Bottles, and packed in good order for shipment to any part of the world. Pints in boxes of four dozen each, and Quarts in boxes of two dozen each.

They are also shipped in Lawrence's Patent Reservoirs (Barrels lined with pure Block-Tin), from which they are dispensed by our customers at their counters precisely as they flow from the springs, without being recharged with gas.

Dr. Fordyce Barker, of New York, says of the EXCELSIOR WATER:

I make great use of the various Mineral Waters in my practice, and I regard the "Excelsior" Spring Water of Saratoga as the best Saline and Alkaline laxative of this class. Sparkling with Carbonic Acid Gas, it is to most persons very agreeable to the taste, and prompt in action as a gentle Diuretic and Cathartic.

FORDYCE BARKER, M.D.

The Water of the UNION SPRING also acts as a Cathartic when drank before breakfast; while, at other times during the day, it is a very agreeable and healthful beverage.

ORDERS BY MAIL WILL RECEIVE PROMPT ATTENTION.

☞ For Descriptive Pamphlets, with Analysis, Prices, &c., apply to

A. R. LAWRENCE & CO.,

Proprietors of "Excelsior" and "Union" Springs,

SARATOGA SPRINGS, N. Y

DRS. STRONG'S REMEDIAL INSTITUTE,
Saratoga Springs, N. Y.

Popular Summer Resort, also open all the Year.

It is finely located in close proximity to the principal springs, hotels, and park; with ample grounds, elegant and complete in all appointments. It is the summer home of leading men in church and state, and offers a delightful retreat for rest and recreation, as well as treatment.

Among its patrons are. Rev. Dr. T. L. CUYLER; Ex-Govs. WELLS and BOARDMAN; Bishops SIMPSON, ROBINSON, HARRIS, HAVEN, FOSTER, etc.; Judges REYNOLDS, DRAKE, BLISS, etc.; Editors MONFORT, FOWLER, PIERCE, etc.; College Presidents, HAVEN, FOSS, TUTTLE, CHADBURNE, PAYNE, BARTLETT, etc.; Generals FEARING, SATTERLEE, CASEY, etc.; Medical Professors ARMOR, ROSS, KNAPP, and others equally well-known.

The boarding department is of the highest order.

The proprietors are graduates of the Medical Department of the University of New York.

The Institution is furnished with every comfort and appliance requisite for the Treatment of Nervous, Lung, Female, and Chronic Diseases, such as Turkish, Russian, Roman, Sulphur, Vapor, Hydropathic, and Electro thermal Baths; Faradic and Galvanic Electricity; The Equalizer or Vacuum Treatment; Oxygen and Medicated Inhalations, also Compressed and Rarified Air, Gymnastics and other varieties of Hydropathy and Medicine.

SEND FOR CIRCULAR.

The NEW YORK OBSERVER is the Best Family Religious and Secular paper. Its steadily increasing circulation is now the best and the largest of any paper of its class, and extends throughout the United States and all foreign countries.

It has five Working Editors, and a large Corps of Contributors. It contains all the Religious and Secular News suitable for Family Reading, Vigorous Editorials, Foreign Correspondence, Youths', Sunday-School, Literary, Agricultural, and Business Departments, with a choice selection of Miscellaneous Reading.

SPECIMENS FREE.

Address, 37 Park Row, New York.

TROW'S
Printing and Bookbinding Company,

ELECTROTYPING & STEREOTYPING,

205-213 EAST TWELFTH STREET

AND

15 Vandewater Street,

NEW YORK.

They are constantly adding improvements, both in the

BINDING AND PRINTING DEPARTMENTS,

And offer to Publishers facilities unequalled in this country

FOR THE

Rapid and Accurate Production of Books.

ALL ORDERS FOR

JOB PRINTING

Promptly attended to.

Estimates for Binding or Printing furnished on application.

IRVING HOUSE,
BROADWAY AND TWELFTH STREET.
AMERICAN PLAN.

Newly furnished and fitted with elevator and baths; running water in every room; excellent accommodations for families; transient, $2 to $3 per day.

CHAS. LEFLER, Proprietor.

TRADE MARK.

This highly endorsed Blacking is manufactured near Paris, France. Its superiority consists, briefly, in its entire freedom from acids, which injure leather, and from all sticky substances which soil the clothing. Its cheapness is marked, as less blacking is required to give the most beautiful polish with the least exertion; and as it will keep fresh and good longer than any other blacking manufactured.   **FOR SALE EVERYWHERE.**
☞ **BEWARE OF IMITATIONS.** ☜

GRAND UNION HOTEL,

Persons visiting or leaving New York City for business or pleasure, to visit Brighton or Manhattan Beach, Long Branch, Niagara, Saratoga, White Mountains, Garrison's, or other *Summer* Resorts, will find the GRAND UNION HOTEL, opposite Grand Central Depot, one of the best Hotels in the City to stop at—you save Baggage Expressage and Carriage Hire. Kept on European Plan. 350 Elegant Rooms, reduced to $1 and upwards per day. Elegant Suites for families. The Restaurant, Lunch Counter, and Wine Rooms, are supplied with the best. Families can live better for less money at the Grand Union than at any other first-class Hotel in the City.

W. D. GARRISON, Manager.

BOSTON AND MAINE RAILROAD

THE DIRECT AND POPULAR LINE FOR

Tourists, Pleasure-Seekers, Anglers, and Sportsmen,

TO ALL

THE SUMMER RESORTS

OF

Northern and Eastern New England.

THE ONLY LINE TO

WELLS, KENNEBUNK,

AND

OLD ORCHARD BEACHES.

DIRECT ROUTE TO

LAKE WINNEPESAUKEE,
THE WHITE MOUNTAINS,
RANGELEY LAKES,
MOOSEHEAD LAKE.

—AND—

BAR HARBOR, MOUNT DESERT.

Close connections made at PORTLAND for all points in the STATE OF MAINE and THE PROVINCES.

Passengers holding EXCURSION TICKETS to the White Mountains or points in Maine, are privileged to stop at the above **BEACHES,** and at the attractive city of

PORTLAND,

with its fine harbor dotted with islands, its charming scenery and beautiful drives, which for variety and beauty are unsurpassed.

Descriptive Lists of Excursion Tickets issued by this Road may be obtained at the Ticket Offices of the Company, or will be sent by mail on application.

Station in Boston, Haymarket Square.
Uptown Office, 280 Washington Street.

JAS. T. FURBER,   D. J. FLANDERS,
General Supt.   *Gen'l Ticket Agent.*

THE "AMERICAN"
BOSTON.

CENTRAL LOCATION.
    UNEXCEPTIONABLE TABLE.
        PERFECT VENTILATION.
            PASSENGER ELEVATOR.

PARTICULARLY DESIRABLE

FOR FAMILIES AND SUMMER TOURISTS.

SIX STAIRWAYS FROM TOP TO BOTTOM.
With every security against fire.

PRICES LOWER THAN ANY OTHER FIRST CLASS HOTEL
Furnishing equal accommodations.

RUNNING WATER IN EVERY CHAMBER.

"It is one of the most attractive and best managed of New England Hotels."—*N. Y. Mail.*

LEWIS RICE & SON.

86 Hanover Street.

COLUMBIAN INSTITUTE

FOR THE

PRESERVATION OF HEALTH

AND THE

CURE OF CHRONIC DISEASES,

21 West 27th Street,

SECOND HOUSE WEST OF BROADWAY,   NEW YORK.

Medical Superintendent,   *Business Manager,*
HENRY A. HARTT, M.D.   **F. G. WELCH, M.D.**

The Institute is furnished with all approved medical, curative, and hygienic agencies, embracing the Moliere-Thermo Electric Bath; Turkish, Russian, Roman, Electric, Hot and Cold Water Baths. The Health-Lift, Swedish Movements, Massage, Galvanism, Electro-Magnetism, etc.

The agencies of the Institute will be found especially serviceable in Diseases of the Blood, Skin, Lungs, Throat, Heart, Brain, Nerves, Stomach, Liver, Bowels, Kidneys and Uterus, including Rheumatism, Gout, Rheumatic Gout, Asthma, Bronchitis, Catarrh, Coughs, Colds, Fever and Ague, Neuralgia, Sciatica, Spinal Irritation, Paralysis, Nervous Prostration, General Debility, Melancholia, Insomnia, Hay Fever, Obesity, Dropsy, Vertigo, Constipation, Lumbago, Dyspepsia, Biliousness.

OPEN DAY AND EVENING.

VISITORS WELCOME AT ANY TIME. CALL AND INVESTIGATE OR SEND FOR FULL PARTICULARS.

COLUMBIAN INSTITUTE,
21 West 27th Street,   New York.

Interior Decorations.

Fresco Painting.

THE
EASTERN RAILROAD.

BOSTON TO PORTLAND,

With its connections, the Maine Central R. R., and Portland and Ogdensburg R. R.,

FORMS THE

GREAT THROUGH LINE AND EXCURSION ROUTE,

VIA **BOSTON** TO

THE WHITE MOUNTAINS,

AND TO ALL PARTS OF

MAINE and **THE MARITIME PROVINCES.**

Pullman Cars run on day and night trains, between BOSTON and BANGOR,

AND ON

White Mountain Trains, Drawing-Room and Observation Cars,

BOSTON and FABYANS,

VIA

NORTH CONWAY, GLEN, CRAWFORD,

AND

THE WHITE MOUNTAIN NOTCH.

Trains will leave Boston, during Summer Season of 1880,

For *Wolfboro*, 8.30 A.M., 12.30 and 3.15 P.M.

For *North Conway, Glen House, Crawford*, and *Fabyans*, 8.30 A.M., 12.30 P.M.

For *Portland*, 7.30, 8.30 A.M., 12.30 and 7.00 P.M.

For *Bangor*, 7.30 A.M., 7.00 P.M.

For *St. John* and *Halifax*, 7.00 P.M., with Sleeping-Cars Boston to Bangor.

For all the

Famous Beaches

on the Eastern Shore of New England, frequent trains are provided.

ASK FOR TICKETS VIA EASTERN RAILROAD.

THE SEASHORE ROUTE.

D. W. SANBORN, LUCIUS TUTTLE,
Must. Trans. *Gen'l Pass'r & Ticket Agent.*

THE GREAT
FALL RIVER LINE,
BETWEEN
NEW YORK AND BOSTON,
VIA
NEWPORT AND FALL RIVER.

QUICKEST AND MOST DIRECT ROUTE TO

TAUNTON, NEW BEDFORD, CAPE COD, MARTHA'S VINEYARD, NANTUCKET, LOWELL, LAWRENCE, NASHUA, MANCHESTER, CONCORD, PORTLAND, BANGOR, MOUNT DESERT, WHITE MOUNTAINS, Etc., Etc.

MAMMOTH PALACE STEAMERS
BRISTOL & PROVIDENCE.

Largest, Finest and most Costly Steamers of their class in the World.

SPLENDID BANDS OF MUSIC

accompany each Steamer during the season of pleasure travel.

Steamers leave New York from Pier 28 N. R., foot of Murray St. Train connecting with Steamers at Fall River (49 miles), leave Boston from Old Colony R.R. Depot, cor. South and Kneeland Sts. Brooklyn and Jersey City PASSENGERS TRANSFERRED FREE, via Annex boat to and from Pier of this Line.

J. R. KENDRICK,　　　　　GEO. L. CONNOR,
　　Supt.　　　　　　　　　　　　　*G. P. A.*

PUZZOLINE.

A LIQUID MINERAL GLUE AND CEMENT.

EUREKA SILVER LUSTRE. Not only the best polish made, but will prevent gold and silver from tarnishing.

CIMITOLINE. The best mucilage in the world; will not dry up or sour.

If you want the best, buy PUZZOLINE. A 25 cent bottle, like the above, will save ten times its cost yearly to every family in the land. Try it and you will never be without it.

MANUFACTURED BY

THE PUZZOLINE CO., BOSTON, MASS., U. S. A.

FOR THE
WHITE MOUNTAINS.

BOSTON, CONCORD, MONTREAL, WHITE MOUNTAINS AND MOUNT WASHINGTON RAILROAD.

This, the only all-rail Route to the SUMMIT of MOUNT WASHINGTON, the FRANCONIA NOTCH and JEFFERSON, takes passengers from NEW LONDON, STONINGTON, PROVIDENCE, FALL RIVER, BOSTON, and all Cities and Towns along the main New England Railway Lines, by through trains equipped with ELEGANT DRAWING-ROOM CARS, connecting with the Sound Boats, from NEW YORK, and Philadelphia, and Western Railway Lines. No change of cars between the Mountains and the several Boat Landings. This route leads through the most picturesque portion of New England, giving a succession of RIVER, LAKE and MOUNTAIN VIEWS unsurpassed, passing through the Manufacturing Cities of the MERRIMACK Valley, and the romantic PEMIGEWASSET, CONNECTICUT and AMMONOOSUCK VALLEYS, skirting for thirty miles the beautiful LAKE WINNEPESAUKEE, connecting at WEIRS with Steamer for CENTER HARBOR and WOLFBOROUGH. At PLYMOUTH thirty minutes are given for dinner at the famed

PEMIGEWASSET HOUSE.

The New Railroads to PROFILE HOUSE and to JEFFERSON diverge from and connect with this line, affording the most direct and cheapest route to these Celebrated Summer Resorts. BETHLEHEM, one of the great centres of the mountain region, is situated on the Line of this Road, and can be reached by no other line, making this the quickest, best and cheapest route to this fashionable resort.

Lower Rates for 1880. Parties purchasing through tickets can stop at all points of interest and proceed at their pleasure. Ask for tickets via BOSTON, CONCORD, MONTREAL AND WHITE MOUNTAINS R. R. See Maps and Descriptive Circulars of this Route, to be found at all Ticket Offices, Hotels and Railroad Depots, or send to General Office, 5 STATE STREET, BOSTON, for all information and tickets to all points.

W. R. BRACKETT,   G. W. STORER, Agent,
     Gen'l Ticket Agt.   5 State Street, Boston.

J. A. DODGE, Gen'l Manager, Plymouth, N. H.

THE
UNITED STATES LIFE
Insurance Company
IN THE CITY OF NEW YORK
(Incorporated 1850.)

261, 262, 263 & 264 BROADWAY, N. Y.

ASSETS...................................$4,083,226 81
SURPLUS....................................872,484 06

JAMES BUELL, - - - President.

Examine the New Form of Policy issued by the United States Life Insurance Company before insuring elsewhere.

After the premiums for three or more years have been paid, upon receiving the required notice from the assured, the Company will continue the Policy in force without further payments, for its FULL FACE, for such a period as the ENTIRE RESERVE will carry it.

Should the death of the insured take place during the continued term of insurance as provided for above, the full face of the Policy will be paid—no deduction being made for forborne or unpaid premiums, excepting in the event of the death occurring within three years after the original default.

The new form of Endowment Policy provides: That if the ENTIRE RESERVE is a greater sum than the single Premium required to carry the full amount of insurance to the end of the Endowment term, the Excess shall be used as a single premium to purchase a pure endowment, payable at the end of the term, thus guaranteeing to the policy-holder in every event the full value of his Reserve.

NO SURRENDER of the Policy is required; only a notice from the policy-holder, on blanks furnished by the Company.

AFTER THREE YEARS, ALL RESTRICTIONS and CONDITIONS in regard to travel, residence, occupation and cause of death are removed, thus making the Policies, after three years, INCONTESTIBLE FOR ANY CAUSE EXCEPTING FRAUD.

THE CONVERTIBLE LIFE POLICY

So far as we are aware, is issued by no other Company, and is our own idea. We would also say that it is considered by many business men and financiers as one of the most desirable forms of Life Insurance ever offered to the public.

The advantage of the convertible plan are that it overcomes all objections to Insurance as ordinarily made.

First—**All premiums will cease at the age of 65.**

Second—If, on reaching that age, Insurance is still desired, the policy may continue in full force, without additional cost; the annual dividends will be added to the Policy, thus increasing the amount of Insurance.

Third—If, at the age of 65, Insurance is no longer needed, the Company will retire the Policy if requested, and issue in lieu thereof an "Annuity Bond," stipulating that, during the remainder of the lifetime of the insured, it will pay to the policy-holder a sum equal to—

Seven per cent. per annum, upon the face of the policy and its additions.

The Company will, upon application, send Circulars giving full particulars.

MASSASOIT HOUSE,
M. & E. S. CHAPIN,   SPRINGFIELD, MASS.

The Massasoit House, near Railroad Stations, was established in 1843. It has been twice enlarged, making it three times its original size, and thoroughly remodeled and refurnished. The large airy sleeping rooms, furnished with hot and cold water, are excelled by none in the country. Connecting rooms, *en suite*, for families, elegantly furnished and with bath-rooms attached. Special attention paid to ventilation and all sanitary improvements. The proprietors are determined that the world-wide reputation of the Massasoit shall be maintained in all respects.

BREVOORT HOUSE,
Fifth Avenue, near Washington Square, New York.

A quiet Hotel, with a Restaurant of peculiar excellence.

                         CHARLES B. WAITE, Proprietor.

The BREVOORT House, which is located on Fifth Avenue, opened its doors to the public Twenty-five years ago. The location was then considered up-town, and many predicted failure for such an elegant hotel so far away from business; but, on the contrary, the most favorable results were attained. its patrons, from the beginning, being the most desirable. This hotel has, during these many years, maintained the most enviable reputation for its *cuisine*, and has entertained more of the royalty and nobility of Europe than all the other hotels in the city. The BREVOORT has more real comforts than any European hotel on the American continent. It is the first resort of Europeans, epicures and experienced travelers in the United States. Its reputation is stronger to-day than ever, while the character of its management cannot be surpassed. It is quiet, elegant, refined, and furnishes the best—and only the best—of everything. Mr. WAITE's connection with the new Windsor Hotel of this city does not weaken his interest in or personal attention to the details of the BREVOORT, whose constant patronage testifies to the position it occupies and deserves. This hotel was never better, and its prices for rooms and in the Restaurant are in accordance with the present times

BALDWIN HOUSE,
NEWBURGH, N. Y.

Situated at an elevation commanding a full view of the City, Newburgh Bay, the Hudson River and the Highlands for many miles—8 minutes from the ferry, communicating with the Hudson River Railroad, and the boat-landing for the Hudson River Steamers. Free Omnibus. Largest and best first-class Hotel in Newburgh. Built of Brick, and has all the Modern Improvements. Terms Reasonable. **SMITH & WALTERMIRE, Proprietors.**

MANSION HOUSE,
ORANGE, N. J.

Thoroughly renovated, newly furnished, put in complete order throughout, and supplied with all modern improvements, including perfect ventilation, gas, and electric bells in every room, direct Telephone communication to all parts of New York. No pains will be spared to make it one of the leading hotels in the vicinity of New York. The table is supplied with the best that the New York markets afford. Open all the year. **ATWOOD & CO., Prop's, Orange, N. J.**

TOWER HILL HOUSE,
NARRAGANSETT PIER, R. I.
Will open for the season of 1880, June 25.

It will be newly painted and put in complete order; grounds lighted by electric lights. For rooms and board apply at Mansion House, Orange, New Jersey, until June 20th. **C. E. ATWOOD, Proprietor.**

OVERLOOK MOUNTAIN HOUSE,
CATSKILL MOUNTAINS,

Highest location, finest scenery and best appointed first-class hotel; opens June 15; terms reasonable. For engagements address JAMES SMITH, Proprietor, Woodstock, N. Y., or SMITH & WALTERMIRE, Proprietors, Baldwin House, Newburgh, N. Y., which is now open.

NEW HOTEL DIRECTORY AND TRAVELERS' MONITOR

A Gazetteer and Hotel Directory of the United States and Canada, is published by the HOTEL GAZETTE PUBLISHING HOUSE, 111 Broadway.

All the best hotels and summer resorts announce particulars in the HOTEL GAZETTE. Weekly illustrated. 5 cts. per copy. Offices, Hotel Exchange Bureau, 111 Broadway, New York.

MOORE'S HOTEL,
TRENTON FALLS, N. Y.   **M. MOORE, Proprietor.**

First class. Finest Scenery and Falls in America. Send for circulars.

PAVILION HOTEL,
NEW BRIGHTON, STATEN ISLAND, N. Y.,

First-class. Liberal reduction for the Season.
JAS. R. SANGSTER, Proprietor.

THE COOPER HOUSE,
COOPERSTOWN, N. Y., OTSEGO LAKE

Will open June 19th, 1880. Accommodations for 500 guests. Fine boating and fishing. Driving and mountain air cannot be surpassed. The Cooper House has hot and cold baths, bells and gas in all rooms. There are four bowling alleys, a large billiard room, and fine stables connected with the hotel. Send for circular. Through drawing room cars on all trains between Albany and Cooperstown.
S. E. CRITTENDEN, Proprietor.

GEORGE G. ROCKWOOD,

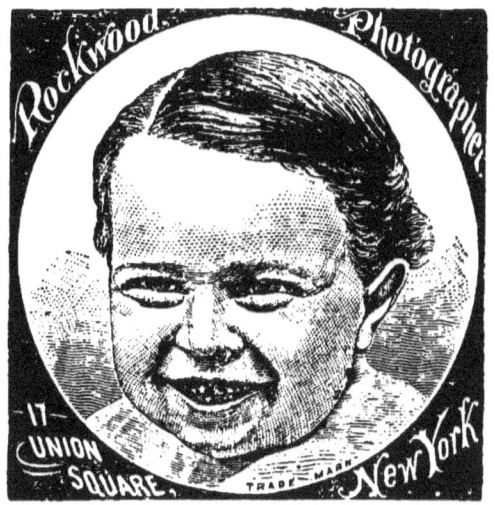

PHOTOGRAPHER,
17 UNION SQUARE (West,)
(Above Tiffany), **New York.**

Established 1859.

Mr. ROCKWOOD is in the Skylight Room from nine till four o'clock daily, and GIVES PERSONAL ATTENTION to the posing of sitters.

Imperial Cards, $6.00 per Doz.

☞ Mr. Rockwood publishes an extensive catalogue of

Photographic Views (Tourists' Series) of New York and Vicinity,

TOGETHER WITH

ARCHITECTURAL STUDIES AND SCENES FROM NATURE,

Celebrated Sculptures, Paintings, &c.

PRICES.—The Standard size is 8x10 inches, and will be sold unmounted at 35 cents each; mounted, 50 cents.

Glass Slides for Stereopticons can be made from any of our publications. One Dollar each.

NOTE.—Almost daily additions will be made to this Catalogue. Parties requiring Photographs of any part of the country, not on our published list, may possibly obtain them by addressing our house.

GEORGE G. ROCKWOOD, 17 Union Square, New York.

Sure Cure for Dyspepsia.

DR. CLARK JOHNSON:—I was afflicted with Dyspepsia for some time, and your INDIAN BLOOD SYRUP entirely cured me, after various so-called remedies failed.   H. P. LIBBY, Prin. Pub. School, Freeport, Queens Co., N. Y.

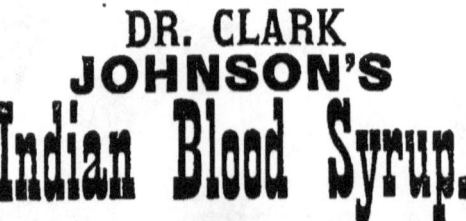

DR. CLARK JOHNSON'S
Indian Blood Syrup.

CURES FEVER AND AGUE.
CURES SCROFULA AND SKIN DISEASES.
CURES BILIOUSNESS.
CURES HEART DISEASE.
CURES RHEUMATISM AND DROPSY.
CURES NERVOUS DEBILITY.

[TRADE MARK.]

CURES Dyspepsia, Liver Diseases, Fever & Ague, Rheumatism, Dropsy, Heart Disease, Biliousness, Nervous Debility, etc.

The Best REMEDY KNOWN to Man !
9,000,000 Bottles
SOLD SINCE 1870.

Dyspepsia and Indigestion.

DR. CLARK JOHNSON:—Suffering for years with Dyspepsia, I was induced to give your INDIAN BLOOD SYRUP a trial, and it completely cured me. I still take the Syrup for the purpose of Regulating my bowels, for which I find there is no equal. Recommend persons seeking reference to me.   CHAS. WEEKS, No. 190 Navy Street, Brooklyn, N. Y.

Sure Cure for Dyspepsia.

DR. CLARK JOHNSON:—I was so badly afflicted with Dyspepsia that I could not keep anything on my stomach. After taking some of your INDIAN BLOOD SYRUP I find myself so well I can retain a hearty meal without distress. I think your medicine is the best I ever used for purifying the blood. I have gained twenty-five pounds in three months.
FRANK N. FREEMAN, Lyons, Wayne Co., N. Y.

For Kidney Diseases.

DR. CLARK JOHNSON:—I was troubled with Kidney Disease for a number of years, and failed to find relief until I tried your INDIAN BLOOD SYRUP, a short trial of which perfectly cured me. I recommend its use to all who are similarly afflicted.   GEORGE E. CARPENTER, Poughkeepsie, N. Y.

REVERE HOUSE,
Bowdoin Square, Boston, Mass.

The most central location in the city. Horse Cars to and from all parts of the city and depots pass the door. **$2.50 and $3.00 per day.**

CHARLES B. FERRIN, Proprietor.

LELAND'S OCEAN HOTEL,
Long Branch, N. J.

Directly in front of the new Ocean Pier. Extensive improvements, 600 new bath houses. Superior accommodations for permanent and transient guests. Address or apply,

LELAND'S OCEAN HOTEL, Long Branch, N. J.

E. D. PINAUD'S
CELEBRATED
PERFUMERY.

SPECIALTIES: Hair Tonic. Extracts for the Handkerchief.

Essence of Violette de Parma. | Essence of Opoponax.
" " Jasra Breoni. | " " Bris de la Pampas.
Essence of Jlang Jlang.

SOAPS OF ALL KINDS SPECIALLY RECOMMENDED.

Lettuce, Jasra, Opoponax, Persian Bouquet, and Rose Buds.
COSMETIQUES. FACE POWDER. TOILET WATERS, Etc.
For sale at all Druggists.

HENRY DREYFUS, Sole Agent for the U. S.,
No. 6 Cortlandt Street, New York.

ESTERBROOK'S
No. 048.   *No. 14.*

STANDARD AND SUPERIOR STEEL PENS

Falcon Pen.   Bank Pen.

The Esterbrook Steel Pen Co.
Works, Camden, N. J.   26 John Street, New York.

COLUMBIA BICYCLE.

100 MILES IN 7 HOURS.

1172 MILES IN 6 DAYS.

Easy to learn to ride. An ordinary rider can distance the best horse in a day's run. Send 3 cent stamp for price list and 24 page catalogue, with full information.

THE POPE MANUFACTURING COMPANY.
87 Summer Street, BOSTON.

Where and How to Shop in New York.

IMPORTERS AND MANUFACTURERS
OF

Fancy Dry Goods,

BROADWAY & 8th STREET.

FIVE IMMENSE FLOORS
DIVIDED INTO

"40 Distinct Departments."

Fresh Importations Daily. Latest Novelties, in

SILKS, SATINS,

VELVETS, BROCADES.

BLACK DRESS SILKS a Specialty.

Great Bargains in Laces and Made-up Laces.

Orders by Mail to any part of U. S. or Canada.
Money by P. O. Order, Reg Letter, or Draft on New York.
Goods forwarded C.O.D., if desired.
Spring Catalogue and Samples forwarded on application.

HOW TO REACH US.

This establishment can be reached by the following numerous conveyances:
All Lines of Stages pass the door. The Crosstown Cars, from 10th St., East River, to Christopher St., North River, pass the door. Broadway, Lexington, Third and Fourth Ave. Cars, pass within one block.
Third and Sixth Ave. Elevated Railroad stations at Eighth St.
Customers from Grand Central Depot, New Jersey, Long Island and Staten Island, are brought by *the above* different conveyances to our door.

HOW TO ADDRESS CORRESPONDENCE.

In all cases to

DANIELL & SON,
BROADWAY AND EIGHTH ST.
New York.

BEFORE YOU START!

FOR THE
Mountains, Lakes, or Shore,
OR ON
Any Trip for Business or Recreation,
SECURE A
GENERAL ACCIDENT POLICY OR TICKET
IN THE
TRAVELERS INSURANCE CO.,
Of Hartford, Conn.
Amount Accident Losses Paid, $3,800,000.

Any regular Agent will fit you out at small cost and short notice. New York Office, Tribune Building; Boston Office, corner State and Kilby Streets. Agents in Principal Cities and Towns in United States and Canadas.

ÆTNA INSURANCE COMPANY,
Hartford, Conn.
THE LEADING FIRE INSURANCE COMPANY OF AMERICA.

Statement, January 1st, 1880.

Unpaid Losses, Fire,	$180,215 64
do. do. Inland,	19,900 25
Re-insurance, Fire,	1,485,685 32
do. Inland,	7,873 10
Other claims,	48,584 21
Cash Capital,	3,000,000 00
Net Surplus,	$2,335,965 97
Total Assets,	**$7,078,224 49**

Agencies in all the Principal Cities, Towns and Villages of the United States and Canada.

WM. B. CLARK,	J. GOODNOW,	L. J. HENDEE,
Asst. Secretary.	*Secretary.*	*President.*

When a Lady Goes Travelling

you will find in her valise, amid her toilet articles, a bottle of

When a gentleman starts for a journey, he never forgets his **SOZODONT**. Why? He and she are well aware that among the most treasured possessions of a human being are **white**, pure, **healthy teeth**, hard, **rosy, healthy gums**, and a **sweet, pure breath**; and he and she are as well aware that nothing so contributes to the possession and retention of these desirable gifts as the free and constant use of **SOZODONT**. This famous **dentifrice** is free from all mineral taint or acid, and is as **harmless** as it is **efficient**. It **purifies the mouth**; **sweetens the breath**; cleanses, whitens, and **preserves the teeth** without injury to the enamel; **hardens the gums**, and keeps them in their healthy and normal condition. The universal popularity of **SOZODONT**, after so **many years of publicity and trial**, is a convincing proof of its merits.

Sold by all Druggists and Perfumers throughout the United States and Canada.

CONNECTICUT MUTUAL
LIFE
INSURANCE COMPANY,
OF HARTFORD, CONN.

Thirty-fourth Annual Statement.

Net Assets, Jan. 1, 1879..................$46,225,182 44
Received in 1879:
   For Premiums $3,750,441.67
   For Interest and Rent.........5,203,848 99
                                                  8,954,290 66

                                                       $55,179,473 10
Disbursed in 1879................................8,063,228 73

    Balance, Net Assets. Dec 31, 1879....$47,116,244 37

Gross Assets, Dec. 31, 1879..................$48,792,334 48
    Liabilities:
Amount required to reinsure all outstanding policies, net, assuming 4 per cent interest, $44,074,325 00
All other liabilities............. 1,277,257 06 45,351,582 06

    Surplus, Dec. 31, 1879...............$3,440,752 42

Increase of assets during 1879 .... $891,061 83
Ratio of expense of management to receipts in 1879, 6.54 per cent.
Policies in force Dec. 31, 1879, 64,504, insuring .$164,585,123 00

JACOB L. GREENE, President.
JOHN M. TAYLOR, Sec.   DAN'L H. WELLS, Asst. Sec.

www.ingramcontent.com/pod-product-compliance
Lightning Source LLC
Chambersburg PA
CBHW031330230426
43670CB00006B/303